Sheffield Forged and Tempered

Memoirs of
BARRIE COTTINGHAM

Grosvenor House
Publishing Limited

This book is published by
Grosvenor House Publishing Ltd
Link House
140 The Broadway, Tolworth, Surrey, KT6 7HT.
www.grosvenorhousepublishing.co.uk

Any royalties arising from the sale of the book will be donated to
St Luke's Hospice, Sheffield.

A CIP record for this book
is available from the British Library

ISBN 978-1-83975-524-8

SHEFFIELD FORGED AND TEMPERED

(1) To Forge – shape metal (especially steel) by heating in fire and hammering.

(2) To Temper – bring to proper hardness and elasticity by successive heating and cooling.

Memoirs of
BARRIE COTTINGHAM MBE

"I dedicate this book to my lovely wife, Nicola,
who has listened patiently to my readings of each chapter
as produced and made many helpful comments.
Of course, as stated in the Introduction,
the book has been written primarily for my grandsons,
Jack, Sam and Ned, and I hope that they
will find it of interest in years to come."

Contents

Introduction   ix

I   A Happy Childhood   1

II   Growing Up   15

III   From Schoolboy to Man   27

IV   The Royal Air Force –
    A   Initial Training   39
    B   Officer Cadet Training   45
    C   RAF Leconfield   53

V   Kenya – Mombasa and the Coast   68

VI   Kenya – Kilimanjaro   87

VII   Kenya – The Winds of Change   98

VIII   Return to the United Kingdom   115

IX   Michelle, Mum and Dad – Saddest of Times   134

X   Michelle and Nigel – Happier Days   149

XI   Partnership in CB&Co – The Early Years   166

XII   Partnership in CB&Co – The Second Phase   187

XIII   Partnership in C&L – The Final Years   201

XIV   Home and Play   220

XV   London   237

XVI   A Second Career   243

XVII   Family, Colleagues and Friends   260

XVIII   The Coronavirus (Covid-19)   283

XIX	Interesting Experiences	295
XX	Sheffield United FC	307
XXI	Miscellany	315
XXII	Concluding Remarks	322
	Photographs –	
	First Group	107
	Second Group	209
	Third Group	324
	Descriptions	336
	Bibliography and Additional Sources	341
	Index	346
	About the Author	349

Introduction

I am a little concerned that setting down my memoirs in this book may seem rather pretentious as I cannot claim to have achieved anything of real importance during my lifetime. However, over the span of years, I have experienced some events of significance which could be of interest to others, for example, my years spent in Kenya as the British Empire hastened towards its extinction. There have also been numerous incidents of much less importance which, when related to my wife, Nicola, (more than 28 years my junior) she would comment, "You should write that down." Only now at 87 years, my business career having come to an end and with free time available, have I decided to take up Nicola's suggestion.

However, probably my main reason for embarking upon what may prove to be a wasted exercise is that I now have three grandsons (at the time of writing, aged 11, 10 and 7 years, respectively) all of whom were born in Australia but have recently moved to New Zealand where their father (my son, Nigel) has taken up a new appointment. I hope that my grandsons will grow up to be proud Australasians, whichever of the two countries in the continent gains their allegiance, but I think it is important that (although their mother, Lisa, is Australian) with a father and three grandparents who are British they should, in due course, learn something about their heritage and forebearers. Hopefully, they may even conclude that "Pops", the old man who, together with Aunty Nicola, visits them for a few weeks each year, was not always as boring as he may now seem!

I know that my son does his best to stimulate my grandsons' interest in "the old country" and maybe my jottings will help him in this task. In the longer term, if my words encourage the three boys to visit Britain in order to explore matters for themselves, extend their education or even spend a period of employment, it would please me a great deal – although I suspect that I will not be around to bear witness.

In the main, my memoirs are intended to be lighthearted and, in places, amusing. I have never kept a diary, except as a record of appointments and commitments, and consequently I accept that some detail of my recollections could be challenged. Nevertheless, I believe that my words accurately portray my thoughts, actions and, sometimes, immaturities when the events took place.

Before concluding this introduction, I would also mention one area where, at the time, I was not conscious of changes taking place but from which my generation would ultimately benefit. This was when, as a teenage schoolboy, moving towards a decision on future employment and the first steps in building a career, I was fortunate (but unaware) to be in an early phase of the major social change in Britain which followed the Second World War.

To the best of my knowledge, up to this time, while my parents, grandparents and other ancestors had been hardworking, honest and highly principled people, their opportunities for education (still fee paying for secondary schools until 1944) and development had been limited. The norm had been for them to follow similar employments as their forebearers – manual jobs in the mines and steelworks, small shopkeepers, holders of routine clerical positions or, at best, to be engaged in semi-skilled occupations. None had attended university, gained entry to the professions or achieved commissioned rank in the armed forces (although several relatives had served with distinction and one, my uncle Frank Darley, had been awarded the Military Medal for "Bravery in the Field").

Although there must have been prior exceptions, my generation appears to have been the first when, more generally, if one had ambition, energy, good health, determination and, admittedly, a degree of good fortune, it was possible to move up the social ladder and achieve a different lifestyle to that of one's ancestors.

Although I now recognise that, had I been born 10 years or so earlier, my life might have turned out very differently, none of the matters referred to in the previous two paragraphs were in my thoughts at the time of leaving school at the age of 15. I had already set my ambitions and objectives for the future and believed that, as I moved into the adult world, I had the necessary drive and enthusiasm to carry them out. Fortunately, the required final ingredient of "good luck" duly arrived, although there were occasions when I feel that I had to help this along.

I

A Happy Childhood

October 1933 to December 1940

I was born in the Park District of Sheffield on 5 October 1933, where I spent the early years of my life. This was also the area where both my parents had been born and bred.

Close to the city centre, the Park District was bounded on the west by a railway line, over which a pedestrian bridge (still in existence) provided access to the Midland Railway Station. Sheffield (like Rome!) is built on seven hills and to the south-east was high ground known as Sky Edge, which in the depressed 1920s had been famous for its "Pitch and Toss" rink – controlled by the notorious Sheffield gangs, and was conveniently located for lookouts to warn of any potential police raid. Although the name remains, Sky Edge was eventually excavated, and the area used for council housing.

For the decade before my birth, unemployment in Sheffield had been high and the Board of Guardians, responsible for administering the Poor Law, had steadily reduced the scale of relief as cash ran short. This was reflected in the poor standard of living of many Park residents, where careworn housewives, living in the back-to-back terraced houses, brought up families as best they could, while attending to the daily chores of cleaning, blackleading the coal-fuelled kitchen ranges and donkey-stoning the outside steps to demonstrate that they still retained some pride.

All the above is social history, my first recollections as a four or five-year-old child are all happy ones, of a cosy home, kindly neighbours and parents who could not have been more loving.

The lower Park District itself was redeveloped after the Second World War, under Sheffield Corporation's priority for clearing terraced housing, and much of the area was given over to impersonal high-rise flats. The former Park residents were relocated (often with reluctance) to newly built council estates on the city outskirts, thus ending many close neighbourly relationships between families, who had resided close to each other for many years.

My father, Jack (born in 1907), worked as a collier at the Nunnery Colliery, the last surviving mine in Sheffield which was eventually closed in 1954. He had started work at the age of 14 years as a "filler" for his brother in law (Albert Needham), a "ripper". In those days, colliers hewed the coal using pick and shovel, sometimes in seams only 18 inches high. The rippers followed, hacking away the rock and widening the seams in readiness for the next shift of colliers. Colliers and rippers were paid for a measured "stint". They personally employed and paid fillers, using boys learning their trade, who would fill the trucks with coal or rubble.

During his time at the "Nunnery", Father was involved in the "Paddy Mail Accident" in December 1923 when seven miners were killed and 46 injured, some very seriously. Father was unscathed, but apparently returned underground as a volunteer with one of the quickly assembled rescue teams which were sent to bring out the injured.

At the time my father joined the coal industry there was great camaraderie between the miners, partly I believe because of the terrible working conditions and physical dangers they shared from toiling underground, when up to 1,300 men were killed and 160,000 injured each year – not to mention those becoming invalided with such complaints as pneumoconiosis and nystagmus. However, the main unifying bond was probably their battle against the mine owners. The economic effects of the 1914/18 war were gradually pushing much of the world towards the Great Depression. The coal industry was out of date and the owners' response was not to modernise, but to cut wages and increase working hours.

The first cuts had taken place in 1921 and resulted in a miners' strike. Despite a "Triple Alliance" with the railway and transport workers, these unions failed to support the miners and the strike fizzled out. Matters came to a head in 1925 when the owners tried to cut wages once more, this time by 13 per cent but with an increase in shifts from seven to eight hours. The miners again withdrew their labour and, this time, in May 1926, the Trade Union Congress gave support by calling a general strike involving 1.5 million workers. The support lasted only nine days, leaving the miners to struggle on alone for a further seven months without pay or benefits until eventually forced back to work by hunger for less pay and longer hours.

No doubt my father always voted Labour but, in common with many of the miners of his generation, his bitterness against the trade union movement never left him.

I believe that, in his heart, my father remained a coal miner all his life, but in his late twenties he was compelled to leave the industry because of duodenal ulcers which made him unfit for underground work. The ulcers perforated soon afterwards requiring what, in those days, was a major operation, leaving him unable to work for many months and needing to exercise care in his diet for some years. He gradually regained his strength and in due course obtained employment labouring with Sheffield Corporation Waterworks Department.

Broad of shoulder, possessing strong arms but wiry in build, my father had the appearance of a miner of his time but in many respects he was untypical. He was teetotal until the age of 35, from when he started to have an occasional "social" glass of milk stout. He could be quick-tempered and would always stand up for his rights, but he cooled down quickly and had a sensitive (even gentle) and generous nature. Despite his rather gruff manner, he liked and was always popular with children. My mother and father had married in 1931 at the ages of 22 and 24 years, respectively. I understand that in the early part of their marriage, after my birth but before the existence of pit-head showers, Father would arrive home in his blackened state and pick me up, to mother's annoyance, before carrying out his "tin bath" ablutions.

However, Father was not without vices. He smoked (Woodbine cigarettes) and, in common with many working-class men of his generation, he gambled on horse and greyhound racing. This was sometimes the cause of arguments between my parents, which would usually be conducted when I was in bed and thought to be asleep. If awakened, I found this conflict between my parents upsetting, and I would get up and go downstairs. While this usually quietened both parties, it probably did nothing to resolve the issues.

In fairness, my father always handed over the housekeeping allowance to Mother on payday, but he was quite capable of losing his remaining "spending money" within a day or so and hoping to borrow back from Mother money for cigarettes and to carry him through the rest of the week. On occasions when his gambling was successful, he would be overgenerous with family and friends and nothing remained in his pocket for long.

As I grew up and, at a time when some physical chastisement of children was the norm, I cannot recollect even a slap on the backside from either of my parents – although I can think of many occasions when one would have been well justified.

Father had five older sisters and a younger brother, all of whom lived in Sheffield, but were dispersed around the city. I have little recollection of my paternal grandparents, both of whom died when I was quite young and, in general, with the exception of two aunts (Clara and Elsie), I had much less contact as a child with my father's family than with my maternal relatives. Nevertheless, on the appropriate Sundays at Whitsuntide and Easter it was expected that my father would take me to visit all his siblings. We travelled around the city by tramcar, bus or "Shank's pony", visiting one house after another, and I would be rewarded at each with a half-crown or florin for sight of my new clothes, or by a chocolate egg according to the occasion. Those of my paternal cousins who were still in their childhood were expected to make similar pilgrimages and woe betide anyone who failed to attend.

While during my younger childhood, I cannot recollect attending many events with my father, he did take me to Bramall Lane to see Sheffield United on a few occasions and established the foundations of my lifelong support of the Blades. His stories, told with obvious partisanship, of footballers such as Jimmy Hagan and of the famous cricketers of Yorkshire (regular County

Champions at the time and providers of the backbone of the England side), stimulated my interest in sport and pride in being English, from Yorkshire and a Sheffielder, which feelings have remained with me all my life.

My mother, Eleanor, was an attractive woman, always nicely turned out, well spoken (certainly by Sheffield working-class standards) and pleasant of nature. She rarely had a bad word for anyone and in later years I would be amused at her kindly descriptions of people. For example, someone clearly overweight would be referred to by Mum as "bonny" or "having good limbs on them". So far as I was personally concerned, she was always selfless and loving; qualities I took for granted throughout my life. Mother suffered from phlebitis in her legs, which I believe had developed shortly after (and possibly as a result of) my birth. This may explain why I was the only child – although I never enquired about this.

Mother shouldered the main responsibility for running the home and balancing the budget, which at times must have been difficult. She was hard working and conscientious and, apart from her duties as a housewife, for much of her adult life she also had part-time employment to supplement the family finances. Through Mum's careful management, we always enjoyed a reasonable standard of living and, to the best of my knowledge, were never in debt. I cannot remember any time in my childhood when I did not have everything that I wanted – although even as a child I think I had enough sense not to want what I would be unable to have.

My mother was very close to her family, visiting her parents most days (and for part of her life working in their fruit and greengrocery business). They also lived in the Park District but in a "posher" area in a semi-detached house in Essex Road, quite close to Norfolk Park. Her two sisters (Amy and Connie) and brother (Walter), all younger than my mother, were unmarried at the time of my early childhood and, excluding Walter who was called up to the army, lived at home. With the intervention of the Second World War, which delayed first the marriages and secondly the starting of families by Mother's siblings, I was the only child in the family until about the age of 12 and probably spoilt by all the attention bestowed upon me. I remember being taken on holiday by my grandparents several times and on one occasion of insisting that we found a café that had my favourite rice pudding (made with lots of milk but with a skin) on the menu! This was another time when a slap on the backside might have done me good.

Because of my father's dietary problems, he would not risk going on holiday for several years after his operation and, on occasions, Mother and I joined up and holidayed with her sisters, Amy and Connie. One such holiday was at Squires Gate Holiday Camp near Blackpool in August 1939, as the world stumbled towards war. By this time Amy (the next in age to my mother) had suffered a personal tragedy in the death of Frank, her fiancé, from meningitis, only a few months before her planned wedding.

Amy was probably the least good looking of the three sisters, but she was acknowledged within the family as having the nicest and kindest nature. Frank's death devastated her, and she gave up all thoughts of romance for several years, becoming almost a second mother to me. In her leisure time, Amy would take me on outings to the cinema, theatre or wherever I chose. She had her own "lock-up" fruit and greengrocer's shop in Clarence Street (now demolished) and in school holidays, as I became older, I would sometimes go along with her to help.

On Ecclesall Road, close to the shop, was an excellent toy store, which Amy would visit every Friday evening after work in order to purchase a present for me and for which I would be waiting. Initially the gift would be lead soldiers, which, after war broke out, would be deployed around the furniture at home in make-believe battles as the British forces fought the Germans. Later on, she would bring an addition to my extensive collection of Dinky cars and vehicles. Because of my collector's instinct, these were never played with, but were kept in pristine condition in several shoeboxes. Mother gave the collection to a rag-and-bone man without consulting me in my teenage years on the assumption that I had outgrown such things. I discovered the loss of my collection only weeks later and never quite forgave her! These days they would be worth a small fortune at auction.

In December 1939, less than three months after my sixth birthday, Britain had entered the Second World War. My favourite uncle, Walter (the youngster in Mother's family) having reached 21 years, had already received calling-up papers for national service. This process was speeded up and he was conscripted and sent to France with the British Expeditionary Force. Fortunately, Walter was one of the 340,000 troops who were evacuated from Dunkirk in June 1940. However, some time in the following year, he was sent to North Africa, where he remained with the "Desert Rats" for most of the war.

Before embarking for North Africa, Walter married his sweetheart Doris (another Park District lass). Doris continued to live at her parents' home but became a regular visitor to my grandparents' house and a close friend of Connie, Amy and the family. I had acquired another aunt – whom I considered to be very beautiful.

Walter and I corresponded throughout the years he was away. He always found time to enquire about my progress at school or with the Boy Scouts. Walter also sent me gifts from time to time, including my first ever pair of football boots – handmade by an Egyptian shoemaker. These were light brown (almost yellow) in colour and about two sizes too large! Nevertheless, with the toes packed with tissue paper, I managed quite well and enjoyed the envy of my schoolmates, few of whom had football boots in these days of clothing coupons. I assumed that the question from my school friends – "Are yer wearing canal barges today?" – was asked out of sheer jealousy.

Being so young when hostilities broke out, I could not at that time or for a year or so, understand or appreciate the significance and implications of war against Germany. I think I felt that something exciting, but quite normal, was happening. After all, both my grandfathers had fought against the Germans in the Great War. In fact, Grandfather Cottingham had survived as a regular soldier in the King's Own Yorkshire Light Infantry (the "pride of the line") taking part in the Boer War and WWI. Grandfather Price had volunteered on the outbreak of hostilities and was sent to France in April 1915, serving with the Hallamshire

Battalion of the York and Lancaster Regiment. He was wounded only five months later and eventually honourably discharged.

Even as a child, I could tell that there was much activity after war broke out and that many changes were taking place. My father, largely back to physical strength, but unfit for military service and probably too old, dug out the foundations, bolted together and erected the corrugated steel sheets which comprised the Anderson shelters at both our house and my grandparents'. Even as a child, I could see that this involved much hard work. Gas masks were issued to everyone and for a time had to be carried everywhere. There was food rationing, with restrictions on the sale of sweets, chocolate and confectionary, and shortages of fruit and many other goods. Clothing coupons were issued and, as the war progressed, inspectors visited school every few months when we were required to line up, a class at a time, without shoes and have our feet measured to see if we justified extra coupons.

To hinder German air attacks, all street lighting was extinguished at night. Houses were required to fit blackout curtains and, in most cases, had fitments to external doors which turned off the house lighting when opened. Air Raid Precaution (ARP) Wardens patrolled the streets to ensure that the blackout requirements were observed. Where people had not been conscripted into the armed forces, there was direction of labour of younger adults of both sexes into essential employments. For example, Connie became a bus conductor – public transport being essential to ensure that the munitions workers could get to and from their factories. Working shifts, which sometimes commenced very early in the morning or continued until one or two am in blackened streets, could not have been pleasant for a young woman, especially in the winter months. However, I have no recollection of Connie complaining.

At the outbreak of war, Grandma Price started to build up a store of tinned food and (based upon advice from a magazine) large quantities of eggs were pickled in pails, which were then stored in the roof void. As the war progressed, sirens would sound on many evenings, warning of an air raid. I believe there were 130 such alerts in the two years August 1940 to July 1942 but only 16 of these were actual raids on Sheffield. The others related to hostile planes travelling over the city to other targets. Nevertheless, we would all traipse into our Anderson shelter (except for my father, who would either be on duty with the Sheffield Waterworks Department, often at Redmires where the dams which served Sheffield were situated, or wandering around "keeping an eye on things"). We would remain in the shelter until the "All-Clear" sounded, which would usually be after a couple of hours or so.

As a young child, I was often asleep when the warning sirens went off and I would be carried in pyjamas and blanket to the shelter. I would also have the privilege of a bunk to sleep in. Therefore, my recollections of this period are scant. However, I do remember the excitement of the first occasion when we went into the shelter at my grandparents' house – six members of the family – all women, except my grandfather and myself, together with Rex, the Alsatian dog. On high ground, about half of a mile from my grandparents, an Ack-Ack battery was located and, shortly after entering the shelter, a regular popping sound began. Grandma announced that the Germans must be overhead as the guns had opened up. We sat in silence and apprehension, until it was discovered that Rex was wagging his tail enthusiastically against the side of the shelter and creating an impression of gunfire.

History records that following our defeat in France and the evacuation of British and some French troops at Dunkirk in June 1940, with great damage to morale and, more importantly, massive loss of weaponry and equipment, Britain was at its most vulnerable and an invasion by the Germans seemed inevitable. Hitler recognised that the main obstacle was Britain's superior sea power, which he believed could be nullified by obtaining control of the air. Consequently, the Battle of Britain commenced in July 1940 and continued to the end of October.

The German tactics were to bomb London on an almost nightly basis with the objective of devastating the city and damaging civilian morale. By drawing the Royal Air Force into the battle in defence of London, it was believed that our planes could be destroyed. My father spent several months in London during this period with a Sheffield Waterworks team, which was sent to help repair the water mains and pipes and keep supplies running. He returned with great respect for the courage of the London East Enders, who suffered the brunt of the bombing, but despite massive damage and heavy casualties showed even greater resolve to stand up to the Nazis.

As the world knows, the RAF, despite great loss of planes and aircrew (including many very young men with a minimum of training and experience), gradually gained the upper hand to a point where the losses of the Luftwaffe were too great for them to continue with their plans. The Germans gave up their ideas of an invasion of Britain to concentrate on the Russian front. They also switched their bombing focus away from London to the major British industrial cities, where the armaments of war were being produced. Sheffield's turn to be blitzed came on 12/13 and 15/16 December 1940.

On 12 December 1940, my aunts, Amy and Connie, took me for a belated seventh birthday treat to the Rex Cinema at Intake, a district about two miles farther away from Sheffield centre than my grandparents' house. We travelled by tramcar to attend the first house performance which commenced about 6.30pm and was scheduled to end at 8.30 or so. However, halfway through the performance, a message flashed onto the screen to the effect that an air raid was in progress and patrons were advised not to leave the cinema until the all-clear had been sounded. The film ended and was shown again to the same audience for a second time, but still, by the end, there had been no all-clear. In fact, it was 4.30am before we were able to leave the cinema, and by then I had spent several hours sleeping across the knees of my aunts.

When we eventually emerged from the cinema in what should have been dusk, the sky was bright – illuminated we discovered by the fires burning in Sheffield. The power wires were down, and no trams were running (we subsequently learned that many had been destroyed), neither were there any buses nor, for that matter, much moving traffic of any type. We therefore set off on the longish trek towards my grandparents' house (where my mother was also staying), my aunts on either side holding my hands. It all seemed very exciting.

The nearer we moved towards the city centre, the greater the evidence of damage and, every now and again, there would be a burning house. I could sense the concern of my aunts by their tightening grip on my hands. As we got to within a few hundred yards of my grandparents' house, great relief all round. Grandparents and my mother were there waiting in the street in hope that we would arrive. However, their house on Essex Road had been quite badly damaged. Something had gone through the roof and smashed its way through each floor into the foundations (taking Grandma's pails of pickled eggs with it!). The fear was that it was an unexploded bomb and houses nearby were being evacuated. It eventually turned out to be rubble, blown into the air by a landmine that had destroyed a nearby building, but we were not to know that, and, in any event, the house was not habitable.

Our party set off for the house of Aunt Nellie Fairbrother, my grandmother's half-sister. This was closer to the city centre. We had not been walking for long when we met Nellie with her husband, Arthur, and their two sons, Ron and Alan, aged about 15 and 4 years, respectively. Their house had been damaged beyond repair and they were hoping to stay at my grandparents.

Our enlarged number of 10, which would be increased to 11 when my father returned the next morning, set off for a new destination. We were now hoping to take up residence in my home. This was even nearer to the city centre and the main area of bomb damage, but, thankfully, when we arrived, the house was found to be intact. However, there was no electricity and for some time water had to be obtained by buckets filled from tankers which came round daily. Our house comprised one room downstairs, two bedrooms, an outside toilet and no bathroom. However, there was a fireplace with oven and a cellar full of coal. It could have been worse.

Alan and I, as the young children, had the privilege of sharing my bed in the smallest bedroom. Ron, at 15 years, was treated as an adult. By the end of the war he was a sergeant with Observers Wings in the RAF. How or where the adults slept, I have no idea, but we managed for several weeks. On Christmas Eve, less than two weeks after the Blitz, Father Christmas arrived as usual. Alan and I pretended to be asleep until the pillowcases had been filled – getting out of bed as soon as the bedroom door closed. We had previously searched the upstairs wardrobes and I was satisfied that my chosen chemistry set, although rather dusty, would be delivered.

How long we were all together in the Lord Street house, I cannot remember. I think my grandparents were the first to leave. Grandma had decided after her experience that she did not wish to return to Essex Road. Some semi-detached houses, where building had commenced before the start of war, were being completed at Intake. My grandparents managed to purchase one and, shortly afterwards, the Fairbrothers obtained the next-door-but-one property. To my delight, it was decided that when the Essex Road house was repaired, we would move there. The house still exists today and from the outside seems a smallish drab semi, but at the time, in my eyes, it was a little palace.

My foregoing comments are running rather ahead of the events. The second part of the Sheffield Blitz took place on 15 December 1940, only three nights after the one I have referred to. Although this raid was shorter, the Luftwaffe found the Attercliffe and Brightside industrial areas of the city and several steelworks were hit, although the damage was not sufficient to badly affect production.

In the two raids, both of which were conducted in perfect conditions with a full moon and a cloudless sky, the German aircraft dropped in the region of 450 high explosive bombs, land mines and incendiaries. 693 people were killed, 1,586 injured and 40,000 made homeless.

Some years after the events, it was disclosed that the Germans flew by a beam (an early kind of radar) that was fixed on a point for the bombers to fly down to their targets. The British had found a way to bend the beam and this had been done on the 12 December raid, so that instead of reaching the industrial area, the Germans flew straight to the city centre. This saved the steelworks to the detriment of the city and resulted in many deaths and injuries.

Prior to the 12 December raid, it appears that Lord Haw-Haw (the traitor, William Joyce, later hanged for his deeds) had announced in one of his infamous "Germany Calling" propaganda broadcasts that "the seven sisters of Sheffield" would be hit. The seven sisters were the seven chimneys of the Brightside steelworks of Steel Peach and Tozer. Whether Joyce was aware that these were targets (which were saved by the bending of the beam) or whether it was merely a statement of propaganda, one can only speculate.

I can remember being present as a child when some of the "Germany Calling" broadcasts were on the radio. My impression is that the adults regarded them as amusing propaganda to be laughed at and ignored. I can still hear grandmother's words "I should think so" said with a chuckle at some of the claims made by Joyce. Looking back and now appreciating the perilous position Britain was in following Dunkirk, I feel surprised but proud of the defiance and resolve the adults displayed despite all the hardships and tribulations they were experiencing. Probably the stirring rhetoric of Winston Churchill was a factor in this.

An amusing sequel to my recollections of the Blitz is a story told to me by a friend of about my age, who is a former president of the Institute of Chartered Accountants and was brought up in Pudsey, near Leeds. Although, I believe, Pudsey was never bombed, in the early years of the war, the sirens would be sounded, and people would go to the shelters whenever hostile aircraft were passing over or in the area. Consequently, my friend and his family, including his slightly older brother, would adjourn to their shelter several evenings each week in the same way as we did in Sheffield. The ARP wardens would do their rounds, checking that all was well and often speculating as to where the hostile planes were heading. Apparently, a frequent suggestion was that "Sheffield will be copping it tonight". Eventually, my friend's brother enquired of his father, "Why do the Germans keep bombing Sheffield?" To which the reply came, "Well, Sheffield is an important place. There are steelworks and that in Sheffield."

Full of local pride, my friend's brother responded, "Well, Pudsey is an important place. Len Hutton (see below) was born in

Pudsey." This time there was a short delay before father responded but eventually, he said, "I don't think Hitler knows that." My friend said that for some months afterwards, he and his brother were terrified in case Hitler found out that Len Hutton had been born in Pudsey.

For younger readers of these memoirs or anyone not interested in cricket, Leonard Hutton was a famous opening batsman for Yorkshire and England. For many years he was holder of the record highest score in a test match innings (364). Hutton became the first professional player to captain England – previously the tradition had been for an amateur captain. He subsequently received a knighthood.

II

Growing Up

January 1941 to August 1949

Inevitably, after the Blitz, it took time for things to return to normal. I had originally started my education at the age of five at Manor Council School, but this had been badly damaged in the bombing and never reopened for the duration of the war. I therefore needed to find a new school. My parents decided that Intake Council, a "village school", about three miles farther away from Sheffield centre and close to my grandparents' new home, would be appropriate and may be safer with regard to any future bombing. The school was accessible from Essex Road, where we now lived, by tramcar in a journey taking about 20 minutes, and I could walk from school to my grandparents' new house for lunch in about 5 to 10 minutes. Therefore, it was at Intake Council School that I recommenced my education from March 1941.

In these early years of the 1940s when the Second World War was still in progress and TVs, computers, iPads, mobile phones, etc., were not in existence, most of our leisure time as schoolboys in holiday periods was spent outdoors. However, in contrast with the present day, when facilities such as playing fields and tennis courts tend to be made available for wider public use, in holiday periods the school gates were locked and barred, and everything was restricted. There were even regular security visits by the police to check for signs of damage or trespass. None of this deterred us from using what we regarded as "our" playing fields. While the sports ground was bordered by the school on the main-road side, on the other three sides were the terraced houses, back yards and occasionally gardens of the homes where many of the pupils resided. Therefore, in holiday periods we would climb over the walls and fences and make use of the sports pitches to play football or cricket for hours on end. On the occasional police security visits, we could disappear from whence we came in minutes, but return just as quickly to continue our contests as soon as they had gone.

During these years, as the war progressed and Britain and its allies started to build up forces for an invasion of Europe, troops from a variety of nations congregated in the UK. As a boy of about 10 or 11 years, I remember a visit from a Canadian soldier named Milner (I forget his first name), a relative on my grandmother's side of the family. Unfortunately, he had no spare cap badge, which I could beg for my collection, but I recollect that he gave me a florin, or what I would have referred to as a two-shilling piece.

Another visitor was Albert Cox of the US Army Air Force. His parents had emigrated to America from the Park District of Sheffield, where they had been good friends of my grandparents. Albert had no spare badges but said he would return. He was as good as his word and there are two US Army Air Force badges in the collection which I still retain from these childhood years.

I hope that these two servicemen survived D-Day and the conflicts which followed. I suspect that my parents would not have informed me at the time if they had been lost.

It was during the years of living at Essex Road that I became involved with the Scout movement. My mother's youngest sibling, Walter, was something of a hero to me. He had been a Boy Scout, and this had stimulated my interest.

The local church, St. Aidan's, where I attended Sunday school, was situated only a hundred yards or so from my home, and its adjacent church hall was the base for the 143rd Sheffield Boy Scouts. On my first attempt to join, I was too young and became a Wolf Cub, but moved into the Scouts at the earliest possible opportunity. I was enthusiastic and progressed rapidly to become leader of the "Ravens patrol" which I regarded as the best in the troop, with members of other patrols wishing to transfer to join us as vacancies became available.

I felt (and still feel) that the Scouting movement with its high principles and objectives is the best of all major youth organisations, and my involvement over a few years helped my self-confidence and provided many challenges and opportunities for outdoor activities. No doubt the organisation has had to change with the times, but I suspect that even in his wildest dreams, Baden-Powell could not have envisaged the success and growth of the movement since its conception in the United Kingdom in 1907, to become established in over 200 countries and territories around the world with a membership of over 38 million.

Of course, like most young people, my focus at the time of joining was not on principles and objectives but the enjoyment of fellowship with similar minded people and the opportunity for new adventures and activities. In Sheffield, we were fortunate with the Peak District on our doorstep and use of the Nottinghamshire Association's excellent Sherwood Forest camping site facilities at Walesby.

My first annual fortnights camp was at Matlock in Derbyshire. Following arrival, while holding a tent peg to be hammered into the ground, I was struck in the eye by a colleague swinging back a wooden mallet. This resulted in a splendid black eye, which (to my mother's concern) was still visible when I returned home two weeks later. It was at this camp that we experienced some days of torrential rain and were compelled to evacuate in the middle of the night on one occasion when the tent became flooded. However, neither of these incidents affected my enthusiasm.

After Matlock, and as momentum in the Second World War moved in favour of the Allied Forces, we gradually became more ambitious and held annual camps at Skegness and Scarborough, interspersed with occasional weekends away, usually at the Walesby site previously mentioned. It was on one of these that I suffered a potentially serious injury. While trimming dead branches from a pine tree for the campfire, the branch upon which I was standing gave way. I fell about 15 feet, ripping open my right forearm on the jagged remnants of another branch on the way down. This resulted in a large and dirty wound. The Scoutmaster drove me straight to Mansfield Hospital, where a surgeon cleaned and stitched the wound while I looked the other way and held the hand of a pretty nurse. I was lucky. The surgeon did an excellent job, but I still bear a V-shaped scar about six inches long, which shows up especially if my arm becomes suntanned.

Probably my most memorable experience came on another camping holiday as I moved towards the end of my period of involvement with the Scouts. The war had ended, but there was still rationing in Britain and various other restrictions continued. Becoming a little more daring, arrangements were made for the annual camp to be on the 3,500-acre Curraghmore Estate of the Marquis of Waterford in Southern Ireland. This was an exciting proposition, as most members of the troop (including myself), had grown up during the war and never been out of the United Kingdom. I was particularly elated when it was decided that I should be part of an advance party of four, comprising two Rover Scouts (who assisted the Scout leader) and one of the other patrol leaders. Our role would be to establish the campsite, erect tents and prepare a field kitchen in readiness for the main party, which was not expected to arrive until late in the day.

Quite early on the appropriate day, our advance party set off for Liverpool, from where we would take the ferry to Dublin. We were travelling in an open-backed truck with two seats in front (including the driver) and the tents and other equipment in the rear. The other patrol leader and I sat in the rear on top of the tents. Of course, there were no seat belts in these days, but we had no thoughts of danger. The weather was good, and our main concern was that this should continue – otherwise we were likely to get a soaking.

The scenery as we travelled over the Pennines was magnificent as always. We skirted Manchester and duly arrived in Liverpool. It was my first visit to the city, and I was impressed to see the famous Cunard headquarters and the Liver Building as we moved towards the harbour. I remember little about the crossing itself except that, at the time, everything seemed interesting and exciting.

We duly left Dublin and made the drive of about 80 miles or so to the south coast and the Curraghmore Estate, ancestral home of the Beresford family. We found our campsite and, while my colleagues set about erecting tents and making preparations for the main party, I was chosen to visit the stately home (which we had passed as we arrived) to announce our presence and find where we could obtain drinking water and purchase milk and other food products.

At the time, I was not aware of the superstition that the Beresford family was the object of a malevolent curse following several violent deaths and tragedies over many years. Neither did I know that the 8th Marquis of Waterford was only the same age as me (and probably still at Eton) having inherited the title when a one-year-old on the death of his father in a shooting accident.

I made my way to the house and, noticing what appeared to be a gardener, enquired if His Lordship was at home. He replied that he was. Therefore, I rang the bell on the impressive door which, after a short delay, was answered by a uniformed servant. I asked if I could see His Lordship and was instructed to wait in the library. He also informed me that, if I made any future visit, this should be to the tradesmen's entrance at the rear of the house!

After a short wait, the "gardener" who I had seen outside arrived. I now believe that this was Lord Beresford, uncle of the 8th Marquis. He was most friendly and helpful, taking me in his estate car to see where we could obtain water and purchase milk. He even drove to the nearby village to show where a general store could be found. I returned to our campsite "mission completed" having missed out on much of the hard work.

Returning to the subject of my early schooling, apart from recollections of happy times, it is difficult to think of anything of real interest in the four years spent at Intake Council School. However, I do remember two occasions when I had contact with the police – in my view for the best of reasons.

The first came a couple of years after I had become a pupil at the school. By this time, my grandparents had sold their house and acquired a fruit and vegetable store with attached living accommodation. This was farther away from the school but still just near enough for me to go for lunch each day (rather than stay for the dreaded school dinners). As one of my friends lived part way towards my grandparents, my routine was to walk with him on my way to lunch but to catch a tramcar for the return journey.

For fun, rather than walk, my friend Albert Kay and I used to run along the top of the stone garden walls of the cottages which lined the road up to his home on the first part of my journey, jumping across the gaps for gates and, where possible, driveways. The challenge was to keep off the pavement as much as possible. I suspect that our "fun run" might not have been appreciated by all the house owners, but I cannot remember anyone complaining. All this sounds rather infantile these many years later, but, of course, we were only about nine years of age at the time.

After reaching my friend's house, there were few suitable walls for me to continue the fun run, but I would sometimes climb and walk along the much higher wall of a churchyard, situated before the junction with Woodhouse Road, before eventually jogging the remainder of my journey.

One day, while on the churchyard wall, I noticed a package inside the grounds which I felt warranted investigation. This package proved to contain two solid silver salvers and two tankards, all bearing the engraved name "Grand Hotel, Sheffield".

My thoughts, as a schoolboy, were that these items must have been stolen and jettisoned over the wall by the thief into the churchyard when in danger of being apprehended. I decided to go straight to a nearby police box and, if possible, hand over the items. I was lucky, a policeman was "in residence" having just completed traffic control duties. He seemed pleased with me and said that the items would be returned to the Grand Hotel, together with my name and address. He felt that the hotel may wish to send a letter of thanks or even a reward! I waited in expectation for several weeks but heard nothing from anyone.

However, I did receive "a flea in my ear" from my grandmother, who had been worried by my late arrival for lunch (which had gone cold). Such is the reward for honesty.

My second encounter with the constabulary came about two years later (it may have been shortly after I had moved on from Intake Council School) – age about 11 or 12. By this time I was an enthusiastic Boy Scout and had developed an interest in hiking and rambling, usually in the beautiful Derbyshire Peak District, which borders on to Sheffield. It was on a Sunday, and a friend and I had been walking over the moors near a famous beauty spot "Toads Mouth" at Fox House on the outskirts of Sheffield. These moors had been used a few years earlier for military training manoeuvres. I came across a cardboard carton, wet and disintegrating from exposure to the elements, from which the contents were bursting out. These contents proved to be live .303 rifle cartridges. I felt that these could be dangerous in the wrong hands and particularly if found by small children. Therefore, I packed the bullets into my rucksack, bade goodbye to my friend and made for the bus terminus for transport to Sheffield City Centre.

I was aware on this occasion that the police box on Surrey Street next to Sheffield Town Hall was normally manned and this was my destination. I expected my public-spirited action to be praised, but the officer on duty gave me a dressing-down for touching live ammunition and even worse in his view "endangering life by taking the bullets onto public transport".

At this period in time (the 1940s), all primary school children were required to sit the eleven-plus scholarship examination (the 11+) at the appropriate stage. Success in the 11+ enabled them to move school (usually to a grammar) where, in due course, they could obtain the School Certificate and have the possibility, if desired, of staying on for a Higher School Certificate and eventual university entry. Furthermore, a School Certificate in relevant subjects with good grades was required as a minimum educational qualification for entry to articles (training contracts) by the professions such as accountancy and law, etc., and for pursuing many other career opportunities.

Those failing the 11+, the substantial majority of pupils, would remain at primary school until age 14 (I believe this was increased to 15 in 1947) when they would normally leave school and seek employment opportunities.

I have probably oversimplified the situation above and have not made any detailed study of the subject. I also recognise that there would be evening classes, correspondence courses and various other sources for further education and training after leaving school. Nevertheless, I think it seems clear that late developers or those who, for whatever reason, failed to pass the 11+, commenced their after-school life with a great disadvantage.

I make the above observations because a possible downside of attending a small village school, as compared with the large city primary schools, emerged in my mind only at the 11+ stage. Out of my class of about 40 who sat the examination in 1945, only eight were successful in passing and none gained a place at their first-choice grammar school. Nevertheless, I was pleased to have been awarded a place at Carfield Secondary School (not to be confused with the secondary moderns).

My impression now is that the standard of teaching at Intake Council School may have been inferior to that at the large city primary schools, or perhaps there was a different awareness and knowledge of the requirements in passing the 11+. It would have been a great pity and possibly made a major difference in my life (and the lives of others in the same situation) if because of these factors we had missed the opportunity for higher education.

I was proud and excited to have secured a place at Carfield starting in September 1945. The first year's intake comprised three forms A, B and C, each of about 40 pupils (generally classes were much larger in these immediate post-war days). However, I was a little disappointed to find that I was in C form, indicating that my 11+ marks had been in the bottom third of those selected. In the examination at the end of the first year, which was taken by all the 120 students, I obtained the second highest marks and was rocketed into the A form.

I could not get home quickly enough to announce to my parents that I was second in the year. Mother said something like "that's nice". Her concern was always that I should be happy, and examination performance was of little importance to her. Father said, "Who was first?" He always expected me to do well. I got the message, and at the end of the second year I was able to report that "I was first".

Comparisons of results obtained by students in the next two years in the run-up to School Certificate were difficult, as choices had to been made on subjects to be taken. In order to obtain the School Certificate, one had to take and pass in a minimum of six subjects, while the maximum number of subjects that could be taken was nine. As I was studying 11 subjects, this meant that I had to drop two. All students had to pass in English language and either mathematics or general science – I chose to take both. I also chose history, geography and scripture knowledge. As my ambition at this time was to become an architect, I also chose to study art (which comprised exam papers in architecture, design and poster), technical drawing (papers in machine and geometrical drawing) and handicraft (woodwork drawing and theory). This gave me a total of nine subjects, and with regret, I had to drop English literature and French.

Surprisingly, there was no guidance to students available at school and, as neither of my parents were academic or knowledgeable on the requirements of the various professions, the choice on subjects to take or drop was left to me. In retrospect and with the benefit of current knowledge I may have chosen differently. However, I achieved the best School Certificate in my year at Carfield with distinctions or credits in every subject except general science (only a pass). This result, together with a written commendation from the headmaster for my conduct and academic performance throughout my years at Carfield was good for my self-confidence and, as will be seen from later paragraphs, it also gave rise to an opportunity which had a significant influence on my longer-term future.

At this stage, it is probably worth a few words on the physical aspects of Carfield School in the mid-1940s. The building was old and, after six years of war with little attention, it was generally run-down and in need of updating. Accommodation was cramped for the number of students, and fittings and furniture would have benefitted from a programme of replacement.

In my view, the quality of teaching was quite good although, as one would expect in a period where there been conscription to the armed forces, the average age of teachers was probably higher than it would be at the present time.

The students comprised boys and girls. Classes were mixed but each sex had its own playground, which was strictly out of bounds for the opposite sex. Fraternisation was not encouraged – but sometimes occurred!

There was a gymnasium (of sorts) but little equipment and there were no playing fields. Sports activities took place each Wednesday afternoon for my year. On alternate weeks we would travel by bus (a 20-minute journey) to make use of the Sheffield Training College sports pitches. The other week would be basketball or shinty (played with a wooden ball and heavy wooden stick – murderous!) in the school yard. The girls would play rounders or netball in their yard.

Despite the above lack of facilities, Carfield had quite a good football team (of which I was a member), which competed successfully against other Sheffield schools. It was at such a game, against High Storrs Grammar School, 74 years ago, that I first met Bryan Hancock, still one of my best friends. We were sent off for fighting but found ourselves waiting at the same bus stop after the game. By this time, all aggressiveness had dissipated and been replaced by fear and concern at the possible reaction of our respective headmasters for the disgrace brought upon our schools. Happily, it appears that the sports masters decided not to report the incident and Bryan and I became firm friends.

Corporal punishment was still exercised by most schools in the 1940s and this included Carfield, where caning, detention, writing lines or extra homework were all possible punishments, according to the type or severity of the misdemeanour. However, only the latter three punishments applied in the case of girls. Caning was normally on the hands and, in fairness, was usually deserved. If given a choice, most boys would choose caning (and get it over with) rather than detention etc.

Carfield Secondary School disappeared many years ago when the old buildings were replaced by modern premises and facilities with a new school name and in a different location of Sheffield. However, my above six paragraphs probably give the impression that the "old Carfield" was a miserable and foreboding institution. This was never my feeling. I got on well and respected most of the teachers and felt that I substantially extended my knowledge under their tutorage. I also made many friends and progressed my sporting abilities. I was, and still feel, proud to have been a pupil of the school.

In the summer of 1949, at the age of 15 years, my School Certificate results having become available and my departure date from Carfield imminent, I started to give urgent consideration to the next stage of my life. I had already made the decision that I would not seek to continue academic studies with the aim of university. I felt that my parents had supported me long enough and that I now needed to make at least some financial contribution.

In practice I believe that (at this time) only a small proportion of those obtaining School Certificate at both grammars and secondary schools (who were mainly children from working-class homes) had any desire to continue towards university. Grants were difficult to obtain and some financial support from family would usually be required for several years while aiming for a degree. Certainly, none of my friends or acquaintances went down this route. Furthermore, even in the professions there were only a smallish percentage of graduates. Most professional bodies preferred to see their members study for the relevant examinations, usually through correspondence courses and attendance at "crammers" during long periods of articled clerkship.

Nevertheless, I was very ambitious and had become even more focussed on my longer-term objectives since reading an article recommending that in one's teens it was important to identify long-term ambitions and to keep these firmly in mind as the years progressed. I formulated my ambitions which could be broadly summarised as:

- Gain membership of and success in a respected profession.
- Serve with commissioned rank in one of the armed services. (I was aware that, at some stage, I would need to serve two years national service).
- See something of the world, including a period of working abroad.

I felt that I had some artistic abilities and that architecture or something similar might be a suitable profession if an opportunity could be found.

Unlike the present day, my school at that time had no careers advisors and neither my parents nor other relatives had much knowledge about architecture or any of the other professions. My father managed to arrange for me to have an interview at an architect's office, but the interviewer was most uninspiring. I also had an interview at the personnel department of a Sheffield steelworks, but the thrust of the discussion was towards apprenticeships in areas such as pattern making or for joining the drawing office with a view to becoming a mechanical engineer in due course. None of these seemed very attractive to me.

At this stage and out of the blue, I was summoned to see Mr C.V. Kay, the headmaster. He said that he had been contacted by a Sheffield firm of accountants (Carnall Slater & Co.) which had a vacancy for a student to whom, if suitable, they would grant five-year articles to train and qualify as an accountant. They would be prepared to pay a small but progressive salary over the five years and would not require the premium, which (at the time) most firms demanded for accountancy articles (usually between one hundred and two hundred guineas). However, the person would be required to accept normal office hours, conditions and holidays and would not receive any special concessions such as leave for study or attendance at courses before examinations, etc., which were customary for premium paying students. The headmaster explained that about two years earlier the firm had taken a Carfield student (named Alan Hall) on similar terms and the arrangement was working satisfactorily, hence this further request.

Neither I nor my father had much idea about the role and duties of chartered accountants. However, the opportunity seemed a good one. Furthermore, the five-year articles (training contract) would mean that I could obtain deferment from national service for that period and hopefully, therefore, obtain my qualification without interruption. I grasped the opportunity for an interview and when the offer was confirmed, I accepted with enthusiasm. Although still aged only 15, my adult career had commenced.

III

From Schoolboy to Man

September 1949 to October 1955

St. James Row runs along the side of Sheffield Cathedral at the start (at least at the time) of the city's professional district, where most of the firms of accountants, lawyers and architects, etc., had their offices. Carnall Slater & Co (CS&Co), my new employers, were located at Number 11, an impressive address, but internally (and particularly in the general office, where I and most of the staff spent our time) it did not live up to the image portrayed. Dusty, poorly decorated, with ancient furniture and a dismal outlook over a grubby back yard, the general office was not what one might have expected. However, none of this was of concern to me, neither was it a deterrent to my objective of qualifying as a chartered accountant in the shortest possible time.

The staff of CS&Co comprised two partners (Cyril Carnall, the senior partner and Walter Wingfield, to whom I became articled), one other qualified accountant, an experienced but professionally unqualified office manager and four or five others. These included Alan Hall, the only other articled student and, as previously mentioned, also a former pupil of Carfield School. Alan and I got on well, although we had little in common in relation to our sporting and leisure interests.

Also on the staff (and the person I liked most of all) was Arthur Fox, who was about 23 years of age and studying for the qualification of the Association of Certified Accountants. Arthur had completed his two years national service in the Royal Air Force (serving in Singapore) before deciding to study accountancy. As he was my senior, I was sometimes allocated to assist Arthur on one or other of the firm's larger audits (we had only a few). This could involve several weeks at the premises of the companies concerned, with work becoming quite repetitive and sometimes tedious. On such occasions, we would take a break from our chores and with my encouragement, Arthur would talk about Singapore or more frequently opera, for which subject he had a passion. He would sometimes hum or even sing a snatch from the aria he was trying to describe to me. Arthur would also encourage me to listen to opera and see the films starring Mario Lanza, who was a massively popular tenor at the time. As a result of his influence I developed an interest in opera, which I retain to this day.

Having jumped at the opportunity to enter accountancy articles and commence studies (and even be paid a salary), I fully appreciated that I would not be granted the usual privileges available to premium paying students, such as study leave before examinations and time off for lectures and crammer courses (although, in examination years, I always kept back one week of my two weeks annual holiday for revision). However, in my ignorance and general naivety, I had not appreciated the high cost of correspondence courses (the main method of study for accountancy at that time) to cover the work required for the intermediate and final examinations. In addition, there was the expense of the numerous textbooks required. From memory, these included publications with such titles as *Book-Keeping and Accounts, Taxation, Company Law, Mercantile Law, Law of Trustees, Liquidation and Receivers, Cost Accounts and Economics* – in total an expensive collection.

I had always been close to my maternal grandparents (particularly my grandmother) and, without even being asked for financial help, they came forward and paid for the correspondence courses and textbooks. Needless to say, this generosity reinforced my determination to get down to studies and qualify as quickly as possible.

My initial salary at CS&Co was one pound and ten shillings per week (£1.50 in current money) or £78 per annum. Taking into account inflation since 1949, this is equivalent to about £2,600 in 2017 values. In all the circumstances, I was not unhappy with this low level of remuneration, although it was much less than most of my friends were being paid serving their various trade apprenticeships.

Out of my weekly salary, I gave my mother 10 shillings for board. I felt quite proud to be making this contribution towards my upkeep, although I suspect that the benefits from living at home substantially exceeded the sum. I kept the remaining one pound of my salary to cover tramcar and bus fares, clothing and for general spending money.

Because of my lifestyle, the financial needs in the first couple of years of my working life were quite modest. My normal routine was to study on Monday, Tuesday, Thursday and Friday evenings. Football training was held on Wednesday evening and on Saturday and Sunday nights I would meet with my friends.

Saturday morning until 12.30pm was part of the normal CS&Co working week. On Saturday afternoons I played football (or, in the summer, cricket – one of my grandmother's classic comments was "Keep away from that hard ball"). Therefore, I would usually take my sports kit to the office and go straight to the match venue on leaving.

Despite my low salary, I have no recollection of feeling hard up during these first couple of years of working life. I did attempt to make financial economies but maybe these were more of an inclination to challenge things rather than a matter of financial necessity.

Office dress at CS&Co required a dark suit (which I purchased from one of the multi tailors), white shirt with double cuffs and worn with detachable semi-stiff collar (I purchased three of each) and black shoes. With only three shirts and collars, my mother needed to be washing and ironing most days. However, I soon discovered that by turning the double cuffs inside out, a shirt could be worn for two days. Furthermore, packets of white paper collars (which looked like the real thing) could be purchased very cheaply at Woolworths – and needed to be worn only once and thrown away.

Another somewhat dubious economy, which I attempted for only a few weeks, was to go to my grandparents for lunch each day. This involved a 50-yard sprint up St. James Row in order to catch the Intake tramcar (which was due at the same time as I was allowed to leave the office). To miss this tram meant a wait of 15 minutes before the next one and left little time for lunch.

In those days, the boarding platform on tramcars was open with only a central pole to encourage passengers to enter either side. However, there was no door to prevent boarding or alighting when the vehicle was moving.

One day, as I concluded my sprint, the tram was on time and had already set off. Undeterred, I leapt for the platform, but it was only in mid-air that I realised that I would land with one foot either side of the central pole, which duly hit me between the eyes and left me sitting in the road with the tram speeding away. With many spectators witnessing the incident, my embarrassment was more painful than the lump on my forehead.

By the time I had reached the halfway point in my articles, several things had changed. I had taken and been successful in the intermediate examination, gained two and a half years' experience in dealing with the affairs of clients, and generally matured from the 15-year-old schoolboy who had originally joined CS&Co. Although in 1951 the voting age was still 21 years, at least at 18, I was old enough to visit a public house where alcoholic drinks were sold. Finding ways to meet girls was also becoming important, with attendance at dance halls presenting the best opportunities.

Playing football on a Saturday afternoon remained important to me and for most of my friends. However, as we played for different teams, with the games at a variety of venues around South Yorkshire, our meeting arrangements for Saturday evenings needed to be flexible. In Sheffield there was a good choice of dance halls, but our favourite (and thus most frequently attended) was located at the Sheffield City Hall, where Bernard Taylor's orchestra was resident. Our usual routine would be to meet at the Sportsman public house, situated only a few minutes' walk from the dance hall, for which we would have needed to queue and obtain tickets in advance.

I believe that Bryan Hancock was friendly with the landlord at the Sportsman and through this we had the privilege of going under a hinged counter into a sort of "speakeasy" behind the bar. This area of the pub was not obvious to the general public, although there were sometimes other regulars in there. It was an excellent and cosy meeting place where we tended to remain drinking for too long before departing to the dance hall to find that most of the attractive girls had been spoken for.

In the 1950s, one would not think of going to a dance unless wearing a suit, soft collared shirt and tie (usually tied in a Windsor knot). Suits were looser fitting (semi-drape) with jackets rather longer than today – although admittedly, there were some exhibitionists, who would wear full drape suits with jackets down to the knees. My office attire was definitely not suitable for Saturday nights out with the hope of attracting girls, but with my meagre remuneration, I could not see how to remedy this. Out of the blue, my grandmother sent me a cash gift – partly, I think, for my birthday, but also because I had passed the intermediate exam. I cannot remember the exact amount, which might have been intended for new textbooks, but I felt that I had greater needs at the time! There was enough cash for me to visit Neville Reed, one of the best and most trendy tailors in Sheffield, to be measured for a semi-drape suit in hopsack and dark brown in colour. Dance hall, here I come.

Having recommenced studies for the final accountancy exams, I found that some of my textbooks were indeed becoming out of date. (Maybe Grannie's money should have been spent in a different way!) The correspondence college was also recommending supplementary reading of books that I did not possess. Therefore, I started spending one (or sometimes two) of my weekly study evenings at the Sheffield Central Library, where the necessary literature was available. On these visits, I became acquainted with several other accountancy students, who used the library for similar reasons as myself. However, on occasions, and particularly when we were at the same stage on our study courses, there was competition for the relevant books, and it became a challenge to be first to arrive at the library.

About this time, CS&Co, in a rare act of generosity, decided that our working hours should be reduced and that we would be required to work only alternate Saturday mornings. However, in partial compensation for this, weekday hours were extended by 15 minutes each day. Of course, this change damaged my chances of winning the race to the library on the relevant evenings.

After one or two wasted visits, I adopted a strategy of calling at the library during my lunch break and moving the books I would require in the evening into the wrong sections. This gave me a good chance of being first to "find" these books even when the other students had arrived before me. I adopted this approach with success for several months and without it ever being challenged.

While the Central Library was excellent in most ways, there was one distraction to studying which is worth mentioning. Located in a classical building close to the city centre, the library enjoyed good natural light from its large windows, a high section of which could be opened or closed only by the use of a long pole with a hooked end. The responsibility for closing these windows in the evening, about 15 or 20 minutes or so before the library itself closed, appeared to rest with two young, pretty and leggy librarians. Shortish skirts were in vogue at the time and the window closure operation involved a certain amount of leaning and upward stretching to correctly manipulate the poles. One sensed an air of expectancy amongst the predominantly male student congregation as "window closing time" approached. Concentration on studies became difficult during this period and we might just as well have given up and gone home early – but no one ever did!

Until my mid-teens, my normal holidays would be two weeks camping with the Boy Scouts and a week away with my parents. However, this changed from the age of about 16 onwards, when I started to holiday with a group of friends. The make-up of the group would vary – these were the days of national service, and because of studies and deferments amongst other things, not everyone would be available at the same time. However, one of the group by the name of Ted Mahon and I had become good friends and always tried to ensure that we could attend the same holiday.

Very few affordable overseas holidays were available in these days and our venues must seem mundane by present-day standards – Douglas (Isle of Man), Butlins Holiday Camp (Filey), Blackpool – an excellent young people's resort at the time where Ted Heath's band were resident at the Winter Gardens and included Dickie Valentine and Lita Rosa, two of Britain's most popular vocalists.

It was at Butlins that Ted Mahon and I became friendly with two girls from Newcastle – Maureen and Marion. On a Saturday evening, a few weeks after returning home, we were dressed in our "finery" queuing for tickets at the City Hall Ballroom when we became aware of a commotion in the crowd behind (where we were known to several people), there was laughter, and I heard the comment "They are up there in front". To our amazement, the two M's from Newcastle had hitchhiked to Sheffield in order to pay us a visit. Wearing jeans, walking boots and complete with rucksacks, they were hardly dressed for the City Hall Ballroom. Somewhat red-faced and to the accompaniment of more laughter, Ted and I exited from the queue. My recollection is that we adjourned to a coffee bar and talked with the girls all evening before eventually escorting them to the YWCA, where they had arranged to spend the night. We never saw the girls again, but the incident gave rise to some subsequent leg-pulling.

For the next two years, life continued much as before – studying, meeting my friends at the weekend and playing football on Saturdays. As regards the latter, there was an age restriction for the league in which I had been playing and I needed to find a new club. I had a brief spell with Sheffield FC, which I mention only because it is the oldest football club in the world, established in 1857. However, I never made the 1st XI and recognised that I would be unlikely to do so. Therefore, I settled on playing for Sheffield YMCA, where I greatly enjoyed the camaraderie and was happy to remain until called up for national service.

One Saturday evening in early 1954, I arrived at the Sportsman pub to find that, in addition to my gathering of friends, there was a party of young women in our usual meeting area. It transpired that this was a birthday celebration and one of those present was my second cousin, Sylvia Wilton, whom I had not seen for some time. Shortly afterwards, the party of girls departed, apparently for the City Hall dance, and, as she was leaving, Sylvia came over to say hello. She also introduced me to one of the girls called Kathleen Morton (Kath).

Later my friends and I also returned to the ballroom and I had a dance with Kath. Dancing ended at 11.30pm. (In these days, all such events had to finish before midnight and the start of the Sabbath!) I found that Kath and I were walking towards the same tramcar terminal, although our intended destinations could not have been farther apart. Kath lived at Shiregreen, about three miles north of the city centre, while my home at Base Green was about four miles to the south.

Before departing on tramcars in opposite directions, I asked Kath if she would like to join me at the cinema the following evening. She said she felt that would not be appropriate, as she was engaged to a boy who was away completing national service. Kath explained that she did not normally go out in the evenings but had made an exception on this occasion because it was the birthday celebrations of one of her best friends.

I said that it was only a visit to the cinema that I was proposing and, just in case she changed her mind, I would be in Fitzaland Square 30 minutes before the start of the performance and would wait for 15 minutes before going to join some of my friends, who I believed intended to see the film.

Fitzaland Square is a popular meeting place, and the next evening I was one of several young men standing around. After a few minutes, another young man arrived and moved from one to another of those waiting. He seemed to say a few words before being dismissed with a curt reply or a shake of the head. Eventually, he approached me and, before he even had chance to speak, I said, "Push off." However, he stood his ground and said, "Is your name Barrie?" When I nodded, he continued, "Kath asked me to find you. She has missed her tram and will be late." Somewhat embarrassed by my previous curtness, I said, "Thank you."

Kath arrived about 15 minutes later and, as this was the start of our relationship of almost 50 years, I think it is appropriate for me to relate the events which preceded her arrival in accordance with my understanding.

On the day following our meeting, Kath made the decision to break off her engagement. With no way of contacting her fiancé, she visited his sister (a good friend of Kath's) to explain. This difficult task done, Kath felt able to accept my invitation to meet for the cinema later that day. However, in course of the walk of several minutes from home to tram stop, Kath realised that she had forgotten her house key. As her parents were going on an evening excursion to Blackpool to see the illuminations (a popular outing at this time) and would not be back until the early hours, Kath turned round and headed back home to try and arrive before her parents departed.

On the way back, Kath met the young man who lived next door (I cannot remember his name). He was heading for the stop to catch the tramcar which Kath had intended to be on but would now miss because of her return home. Kath asked him to "find Barrie" on arrival in town and explain that she would be late. He must have had a soft spot for Kath to accept this assignment.

Kath's efforts to collect her key were in vain – her parents had already left. Therefore, she caught the next tramcar and came to meet me, still without a key. We attended the cinema as planned and afterwards I escorted Kath home. My first task on arrival was to smash a window in the front door in order to gain access to the Yale lock. A week or so later, my introduction on meeting Kath's parents was: "This is Barrie, the boy who smashed the window in our front door." Not an auspicious start!

I qualified as an accountant on 27 July 1955, having passed Final Examinations Part I and II in November 1953 and May 1955, respectively. As my five years of articled service had also been completed, the next step was to await call-up for two years' national service in the Royal Air Force. While I may not have volunteered for military service, I was quite looking forward to the experience – although my grandmother was worried that, going into the armed forces, I might have to wear "those heavy boots"!

At this time, my remuneration at CS&Co had increased to the princely sum of three pounds and ten shillings per week (£3.50 in present currency) and I went to see Cyril Carnall, the senior partner, to enquire how much I would be paid now that I had qualified. Never the most generous of employers, his response was that as I would be called up in the next few weeks, he could see no justification for any change in my status or remuneration.

At lunchtime I visited Sheffield Midland Railway Station where I had noticed an advertisement for porters. I was offered a job at six pounds, nineteen shillings and six pence per week. I returned to the office and informed Mr Carnall that I would be giving one week's notice. My salary was immediately increased to £7 per week. I took the easy course and stayed at CS&Co until call-up, but sometimes think it might have been fun to be a porter for a couple of months.

Although Cyril Carnall may not have noticed any difference in my abilities or demeanour, I was surprised at the increase in confidence and change in attitude following qualification. In the 1950s and 60s, a "professional man" was expected to observe high standards of behaviour towards his fellow professionals, his clients and the business community in general. For example, advertising was not permitted in any form and many present approaches to "practice development" would have incurred disciplinary action by the Institute. Basically, it was expected that a professional person or firm would develop a reputation through "word of mouth" resulting from their ethics and the high quality of service they provided. I felt happy to embrace such standards and confident that I could flourish in this environment.

In the weeks following completion of studies, and while awaiting call-up for national service, I found that for the first time since leaving school, I had a great amount of leisure time available. Kath and I started to see each other more frequently, although (as we resided at opposite sides of Sheffield) the travel from my home to Kath's (or vice versa) involved journeys by both bus and tramcar, taking in total about one hour each way. We, therefore, tended to meet only at weekends and probably on one evening during the week.

As I became more acquainted with Kath's family, I discovered that the two people she called Dad and Mum (Edward and Evelin Morton) were, in fact, her uncle and aunt, who had a daughter of their own (Glenis), a couple of years younger than Kath. Kath's birth mother (Francis Eva) had died in her mid-twenties and her father (John Ernest, brother of Edward) in his early thirties. Although not formally adopted, Kath had been brought up by Edward and Evelin from an early age following her mother's death. However, she remembered her mother and, of course, had continued to see father "Daddy John" for several years until his death.

Edward had recognised my second name at the time of our first meeting and enquired if my father was called Jack. It transpired that both he (for a short period) and brother John had worked at the Nunnery Colliery and John had sustained a broken leg in the "Paddy Mail Accident" to which I have previously referred. According to Edward, my father was one of the rescue team which brought John to the surface. Whether or not this was correct, I am not sure. It is true that my father returned underground with the rescue parties, but in the difficult conditions and mayhem which existed, he told me that he could not remember which of his workmates he had helped to bring out of the mine. Of course, he was only a boy of about 16 years and a relative newcomer, still finding his way in his first employment. However, to Kath and me, it seemed an incredible coincidence that, in a city with a population of over half a million, the paths of our fathers had previously crossed in such a dramatic way.

Much of Europe (including areas of the United Kingdom) and other parts of the world had been devastated in the Second World War. Furthermore, in Britain, the rationing of food and clothing continued for some years after hostilities and currency restrictions existed, which limited the amount of money one could take out of the country to quite small sums. Against this background, overseas holidays and travel, now such normal events for many families, developed only slowly. My first trip outside the UK had been the Scout camp in Southern Ireland to which I have previously referred. In autumn 1955, while awaiting call-up for national service, I made my second overseas trip – a couple of days in Brussels as a member of the Sheffield YMCA Soccer XI, which had arranged to play a goodwill match against a team of British residents.

Why this event had been arranged, I cannot recollect, but at the time, the prospect of crossing the channel and then travelling through France was very exciting. The game took place on the day following our arrival and we had attracted quite a crowd of spectators. The residents' team, having won the toss, chose to kick-off and their centre forward passed the ball to his inside-left (positions which existed in those days). Enthusiastic as always, I streaked across the few yards of centre circle and flattened the inside-left before he could move the ball onwards. This action incurred the wrath of the referee, a booking for foul play and boos from the spectators before anyone else in my team had even touched the ball – not a good start. I felt badly done to but think I had forgotten that this was a goodwill match and not one of my accustomed games against a Sheffield steelworks team or South Yorkshire colliery side.

Our British resident hosts had arranged that, in the evening, we would meet for dinner and entertainment in a Brussels night club. I had never been in a night club and regarded the prospect with interest. However, as I wished to see something of the city, I said that I would join the party a little later. In due course I arrived, feeling quite dashing in my new blazer (complete with YMCA badge), light grey trousers and club tie. To my embarrassment, the doorman refused me entry to the club in the belief that I was a schoolboy! His English and my French were equally bad, and it took a period of argument and gesticulation before he agreed to summons one of our party to vouch for me. The incident provided a source of amusement to my teammates and an opportunity for ribbing. Two embarrassments in one day. I was quite pleased to return to England.

Call-up for national service came a few weeks later, starting with a few days at a reception centre in the Midlands where we were lectured to, subjected to various medical tests, provided with boots and an ill-fitting battle dress uniform and given a short back and sides haircut. Eventually, all recruits were posted to one or other of the basic training centres. In my case, this was Royal Air Force, Wilmslow, in Cheshire. My RAF career had commenced.

IV

The Royal Air Force

November 1955 to October 1957
A: Initial Training

As one of about 50 national service conscripts, I arrived by train at Wilmslow Railway Station in early November 1955. We had previously spent two days at a reception centre where we had been kitted out, medically examined and relieved of much of our hair! Our destination now was Royal Air Force, Wilmslow, one of several basic training centres spread around the UK. We were met at the railway station by three drill instructors (DIs), a sergeant and two large and aggressive corporals. After much shouting and abuse, the corporals managed to herd our party into a fairly orderly squad and, after a roll call, we marched (maybe shambled would be a more accurate description) to the Training Centre.

This was the start of two years with the RAF, my chosen service, motto Per Adua Ad Astra – Through Adversity to the Stars. At this stage, I felt that the stars were a very great distance away.

Wilmslow is now a desirable and expensive residential area, particularly attractive to business people and professionals (including some Premier League footballers) operating in Manchester. Presumably, this also applied in 1955, but during our 12 weeks training we were allowed out for only one 24-hour pass midway through the course and (I think) a couple of days at Christmas. There was little opportunity for sightseeing.

Our accommodation was in wooden huts, heated by a single coal-burning stove and providing living space for about 24 recruits. There were, of course, several "flights" at different stages of the training process and a recruit from the most advanced had been instructed to be available at our billet on arrival in order to "explain the ropes". The routine was that we would rise about 6.30am, shave and shower (the water was usually tepid) in the ablutions block, breakfast in the recruits mess and be standing by our beds, wearing the appropriate dress for the first exercise of the day, for inspection by one of the DIs at 7.30am. An added requirement for this inspection was that our blanket and sheets had to be folded into neat squares and placed on top of the bed to form a base for laying out plate, mug and highly polished knife, fork and spoon.

However, it was not just our personal smartness and equipment which was subject to inspection, the billet as a whole had to be immaculate. The floor, which already shone like glass on arrival, had to be polished daily and was protected at all times by recruits removing their boots before entering the billet. We skated around on felt pads, which were kept in neat piles inside the entrance. Any failure in standards (real or imagined by the DIs) would incur punishment in the form of extra duties for the individual concerned or the group as a whole. My rather cynical view was that, if there were chores which needed to be done, some failure in standards would be found.

Of course, we were subjected to a further inspection, often by a different DI, whenever parading for drill. We slept with our trousers under the mattress in order to maintain a sharp crease. Many hours were spent in the evenings pouring molten polish on the toe caps of our "grain leather" boots and rubbing with a knife handle in order to produce the smooth, shiny surface demanded by the DIs.

For weapons training, which often involved kneeling or lying on the ground, denims were worn. We found that the specialist instructors were less finicky than the DIs and we would hurry first to the barracks and exchange trousers for pyjama bottoms, which were not readily visible under the denims.

As regards the training itself, a good deal of time was devoted to drill at which we became very proficient. Weapons training (rifle and Bren guns) on the firing range was fun, but stripping-down, cleaning and reassembling weapons with cold hands, as we moved more deeply into winter, was not enjoyable.

There were physical training sessions, an obstacle course to be completed and occasional lectures. There were also vaccinations and inoculations to be suffered, which always seemed to be followed by rifle drill when our arms were still sore and aching.

A surprise to me was that, although we had all been passed as fit, not everyone was capable of completing the training. An example was George, a pleasant enough lad from our billet. The first problem was that he seemed to lack normal coordination and when attempting to march had difficulty in moving his leg forward as his arm swung backwards (and vice versa) on the same side of his body. George's efforts on the obstacle course ended in disaster when he fell from a makeshift rope bridge into the water hazard below. However, I think it was when he was ordered to cease fire on the range and swung round with weapon pointing upwards (causing us to dive for cover) that it was decided he was not destined to be a "fighting man" (or, in any event, not on our side) and that he should be "reflighted" and considered for discharge.

I always felt sorry for recruits such as George when they were rejected. This was often after weeks of training and sometimes having suffered a good deal of ridicule.

One of my ambitions as a schoolboy growing up in wartime had been to obtain a commission in the RAF but, having been conscripted into my preferred service, I had no idea how to progress this objective. Fortunately, the RAF procedures solved this for me – recruits with appropriate educational and professional qualifications had been identified for consideration as Potential Officer Material (POMs). Consequently, during basic training, I was summoned for several interviews, starting with the flight commander and steadily moving up the chain of command to seeing the station commander shortly before completion of the course.

Being periodically called away from such "important" activities as drill practice did not endear me to the DIs, but this was a minor concern and I was delighted on my final interview to be informed that I would attend a four-day Officer Selection Panel at RAF Uxbridge.

On arrival at Uxbridge, I found that I was one of a group of eight candidates who were to be reviewed by three invigilating officers – a squadron leader and two flight lieutenants. In what was presumably an attempt for candidates to be considered on equal terms, we were issued with denims to be worn without names or indications of rank and with only an alphabetic letter on our backs for identification. However, strangely, we continued to wear our own berets and cap badges which, together with our different ages, in my view, did much to nullify the attempted anonymity.

Three of the candidates were of quite mature years and in two cases wore warrant officer cap badges (the highest non-commissioned rank). It seemed likely to me that these three were senior NCO's seeking branch commissions as they approached the end of their service in order to obtain the better pension rights which applied to officers. In contrast, two young men already wore officer cap badges and I suspected would hold commissions in University Air Squadrons. They were probably hoping to move into officer training without the need to go through basic training. The remaining three candidates (which included me) were probably AC2's (aircraftmen second class – the lowest of the low) direct from basic training centres. I felt happier having completed this analysis, although I have no idea whether we were regarded as being in competition with each other or could all qualify for OCTU.

The selection process was a mixture of internal sessions and external challenges. One or more of the invigilating officers would always be present to observe or take part. Many of the internal sessions involved candidates being asked to respond to questions as to how they would act in various hypothetical situations (sixty-plus years later, I can still remember most of the questions asked). It soon appeared clear to me that there were no right or wrong answers to the questions so that, whatever reply was given, it could be challenged. The aim appeared to be to see how well candidates stood up to the challenges.

On the whole, I found the selection process enjoyable. Nevertheless, I was relieved soon after returning to Wilmslow to be informed that I had been successful and would be going to the Officer Cadet Training Unit (OCTU) at Jurby, Isle of Man, on a twelve-week training course. My pleasure was diminished to some extent when told that there was a "bottleneck" at OCTU and that I may have to remain in transit flight at Wilmslow for some weeks. However, after only a couple of days, instructions were received for me to report to Training Group Headquarters in Shropshire. No reason for this was given.

I arrived at Group HQ with some trepidation and, still in recruit mode, stood to attention when reporting to the sergeant at reception. This seemed to amuse him, and I realised that life on a normal station (even an HQ) might be more relaxed. I was shown to a two-bedded room, which I was informed would be my billet while at Group HQ to be shared with another person still to arrive! This turned out to be Tony Hodgetts, another Yorkshireman, who had also recently completed basic training but at a different centre to myself. On exchanging details, I found that Tony had qualified as an accountant and had been called up on similar timing to myself – the plot thickened.

In due course, Tony and I were summoned to report to the office of a squadron leader (SL). I feel embarrassed not to be able to recollect the SL's name, but he was friendly and wore pilot's wings and several medal ribbons. I sensed that sitting behind a desk at Group HQ may not have been his chosen posting. The SL told us that one of his responsibilities was the coordination of postings to OCTU, in which role he had details of the education and qualifications of all candidates. He had sent for Tony and me because we were accountants.

The SL continued by explaining that, in common with most officers in administrative roles, he had also been given several extraneous duties. One of these was to form and chair a board to audit and report upon the non-public funds at the station – namely the officers and sergeants mess accounts. This was not a task he relished. His approach, therefore, was to do a deal with Tony and myself – we would carry out the audits and prepare reports for his signature. In return, we would be placed at the top of the list for posting to OCTU.

Obviously, we jumped at the opportunity and completed the work over the next week. We were given a 36-hour pass and, on returning to our basic training stations on Monday of the following week, posting notices to OCTU were awaiting us.

IV

The Royal Air Force (continued)

B: Officer Cadet Training

Before travelling to Jurby (at which station the RAF OCTU and Airfield were based) in February 1956, I had visited the Isle of Man (IOM) on only one occasion. This was for a holiday with a group of friends, when we had stayed in a small private hotel on the promenade in Douglas (the largest town on the island) quite close to the cafés, bars and entertainments and well served for transport by the famous open-sided horse-drawn tram cars.

On that occasion, I recollect that one member of our party (Bernard Gaffney, one of my former school chums) had unintentionally provided us with some amusement when, although accustomed to exiting Sheffield tramcars when still in motion in order to save time, he came a cropper by attempting to drop off the much slower and sedate Douglas vehicle (as it was passing our hotel) on the wrong side and with the wrong foot! The result had been a spectacular tumble, ripped trousers and much loss of dignity.

My visit to the IOM this time was much more important to me than a mere holiday. I was determined to obtain my RAF commission.

Although Jurby (in the north-west of the island) is only 20 miles or so from Douglas, it is separated by high ground in the centre in which Snaefell, at 2,034ft, stands majestically. Therefore, our transport to OCTU travelled first up the east coast, passing Laxey (with its famous wheel) and Ramsey, before forking left. Thereafter, civilisation became much sparser with only small villages and occasional farms to be seen as we approached the RAF station.

On arrival I found that I was to be part of Officer Initial Training Course, Flight No 50/1 Red, for which Sqn Ldr C.E. Bulport was responsible assisted by Flight Lieutenants F.S. Lacey and N.J. Tull, not forgetting Warrant Officer J. Webb (of whom, more comment later). The flight totalled 50 cadets, with a mixture of senior non-commissioned officers (NCO's) seeking branch commissions, student officers from the University Air Squadrons and new recruits (such as myself) selected while at Initial Training Centres. However, despite the different ages and backgrounds, a good camaraderie was soon established.

In the beds around my space in the billet were two NCO cadets – Pete Forrester (who could always keep everyone amused) and Tom Gray; two student officers – "Jock" Gray, a recently qualified dentist, and Denzil De Villiers (Brother of Desmond De Villiers, famous as the chief test pilot for English Electric Company at the time); and three cadets from Initial Training Units – myself, "Rock" Glover (a good athlete and soccer player) and Hugh Davies (just 18 and one of the youngest on the course).

One evening as Peter Forrester was happily cleaning his boots and (for no reason I can think of) humming the 'Eton Boating Song', young Davies piped up with the information that the author, Sir Henry Newbolt, had not even attended Eton but was a pupil at Charterhouse (which Hugh had attended) and was the author of their school song –'The Finest School of All'. "Really," said Pete. "Could you sing it for us?" After two verses of Hugh's tuneless rendering, we could not contain our mirth any longer and burst into uncontrollable laughter. Thereafter, and to Hugh's chagrin, we adopted 'The Finest School of All' as our marching song as we travelled between lectures.

Although some aspects of training were similar to those I had previously experienced, the atmosphere at OCTU was very different, with greater freedom of action but much more responsibility placed upon individuals. Our training programme was clearly set out, but a duty cadet was designated each day with the chore of ensuring that the flight arrived in an orderly manner, complete in number, appropriately kitted and dressed and on a timely basis for whichever exercise or lecture was scheduled.

However, apart from the daily routine, there were several one-off events which took place outside the station, including overnight manoeuvres and a three-day camp under canvas at a north-westerly point on the island. Cadets would be nominated to lead on these events and be responsible for delegating tasks as necessary to others in the team to ensure that everything ran efficiently.

My first experience of the above was in leading a group of about 20 cadets, when we were transported in a covered vehicle into the hilly and relatively remote central area of the island and deposited with no knowledge of our exact whereabouts. I was given a compass, map and reference point with the time for meeting a field kitchen, which would provide us with a meal. Having eventually fathomed our position, I decided that a straight-line route across fields, heath and scrubland was appropriate in the limited time available. All went well until a "small stream" shown on the map proved to be a shallow river. We eventually found a reasonable crossing point, but two of the party (senior NCO cadets) were reluctant to continue on the proposed route and "get their feet wet". I decided that we should stick to the plan. Although conscious that if I arrived with a party short of two men it would be bad for my record, I felt that failure to keep up with the group would not be good for the two concerned. My gamble paid off, we regrouped, and the complete party arrived for lunch on time.

While our supervising officers did not accompany us on these external exercises, they were never too far away and would monitor and observe our performance, whether engaged on special challenges or routine activities, with a view to assessing the extent to which each cadet demonstrated their officer qualities (OQs). From time to time (and particularly in the earlier stages of the training course), a candidate would be deemed to lack the necessary requirements and would leave the course to be "reflighted". Sadly, for those concerned, this ended their officer training and, effectively, any prospect of obtaining a commission.

Although always conscious of the above danger, I found most activities both outdoor or in the lecture room, to be interesting, enjoyable and often a source of humour. The three-day camp reminded me of my Boy Scout days and was my favourite occasion, despite taking place in cold and inclement weather. Sixty years on I cannot remember my specific duties but recollect that one of our number by the name of Blurton was allocated the unfortunate responsibility for digging and maintaining the latrines. He was promptly christened "Bogs Blurton". This nickname (but fortunately not the odour which resulted from carrying out the task) remained with him for the remainder of the course.

Of the more traditional activities, weapons training was provided on the firing range by specialist NCO instructors but, instead of use of Bren guns and rifles (as at recruit training), this was for Sten guns (the officers' personal weapon), of which more than four million had been produced in World War II at a price of only about $10 each. I was amazed at the simplicity of this cheap but very effective short-range weapon, which had been contrived in the desperate days following the debacle of Dunkirk and the massive loss of small arms.

Drill was carried out under the eagle eye of Warrant Officer Webb, who had introduced himself with the words: "While you are here, gentlemen, I will call you sir – and you will call me sir. The difference is that you will mean it." In practice, I found that he usually addressed cadets as mister or master followed by their second name. I suspect that this was to demonstrate, for good or bad, that he was aware of the identity of the person he was speaking to. However, on occasions it also provided him with the opportunity to display his rather caustic wit. For example, Student Officer M R Bates was always referred to as "master-bates", with use of the long "a"!

Although we were free to leave the station in off-duty periods, the demanding training programme and related activities, coupled with a lack of local facilities, effectively precluded this. However, halfway through our course, we were granted a 48-hour pass which, in normal circumstances, would have made it possible for most cadets to visit home. Unfortunately, on the weekend in question, there was a labour dispute involving employees of the ferries which served the island, resulting in cancellations and delays. We were warned that any failure to return on time would be treated as absence without leave (AWOL) with the danger of being "charged" and reflighted. Therefore, except for a handful of cadets who for various reasons could guarantee their return, no one took the risk of leaving the island.

However, a group of us decided that a short break from the training routines and station environment was desirable. Therefore, we clubbed together and hired a minibus with a driver to transport us to (and, in due course, return from) Douglas. Of course, as national service cadets, we were not, by necessity big spenders. My pay as a recruit (after deductions) had been four pence (old money) per day, which, taking into account inflation, is only equivalent to about £160 per annum in present-day money. I think I might have received a small increase in pay when becoming an officer cadet and, of course, there was little need, or opportunity, to spend when on the station. Therefore, at least the small daily sums we received were allowed to accumulate over a period.

Having gathered together our meagre financial resources and made enquiries of more experienced "residents" at the station, we decided that the Saturday evening dance at the Majestic Hotel (referred to by some of the more knowledgeable cadets as "The Magic Stick") was a suitable venue. This hotel was available to cadets but off-limits to other ranks which, according to our advisers, meant that "a better class of talent was likely to be present"!

My experience of dance halls had mainly been in Sheffield where, on a Saturday night, the venues were usually very crowded. The challenge had been to take up a position in the proximity of the girl you hoped to dance with (but had been too embarrassed to ask in advance), so that you had the chance to make your request immediately the music commenced. Of course, there would usually be someone with a similar intent who would be quicker on the draw, by which time your second choice would also have been snapped up.

I found "The Magic Stick" to be much more civilised than my accustomed venues in South Yorkshire. The smallish dance floor was surrounded by tables where snacks and drinks could be served. Each table had a light with a number, which was illuminated, and a telephone. The phone could be used to contact the occupants of other tables. Therefore, one could request the pleasure of a dance without any need for jockeying of position. Rejection of a request was also much less embarrassing.

Our brief escape from routine was soon forgotten and we steadily moved through the next few weeks into the final stages of training. However, despite the hectic schedule, time was always made available for sport, and the main event of interest, in which teams from each of the flights going through training and also several of the resident sections on the station took part, was a knock-out football competition.

I was pleased to be the regular choice at full-back (I suppose that these days it would be called wing-back) for 50/1 Red Flight, in which team we had several very useful players. Consequently, we moved steadily through the rounds to qualify for the final, which was to be played a couple of weeks before conclusion of our course.

At about this time I was summoned to see Flight Lieutenant Tull, who informed me that at a recent meeting of the three supervising officers (which had been held to review the progress of all cadets in the flight) it had emerged that, despite my performance in lectures and on exercises being satisfactory, none of the officers felt that they knew me. Therefore, in these final few weeks, he advised that I needed to take steps to show more of my character and leadership qualities. In this connection, I was informed that I was one of three cadets who were under consideration to lead a challenging overnight exercise to be held in about one week's time.

I felt that the above information was bad news, although in fairness to the supervising officers, it was not entirely a surprise to me. In the early days of the course, I had seen several cadets push themselves forward to assume or volunteer for responsibilities for which they were not suited or capable of carrying out. The result in some cases had been failure, reflighting and removal from the course. Therefore, I had decided to carry out all tasks given to me to the best of my abilities, but to volunteer for nothing and generally keep my head down. This approach appeared to have been successful up to this point, but it was probably of credit to the supervising officers that they had detected a need for me to demonstrate more OQs than I had shown.

Although disappointed about the interview, my immediate concern was the football knock-out final, which took place two days later. As the day's training activities for all flights had ended before the start of the game, there was a substantial crowd of cadets, their supervising officers and NCOs, and also several off-duty airmen from various resident units on the station. To our great surprise, also present in the latter stages of the game was the station commanding officer (the CO), a football enthusiast and strong supporter of the Station XI, which headed the IOM football league.

As the game progressed it was clear that it would be a close contest, but about midway through the first half, I dipped my head to a lowish ball, only to be kicked by an opponent above the right eye. This resulted in quite a bad cut with lots of blood, and my departure to the station Medical Centre for several stitches. It was well into the second half when I returned as a spectator (but still wearing my bloodstained strip), with a large dressing over the stitches and a rapidly developing black eye and swollen nose.

There had been no score in the game but my team of 10 men (substitutes were not allowed in these days) were clearly tiring. After a short time, I could not bear being a spectator any longer and I waved to the referee and obtained permission to return to the fray. As we neared 90 minutes and the prospect of extra time, I had the opportunity to make a run forward, which I finished by making a cross intended for the opposite wing. I was delighted when through a slight miss-kick (I think no one except myself was aware that it was an intended cross and not a shot at goal) the ball flew into the top corner of our opponent's net. The game had ended, and we had won the trophy by one goal to nil.

Next day as we marched around the station in accordance with our programme of activities, I was still wearing the dressing above my eye, which was turning ever darker. Everyone appeared to recognise me, and I received several waves and congratulations. Later that day at drill, even Warrant Officer Webb muttered a few kind words! However, I heard nothing from Flight Lieutenant

Tull, either in connection with the match or, more importantly, the overnight exercise.

On the final evening at OCTU, we attended a dinner, together with our sister Flight No. 50/2 Red. By then we were all aware that we had received our commissions, although I believe that the certificates, signed by Her Majesty Queen Elizabeth II, came only later. It was a happy occasion, concluding with a few words from the CO and the reading out of the stations to which each of us had been posted. The RAF still had several overseas bases, and I would have been pleased for the opportunity to serve at one of these. However, I was more than satisfied with my posting to RAF Leconfield in East Yorkshire, a flying station, home of the Fighter Weapons School and reasonably accessible to Sheffield.

Our passing out parade was held the next day. I thought back to a few months earlier when I had felt proud to qualify as an accountant and take on the principles and responsibilities of being a professional man. This subsequently proved to be a most significant event in relation to my long-term career. However, as a boy brought up in WWII, when many of my heroes had been members of the RAF, to be commissioned into the service, even though only in a non-flying capacity, gave me great satisfaction and a pride which has remained throughout the years.

IV

The Royal Air Force (continued)

C: RAF Leconfield

In early May 1956, I reported to Squadron Leader J.B. Harrison, the senior accountant officer at Royal Air Force, Leconfield. Although I was not fully conscious of it at the time, the next 18 months would prove to be an important phase in my life.

I had been brought up in a working-class environment, with loving parents and kind and supportive relatives. In my school years, I had been fortunate to benefit from conscientious and dedicated teachers, while never lacking an abundance of friends and the opportunity for outdoor activities. At the age of 15 years, I had been granted access, without payment of the usual premium, to a path that would lead to a professional qualification at the age of 21. Finally, after six months of training, I had been awarded a commission in the Royal Air Force, with its responsibility for providing leadership and command (even if only in a modest way), but also with the opportunities for new social experiences, a widening of interests and personal development in several respects. I was well aware of and most grateful for my good fortune.

I liked Sqn Ldr Harrison immediately and felt sure that I would enjoy working for him as assistant accountant officer. The Sqn Ldr briefly explained my duties, which included responsibility for collection of rental income from officers married quarters, payment of certain claims and expenses and officiating at monthly pay parades, where the majority of airman below the rank of sergeant received their pay in cash.

After showing me my office, which was in Station Headquarters next to his, the Sqn Ldr took me through to the main accounts department to introduce me to our staff. The main role of the section was to maintain the loose-leaf records, which contained details of the pay and allowances of all the airmen on the station below the rank of sergeant. Heading the section was a flight sergeant (whose name I now forget but always referred to simply as "Flight"). Second in command was Corporal Jackson and the complement was made up by four senior aircraftsmen (SACs) – Jackson (younger brother of the corporal), Atkinson, Murgatroyd and Metcalf. Finally, we had one civil servant (Mr Linacre) whose role was dealing with local suppliers' contracts. They proved to be a conscientious and likeable team.

After the introductions, Corporal Jackson's first words to me were "Do you play football, sir?" I confirmed that I did, and he invited me to join a practice game of the station team after duties ended the following day. I duly attended and, before the end of the week, had been appointed captain of the station team, which included three members of the accounts section.

Sqn Ldr Harrison (due to retire in about one year's time) had been without an assistant accountant officer for some months and, consequently, unable to take his leave entitlement. Therefore, within a couple of weeks of my arrival, and feeling satisfied that I could manage without him, he departed on holiday. Before leaving, he explained as my first priority, the need to complete and submit to the appropriate Air Ministry department the requisition for monies to pay the month's wages to the airmen, which document needed to be counter-signed by Group Captain R. Deacon Elliott, the station commanding officer (the CO).

I prepared the requisition as soon as the necessary information was available and, through his adjutant, arranged to see the CO. His first comments were, "Who are you and where is Harrison?" My answer, while accurate, did not seem to please him and brought a further question, "How do I know this document is correct?" He appeared somewhat sceptical at my reply, which was to the effect that I was a qualified accountant and had checked the figures. However, with some apparent reluctance, he eventually signed.

My first meeting with the CO had not been enjoyable, but I wondered afterwards if there had been some previous incident of

Sqn Ldr Harrison wishing to take his overdue leave in the several weeks before my arrival, when he had been left without an assistant accountant officer.

A few days later I received the wages cheque, which would enable the cash to be collected from the local bank. For safekeeping, I placed the cheque in my office safe to await pay day. When that arrived, Corporal Jackson and SAC Metcalf, both carrying truncheons, came to my office and informed me that the staff car was waiting outside to transport us to the bank in Beverley and that airmen would already be assembling in two venues for receipt of their pay on our return.

It was only a few miles from Leconfield to this attractive and serene county town of the East Riding of Yorkshire, and it seemed rather incongruous on arrival for me to march into the bank carrying a large leather bag as receptacle for the wages cash, accompanied by one of my truncheon-bearing escorts, while the other remained outside apparently guarding the door! However, as I approached the counter, I broke into a cold sweat – I realised that I had forgotten the cheque, which was still in my office safe!

I asked to see the manager and introduced myself as Sqn Ldr Harrison's new assistant. I then explained my predicament and that, in particular, there would be several hundred airmen congregating in two hangars as we spoke, having been temporarily released from duty to collect their wages. In the circumstances, I asked if I could take the money and send Corporal Jackson back immediately with the public cheque.

The bank manager smiled, and I feared the worst. He commented that it was the first day of a meeting at Beverley Races and hoped that I would not be taking the cash there. We both laughed – although my laugh was rather forced. To my relief, he then instructed the counter clerk to load the cash (which had been prepared and ready for collection) into my bag. I was most grateful.

I wonder if these days (60-plus years on) a manager at a medium-sized branch (if there are any such managers remaining) would have the authority or confidence to act as the one referred to above?

Depending upon their type of duties and sections or unit to which they belonged, not all airmen were paid at the two centres, but there would usually be about 500 men in total congregated and "standing easy" in the hangars. Trestle tables would have been erected and the loose-leaf pay ledgers in place upon these tables. Seats would have been provided for myself, a witnessing officer and my ledger clerk. All this had been done and awaited my arrival.

The procedure for the parades was that my clerk would go through the ledgers alphabetically and call out the last three digits of an airman's service number, together with his last name. The man concerned would come to attention and reply "Sir". He would then march to the table holding-out his Form 1250 (identity card), so that the witnessing officer could check that the last three digits on the card agreed with those called out. As the airman approached the table, my ledger clerk would call out the amount of pay and I would count out this sum (the wages were paid to the nearest 10 shillings – old money, in £1 and 10 shilling notes). The airman would come to attention as he reached the table and salute, and I would hand over his pay.

The procedure sounds complicated but in practice it was straightforward and speedy. In my time at Leconfield there were only two occasions when I concluded the parades 10 shillings short, which sums I paid out of my own pocket. The witnessing officers were usually flyers, given the chore at short notice because of weather conditions or similar circumstances. I never felt confident that they would check the identity numbers as required, so I always made sure of this information myself. It all became a regular and simple routine.

After my disappointing brush with the CO and the trauma (largely self-inflicted) of the first pay parades, I quickly settled into life at Leconfield. My room in the mess was comfortable, and the food and facilities very good. I had a quarter share in a batman, who served myself and three other junior officers. He was a pleasant lad, but other than making my bed, there was not much for him to do. Therefore, he pressed the meagre contents of my wardrobe every other day. Eventually I instructed him to do this only when asked. My only lounge suit of navy blue barathea was beginning to look more like shot silk!

In accordance with RAF custom (and possibly that of the other services) the charges to officers for living in the mess and attendance at official mess functions such as monthly dining-in nights, summer, winter and Battle of Britain balls, the sports day cocktail party, etc., were always related to their pay and, in my experience, never exceed one day's pay. Therefore, junior officers, such as myself, were effectively subsidised by our senior colleagues, which ensured that we were always able to enjoy mess events.

As my pay as a national service pilot officer (a rank not a job) reached only 19/6d per day old money, equivalent to about £10,000 per annum at the present time in current money, I did very well out of the way in which charges were levied. While I never had money to spare, I survived quite comfortably. More importantly, many of the mess functions were of a type which I had not previously experienced and, to an extent, I felt that this helped my maturity and social development.

Apart from their official roles, junior officers were usually given some extraneous duties, which contributed to the smooth running of the station. I was fortunate in the two duties given to me. Supervision of the station post office was a simple task, as it was run by a very efficient corporal and all that was required from me was a periodic visit for reconciliation of stamps held and cash.

Acting as sports member for the officers' mess was even simpler and was little more than ensuring that the snooker room equipment was in good order and the squash court booking sheet maintained. The latter responsibility was particularly helpful to me. Prior to conscription I had had the opportunity to play only two or three games on a squash court. In my new role, I took every chance to play or practice whenever demand on the courts was low. By demob, I had become quite a useful player and continued enjoying the game (in later years playing with my regular opponent and good friend John Swynnerton) until my early seventies. At this stage, John and I switched to racquetball, similar to squash but less physically demanding, of which our last game was after I had reached 80 years. I thank the RAF for initiating this "almost a lifetime" of enjoyment.

Over the following months, I made many friendships with my fellow junior officers, several of whom were national service men like myself, and, usually, either straight from university or having completed some form of professional training. Johnny Lee, Ken Ackroyd and Ray Shearing fell into these categories. However, there were also a number of other young men in our friendship group such as Paul Brink, the admin wing adjutant, and Tom Ridout of the RAF Regiment, who were serving for longer terms. The different backgrounds, educations, professions and ambitions made this an interesting group, and we would often finish an evening in the room of one or other of the crowd, drinking coffee and debating some issue or other.

However, before the above stage was reached, on one or two evenings per week (after dinner in the mess and if any of our car-owning members were available), we would visit one of the hostelries in the area for a change of scenery and beverage. My recollection is that the Pipe & Glass in South Dalton was a favourite venue as was a pub in Driffield (was it the Star?) where a very pretty barmaid added to the attractions. When there were no cars available, we could always catch a bus into Beverley or even to Hull if we needed a wider choice.

Of more senior rank and age were several officers at Leconfield with whom I had limited contact but felt proud to serve alongside. One of these was the Wing Commander Admin A.E. (Lofty) Lowe, MBE, DFC, who in WWII had achieved the unique distinction for an air gunner of becoming an officer commanding a squadron (No. 77 Squadron).

There were many stories about Lofty (of course, I always called him sir) and his courage and fortitude in the course of numerous missions. Whether or not these were true (or completely accurate) I cannot say, and he was too senior an officer for me to enquire – but I never doubted them.

The story I liked best was of an occasion when, flying as rear gunner on a bombing mission, his plane was damaged by flak and the pilot, believing it could not be saved, gave the order for the crew to bail out, while he would try to maintain the aircraft on a stable course. On this order, Lofty wound up the guns and opened the rear hatch but, instead of bailing out immediately, he climbed on top of the guns with the intention of jumping only when some other crew members did so. At this point, the pilot found that he had regained control of the plane and he cancelled the order to bail out, then used the intercom to speak to each crew member to ensure that they were still in position. There was no response from the rear gunner. Consequently, the flight engineer was instructed to crawl down the fuselage in order to investigate. Halfway down, he could see the open hatch with no sign of Lofty. He returned with the news "Lofty has gone". Meanwhile, getting cold and windswept clinging onto the guns and with no sign of a parachute by any of his colleagues, Lofty climbed back into the plane. To everyone's amazement, his dulcet tones suddenly came down the intercom: "What the hell's going on, Skip?"

Probably the most famous of my colleagues at Leconfield (although he would not think of himself as such) was another Yorkshireman, Flight Lieutenant Jim (Ginger) Lacey, DFM and bar and holder of the Croix de Guerre. Jim called in my office each month in order to pay the rent for his married quarters.

In Michael Ashcroft's book *Heroes of the Skies*, he describes Jim as "very understated and proud of his modest roots", a description I can understand as, in some ways, he seemed an unlikely hero. However, flying with 501 Squadron as a sergeant pilot, Jim is credited with the most kills in the Battle of Britain (at least 18 aircraft), including the Heinkel He III, which had earlier in the day bombed Buckingham Palace.

Commissioned later in 1941 and posted to the Far East, by the end of the war, Jim's total kills had increased to 28 confirmed and 5 probables. However, in course of the war years, he had experienced many narrow escapes and had been shot down or forced to land because of combat damage no less than nine times. Ginger Lacey died on 30 May 1989 at the age of 72. I cannot claim to have known him well but feel proud to have served with him, even though only in a very different setting to that in which he had excelled.

My life at Leconfield settled into a busy and satisfying routine. Although the accountancy role was not demanding in a technical sense, my overall duties were varied, occasionally quite challenging and different from anything that I had previously experienced.

After a few months, I was contacted by one of the other junior officers in the education branch, who informed me that, in addition to their required programme of lectures, he and his colleagues wished to provide a wider range of subjects, which would be available to airmen in off-duty evenings and might be of benefit either in their service careers or, eventually, in civilian life.

Subjects which they wished to include were book-keeping, commerce and commercial arithmetic, but none of the education branch officers had the necessary qualifications to give these lectures. He continued that, as a chartered accountant, I would be deemed satisfactory and as I was not part of the education branch, I could be paid a fee for each lecture. I was pleased to take on this role, which was spread over about three months and provided a useful supplement to my pay.

Whether or not I was an effective teacher, I am not sure. There were no examinations to be taken, which might have provided proof one way or the other and, although I always asked if there were any questions, only rarely were there any takers!

A duty which all junior officers had to undertake every six weeks or so (as their turn came around) was orderly officer, which required being in the station on call for one day and night and available at all times in the event of an emergency. It was on one of these occasions that I experienced my only genuinely unhappy event while in the RAF, when one of our Hawker Hunter jets, piloted by a resident officer, crashed when coming in to land, killing the pilot and breaking up the aircraft, which exploded into flames.

I heard the explosion when in my office and, on going outside, could see the plume of smoke on the airfield. However, by the time I arrived on the scene (having travelled by bicycle) it was well after the station fire tenders had done their work and the wreckage was covered in foam.

I feel it inappropriate to name the pilot in casual jottings of this nature all these many years later. I did not know him well, but he was a career officer from an RAF family. I know that he was popular with and well-liked by his fellow flyers and highly regarded as a pilot and instructor. I was not party to any investigation and have no knowledge of what gave rise to the accident.

In accordance with RAF custom (which I assume had originated in WWII when fatalities were a regular occurrence but life had to go on as normal and morale be maintained), it was taboo to mention the tragedy in the mess. However, unlike the wartime years, we current occupants were unaccustomed to such events. Dinner was eaten largely in silence; afterwards the bar was virtually empty, and no gramophone records were being played in the lounge.

I retreated to the orderly officer's room but could not help thinking of the emotions and fears which must have been experienced by the many young men living in RAF messes throughout Britain 15 years earlier when loss of friends and colleagues was commonplace and expected to continue.

Being only about 70 miles from Sheffield, it was reasonably easy to get home for weekends. For my first few months at Leconfield (and until his demob), I shared the cost of petrol and travelled by car with Bill Walsh, another national serviceman, who was engaged to a Sheffield girl. Later on, Sqn Ldr Harrison happily gave me a lift to York (where he had bought a house in readiness for his retirement), from where the train services to Sheffield were quite frequent and speedy.

Between these periods, travel could be less convenient, usually involving a bus journey into Hull and a train, travelling down the north side of the Humber to Goole before branching south, via Doncaster to Sheffield.

About two days before one of these weekend journeys, I had (for fun) volunteered to take part in a practice exercise involving 77 Helicopter Squadron, which was based at Leconfield, and an Air Sea Rescue (ASR) unit which operated down the Yorkshire coast. The volunteers (myself included) were taken out to sea by the ASR boys, dropped overboard and winched up into the helicopters. My "reward" was to be given four large crabs, which had been caught by the ASR people in their leisure time.

As I had no refrigeration in my room, I placed the crabs in a case in my wardrobe until the start of the weekend, two days later, when I set off to visit home. It was a very warm day! When I eventually boarded the train in Hull there were two other passengers in a six-seater compartment and, after about half an hour into our journey, one of my fellow passengers commented, "I can still smell the Hull docks even though we must be 20 miles away." I made no reply. Fortunately, both of the other passengers left the train at Goole (or maybe they just changed carriages!). I removed the crabs from my case, opened the carriage window and threw them out.

Some months later I experienced a similar incident. I should have known better, but as I was travelling home for Christmas and the weather was cold, I felt that all would be well. On this occasion I had won a 24lb turkey in the mess raffle. As previously, the prize had to be kept in my room for a couple of days before departing for home, and I detected no problems before leaving on the journey. However, on arrival when I proudly presented the heavy package to Mum, she opened it, took one sniff, crinkled her nose and hurried outside to the bin!

In my case, one of the most enjoyable aspects of national service was the many opportunities for taking part in sporting activities and I have made several previous references to these. I was delighted, therefore, when a few months after my arrival at Leconfield, Bernard Bellwood, scrum-half of the Yorkshire Rugby Union XV arrived. At last I had someone to join in my training routines and runs around the airfield.

Bernard and I became good friends and we trained together on several evenings each week, often kicking a rugby ball to each other to practice catching. Bernard had, of course, become an immediate star in the station rugby team and, after a few weeks, he suggested that I should consider playing rugby as well as soccer. He considered that I had the necessary speed and ability to kick a ball, and said he would teach me how to tackle, with my head in the appropriate place and making use of an opponent's body weight.

A few weeks later I played my first rugby game, on the wing against an army team from the East Yorks Regiment on their headquarters ground in Beverley. I think we lost but I enjoyed the experience, and after the game, Bernard and I were invited for drinks in the officers' mess. This seemed quite homely with its small number of officers, as compared with our mess at Leconfield where, in addition to the resident establishment of officers, there were usually a dozen or so visiting flyers attending the Pilot Attack Instructor Courses.

Before the season ended, I was selected to play for the station side in three or four more games against rugby clubs in the East Yorks area. Although I appreciated that I was still very much a novice (particularly in a positional sense), this experience proved sufficient for me to obtain a place in the Mombasa Sports Club team a couple of years later.

However, in retrospect, it was neither rugby nor soccer which gave me the greatest sporting pleasure in my time at Leconsfield, but being part of the Administrative Wing Athletics Team, which took part in the Annual Station Sports Day in 1956. The Station Trophy, together with numerous minor prizes and mementos for success in various disciplines, was competed for by teams from the three wings – training, technical and administration (of which accounts section formed part).

The problem for admin wing (with its 90 or so members from which to select a team) was the mismatch in size compared with the other two wings. Although I cannot remember the exact figures, training had something like 800 plus members and technical wing (including a Resident Aircraft Modification Unit) about 400. I was surprised, therefore, when Corporal Jackson came to see me to ask if I would become involved in selecting a team – as he believed we (admin wing) could win!

Until this meeting, I had not been aware that the corporal had made a jump which was only a few inches short of the Olympic qualifying distance for the triple jump event and that he was also a good performer in the long jump. Furthermore, his brother, SAC Jackson (wise enough not to compete in the events in which his bigger and stronger sibling excelled), was one of the few pole vault specialists on the station and was proficient in the high jump. I also found that we had other athletes in accounts section capable of competing well in the sprints and the javelin-throwing events. Finally, Corporal Jackson said that he had my name pencilled-in for the 400 and 800 metre races. With this nucleus of a team in our own small section plus a few other known athletes in the wing, I agreed to become involved.

Sports Day arrived a couple of weeks later and the corporal's prediction proved to be correct. To the great surprise of most people on the station, admin wing won the trophy with 142 points compared to 139 and 129, respectively for training and technical wings. Accounts section had an excellent haul of prizes (I still have the photographs to prove it) and I was pleased to have avoided any personal embarrassment by obtaining points for second and third places in my two events. The cocktails tasted especially good to me at the mess party, which always concluded annual sports day, although I would have enjoyed it more if I had been able to celebrate with my team in the NAAFI.

Probably the major international event during my period of national service was the Suez War. At the time there were two Egyptian officers on a training course at Leconfield. I recollect seeing them in the mess in the evening, but by the time I heard the announcement of hostilities the next morning, they had disappeared, presumably returned to Egypt.

Despite the political and international controversies regarding Suez, no doubts appeared to exist in the minds of the aircrews. Keen to demonstrate their abilities, I believe that all members of our 131 Squadron volunteered for the new squadrons which were being formed but so did many of the pilots throughout the RAF. Out of our squadron of "ace" pilots, only one was selected. Of course, the "war" lasted for only a few days.

With Sheffield being so accessible, I probably saw as much of Kath when stationed at Leconfield as in the days before call-up when I was still studying for the accountancy exams and, as I moved towards my final months of RAF service, we decided to become engaged. However, as it was still uncertain as to exactly what I would do or where I would be located in civilian life, we did not fix any date for marriage.

At this time, I was not even sure that I wished to continue in accountancy, but I recognised that this was likely to provide the highest level of remuneration, at least in the short term. Therefore, I decided to remain in accountancy but with a job in industry or commerce. After two or three interviews, I provisionally agreed that, on leaving the RAF, I would take up a position as deputy chief accountant of Mardon, Son and Hall, a company based in Bristol and part of the Imperial Tobacco Group. However, almost as soon as I had notified this decision, I realised that it was the wrong one.

Ever since my days as a schoolboy, I had intended to spend some time overseas and see something of the world before settling down. Therefore, I informed Mardons that I had changed my mind and would not wish to join them. I then wrote to three of the major accountancy firms, all of whom were advertising for staff for their overseas offices –

Peat Marwick Mitchell – for Johannesburg

Price Waterhouse – for Buenos Aires, and

Cooper Brothers – for Mombasa

All these firms (which with different names, still today remain part of the "Big Four" accountancy organisations) replied offering interviews and, in due course, employment opportunities.

Other than an awareness that all three were major players in the accountancy profession, I had little knowledge of the firms concerned, and even less of the countries where the job opportunities were available. I am not a linguist and decided to rule out South America but the choice between South Africa and Kenya, both countries with strong historic connections with Britain, was difficult. However, Sqn Ldr Harrison mentioned that he had spent a tour in Kenya, which he had greatly enjoyed. This was the "scientific way" in which I made my choice of Coopers, and the start of a career of almost 38 years with the firm.

I conveyed my decision to John Perfect, a senior partner in London who had interviewed me. He said that I would need to spend six months being "Cooperised" before going to Kenya and that this could be arranged in Sheffield office. I spoke to Kath and told her of my change of plan. She confirmed that she would be happy to go to Kenya or wherever I chose and we agreed that, as I had 10 days or so leave entitlement, we would use this to get married just before I left the RAF so that my Cooperisation period could start on demobilisation.

We eventually settled on 5 October 1957 (my 24th birthday) as the date for the wedding to be held at St Cuthbert's Church in Sheffield. I returned to Sheffield the day before to make a few final arrangements, but most of the work had already been done by Kath. Kath looked stunning in her white bridal dress and was supported by four bridesmaids. The best man, Frank Gunby, had been a friend from my primary school days. I wore RAF dress uniform, complete with sword, to the excitement of a couple of small boys who witnessed my departure from home for the church. It was not a particularly posh wedding and the male dress was lounge suits (which suited our families and friends at the time), but everything seemed to go well.

After the wedding, Kath and I caught a train to Edinburgh for a week's honeymoon (it rained much of the time, but this was of no real concern). I then returned to Leconfield for my final week in the RAF.

A few weeks before the above, it had been announced that the Fighter Weapons School (the FWS), with aircraft, pilots and supporting staff, was to be transferred from Leconfield to RAF Leuchars, a station in Scotland situated about five or six miles from the famous St Andrews Golf Course. Although not directly involved with the FWS, many of the other officers and airmen would no longer have a role at Leconfield and were to be posted elsewhere.

These events had taken place in the time that I was on honeymoon and I returned to a virtually empty mess and a "ghost" station with few of my friends and colleagues remaining. There was little for me to do except tidy up a few loose ends and prepare for demob. This was a rather sad and disappointing end to two years in the RAF, which, on the whole, I had enjoyed and, I believe, benefitted from.

I joined Cooper Brothers & Co Sheffield office on 21st October 1957. The office was headed by a young, energetic and charming but very new partner – David Corsan, nephew of John Pears, one of the firm's two senior partners. David was supported by two managers – Ray Emmitt and Joe Chopping. More about Ray is mentioned in later paragraphs, but he became a good friend to me over many years and played an important role in my future progression in the firm.

The office numbered only about 25 staff at the time, including two people working from their homes in Leeds and reporting into Sheffield office on Saturday mornings to submit timesheets and collect their expenses.

Most of my work in this period was at clients for which Joe Chopping was responsible. He was a good man to work for and one of the most trustworthy people I have ever met. Joe left Coopers while I was in Kenya to become managing director of a major Sheffield office client, but he remained a good friend to both the firm and myself for the rest of his life.

Probably the only amusing incident worth mentioning in this period is a Coopers' internal assignment, which I was given to complete in respect of a major client, one of the first internal control questionnaires (ICQ), a new document being developed by the firm with the object of having available from year to year valuable information on the client's systems and controls. It was believed that this document would put us ahead of the competition in the understanding and information we would have available on clients' processes, systems and procedures. Completion of the ICQ, with all the supporting documents, took several weeks of work, and on completion I handed it to Joe Chopping for review. He accidentally left it on a bus – never to be seen again!

V

Kenya – Mombasa and the Coast

April 1958 to April 1961

On 9 April 1958, Kath and I travelled to London on the first stage of our journey to Kenya. There was still a sprinkling of snow on the ground in Sheffield and London was cold and icy. We were wearing winter clothing despite our eventual destination being less than five degrees south of the equator.

We spent the night at the Grosvenor House Hotel on Park Lane (very posh by our standards at the time but arranged and paid for by Coopers). We were also taking the opportunity to see a West End musical – *The Boy Friend* – as we thought this would be the last chance to see a London show for some time.

With the insensitivity of youth, we had said goodbye to our families without any thought that we may not see them again for three years or (as neither family had a home telephone) even have the opportunity to speak.

The next morning, we travelled to Heathrow to commence our flight. Of course, 60 years ago, airliners were much smaller, slower and with a shorter range than at present. On the credit side, airport formalities were less stringent, and to the best of my recollections, there were no baggage or security checks. After refuelling stops in Frankfurt, Rome and Khartoum, we landed in Nairobi 20 hours later as dusk was falling. The coach journey into the city gave us our first experience of the sights, sounds and smells of Kenya – our excitement steadily increasing.

Our destination in Nairobi was the famous (notorious may be a more appropriate adjective) New Stanley Hotel, a haunt in the 1920s of the so-called Happy Valley set. A reminder of these days was the statue across from the hotel of Lord Delamere, one of the set founders and the most distinguished member. We had dinner, followed by a nightcap in the Long Bar (once available to men only) before retiring and looking forward to the next day and the internal flight by Dakota to Mombasa.

Arriving at Mombasa airport about mid-morning, we were met by Peter Pleasance, a member of Coopers staff. Peter transported us to Nyali Beach Hotel, one of the best hotels in the area, situated in attractive gardens flowing down to a beautiful white sandy beach. We had been booked into the hotel for a few weeks ahead to give time for us to get organised. Our impressions could not have been better. However, in accordance with his instructions and in typical Coopers style, having dropped off Kath and the luggage, Peter drove me to an Indian tailors in order to purchase white short-sleeved shirts, white shorts and long white stockings (the business uniform at the coast). I bought several sets of each, changed into one of them in the shop and, within the hour, arrived in Coopers office. I spent the rest of the day meeting the partner in charge and senior staff and being briefed on my responsibilities. It all seemed very familiar!

MOMBASA – even the name sounded mysterious and exciting to me and I soon fell under its spell.

Situated on an island of five and a half square miles approximately 300 miles south-east of Nairobi, Mombasa was the second-largest city in Kenya and the most important commercial port in East Africa (the Confederation of Kenya, Tanganyika and Uganda, all under British control). The road to Nairobi (and thus to the upcountry areas of Kenya) was accessible over a causeway to the mainland but, at this time, had only about 45 miles of tarmac – mainly at the Nairobi end. The remaining 250 miles or so was murram (gravel, soil or sand) and one could complete the drive to Nairobi only after many hours and probably be covered from head to toe in red dust on arrival.

Fortunately, in addition to the daily Dakota flight, there was the option of travelling to Nairobi by train, on which sleeping facilities were available. This was the choice of travel on several visits by the Mombasa Sports Club football and rugby teams of which I became a member. We would leave Mombasa in the evening (usually on a Friday) and, fortified by a couple of Tusker beers, retire to be awakened in the early morning six hours later on arrival in Nairobi. Members of the opposing teams would pick us up at the station and provide transport, accommodation and hospitality until finally returning us to the station (often worse for wear in several respects) on Sunday evening to arrive in Mombasa in time for work on Monday morning. We would return the favour for any upcountry teams visiting Mombasa.

Both north and south of Mombasa were many miles of beautiful white sandy beaches but access to these was not always easy. To the north, one would leave the island by crossing a pontoon bridge for which a toll was payable. The articulated sections of the bridge would rise or fall in accordance with high or low tide. I recollect an occasion, some weeks after we arrived when Kath found that controlling the car clutch at low tide while attempting to pay the toll was quite a challenge (which she overcame) when preparing for her Kenya driving test.

Over the pontoon bridge was Nyali (previously mentioned), a pleasant area where some of the more affluent members of the business community chose to live. The road here was tarmacked but soon deteriorated to murram as one travelled along the coast. Although there were a few hotels standing back from the beach (in addition to Nyali, I recollect Shanzu and Whitesands), there was little civilisation until the town and tourist resort of Malindi about 80 miles away.

The beaches south of Mombasa were even less easy to access. The murram road to these was reached by using the Likoni car ferry to the mainland. Again, there were several hotels amongst the palm trees and vegetation which lined the beaches – Shelley Beach, Trade Winds and Jadini come to mind. However, there was no settlement of any size to the south until the town of Tanga, about 80 miles away and over the border in Tanganyika (now called Tanzania). However, I doubt if there was passable road access to Tanga along the coast and for my journeys over the years on client affairs, I would travel approximately 20 miles up the Nairobi road before branching off.

The office of Cooper Brothers & Co in Mombasa was quite small. The complement comprised one partner (Malcolm Pedlow), a senior manager (Tom Winning, with whom I developed a good friendship) a manager (who I was replacing), three senior grade clerks, including the previously mentioned Peter Pleasance, a female secretary/typist (English), an African typist (male and very efficient) and two other Africans – a driver and an office junior.

The Coopers office was located on the third floor of a fairly new block quite close to the city centre and I remember, when looking out of the window on my first day, noticing an attractive young woman walking across the car park to her vehicle. Peter Pleasance commented, "Poppy is leaving the office. She works for the company on the floor above." By chance, the next morning, I found myself in the lift with the same young woman. I said, "Good morning, Poppy. Let me introduce myself, I'm Barrie Cottingham and have joined Coopers on the floor below your company." She replied, "Very pleased to meet you but my name is not Poppy. I'm Annabel, Annabel TUPPER!" Fortunately for Peter Pleasance, he was working away from the office that day.

Mombasa itself had great character. Fort Jesus, a Portuguese stronghold until stormed by the Omani Arabs in 1698, looked out over the Old Harbour where dhows from Aden and the Persian Gulf could be found on their journeys up and down the east coast of Africa. On a greater scale, in the major commercial harbour of Kilindini, one might find the cruise ships of the Union Castle or Lloyd Triestino lines, which, while in port, provided customers for the bars and souvenir shops. There were also periodic visits by vessels of the Royal Navy, particularly the commando carriers *Bulwark* and *Perseus* which provided a reminder that highly trained marines were readily available for action if ever required.

Tourists would also find the Arab town of interest. Small bustling shops and old houses, often with low balconies and heavy wooden doors, set in streets too narrow for motor vehicles.

A week or so after arriving in Mombasa, I was given an assignment (acting for our Nairobi office) to work jointly with a manager from Peat Marwick Mitchell (now KPMG) in obtaining information for the valuation of a hotel in Malindi – the Eden

Rock Hotel. The information was required in connection with the possible sale of the hotel and was expected to take four or five days to obtain.

I was delighted to have this opportunity to see some of the country to the north of Mombasa, including the ancient town of Malindi itself. Furthermore, as I would be staying at the Eden Rock, all the facilities of the hotel would be available, together with direct access to the excellent beaches, although in practice I found that there was little time for leisure.

At this stage I had still not acquired a car, but the office vehicle and driver were made available. On arrival at the hotel, the Peats manager and I agreed a programme of work with an allocation of duties between us and everything went smoothly.

Kenya has two rainy seasons, the longest taking place from about mid-April to June. The usual pattern is for heavy rainfalls each day in the first few weeks but becoming less frequent and gradually petering out over the period. On this occasion, the rains started on the day before my return to Mombasa. The effect was dramatic. The foliage turned to a brighter green, but blossoms and flowers were being washed away. However, of more concern was that dried-up stream beds, which I had noticed on the outward journey, had become raging torrents. At one point, we were delayed by a river, which now ran across the road. Fortunately, the heavy rains stopped about mid-morning before returning again in the afternoon. During this break, the driver waded in periodically to assess the water level and judge when we could cross. It was fascinating to experience another side to Kenya.

Back in Mombasa, I learned two important lessons over the next few weeks. Tom and Nancy Winning had returned to the UK for six weeks "end of tour" leave, and Kath and I had taken over their second-floor apartment on Mombasa Island. The Winnings were moving to a house in Nyali on their return, thus giving us the option of continuing to remain in the apartment or finding an alternative. However, as the Winnings would require their furniture and furnished accommodation was not readily available in Mombasa, we would need to purchase our own replacements.

Shortly after moving into the apartment, we were invited out for dinner and arrived back quite late. We had locked all doors but left open the windows to try to keep the apartment cool. However, as the windows were protected by a diamond-patterned steel mesh, this did not seem a concern. Therefore, we were shocked on return to find that we had been burgled. No one had warned us about the infamous pole robbers of Kenya who, armed with bamboo poles (with a hook on the end), which were thin enough to go through the holes in the steel mesh, could even strip sheets from a bed without waking the occupant. With no one in the apartment, the robbers' task had been made much easier. Almost all Kath's dresses had been stolen and also my new lightweight suit, purchased specifically for wear in the tropics. Lesson one – a requirement to pay more attention to security.

I have mentioned above the need for us to purchase furniture in time for the Winnings return. We found that there was little imported furniture on sale in Mombasa, but several shops owned by Indian tradesmen would make furniture to order. We decided upon such a shop, made our selections based upon items we could see in course of production or awaiting collection, and agreed the date for delivery – this being the date of the Winnings return. At this stage of our life we had quite limited funds and, as I wished to determine how much money would be available for the purchase of a second-hand car and certain other expenses, I paid for the furniture there and then. Looking ahead I felt confident that my salary from Coopers, which would be supplemented by Kath's earnings from a position she had obtained as a supervisor at Mombasa telephone exchange, would steadily improve our finances.

On the agreed day for delivery, Kath and I departed to our respective jobs having told Henry, our cook/houseboy (who stayed with us for the whole three years we spent in Kenya) to expect the existing furniture to be removed and replaced by a new batch. However, when we returned at lunchtime, the Winnings furniture had been collected but only one item of new furniture delivered – a small dressing table which had been purchased from a different shop. Henry had used his initiative, this small dressing table had been covered with a tablecloth, plates and cutlery set out, and two packing boxes arranged for seating (at least we were able to have lunch). As soon as I arrived back in the office, I telephoned the owner of the furniture shop. He apologised profusely and promised that delivery would take place immediately.

Feeling a little uneasy despite this assurance, I left the office promptly at 5.30pm, only to find on arriving home that no delivery had been made. I drove straight back into town and arrived just in time to see the shop owner locking the door and about to leave. The penny dropped, I had paid for the furniture and, therefore, in the shop owners mind there was no urgency to produce it. I had learned my second Kenya lesson – do not pay for goods in advance.

I rarely lose control of my temper, but I do not like to be taken advantage of. Therefore, I decided to make a stand. I grabbed the shop owner by his shirt collar at the neck with both hands, pushed him backwards and said, "Open the door." His two teenage sons, who worked in the shop, looked on with interest. I took the owner back into the shop and chose several items of furniture, which I insisted should be loaded (with the help of his sons) into his van. I disregarded his protests that this furniture was awaiting collection by other customers. I then drove closely behind the van as it proceeded to my apartment where, under my supervision, the furniture was unloaded. I told the shop owner that he could recover this furniture when mine was delivered – in fact, this took place about two weeks later.

The following morning, having cooled down (and feeling rather ashamed of myself) I was concerned that my actions might have been too aggressive in what was still a new environment to me. Therefore, I decided to visit the police station, where I asked to see the superintendent in charge. Having related details of the incident to him, the superintendent asked, "Did you actually thump him?" I said, "No, but I bounced him against the door a couple of times." After thinking for a few seconds, he replied, "If he comes here, I will kick his arse."

Over the next few months, I set about establishing my position in the office, making contact with the clients I had been asked to take over and getting to know the strengths, weaknesses and, in some cases, idiosyncrasies of my colleagues on the staff. I had an interesting portfolio of clients, including a number providing services relating to shipping and the movement of goods and produce through the port of Mombasa, but also several located in Tanganyika. Two of these were large sisal estates, owned respectively by German and Swiss groups. While the size of many clients was smaller than might have been the case in the United Kingdom, the level of responsibility seemed greater and, overall, I felt that the experience available was excellent for my stage of development.

My colleagues at Coopers were a generally likeable group and included several interesting characters. One of these was Cyril Carver, but known to everyone simply as CC. He appeared very much older than anyone else in the office, although on reflection, I suppose he was only in his fifties. CC had originally come to Kenya to prospect for gold but had clearly not been successful. He had been married (twice, I believe) but appeared to have no contact with any family members. Someone told me of a cricket game between Mombasa Sports Club and their Dar es Salaam equivalent when CC, as a spectator, had expressed admiration of the style of the visiting opening batsman, only to find later that it was his own son. I never felt able to ask him if this story was true.

CC had no accountancy qualification but, at some time of staff shortages, he had obtained a job with Coopers as an audit assistant. He was a conscientious worker and, after some years of gaining experience and becoming generally more useful, he was given a three-year service contract, which was the normal arrangement for European staff.

Away from the office, CC could be a charming and entertaining companion. He greatly enjoyed a few (sometimes more than a few) gin and tonics and after-dinner brandies, but I learned that his words "I will top up my own glass – an old Kenya custom, you know," should always be taken as a warning. However, before reaching this stage, CC could be an excellent raconteur. His stories of earlier times in Kenya, often including references to attractive ladies who, he would say "rather cared for me", could be hilarious, although, with his bald head, which seemed too large for the rest of his body, it was difficult to imagine him as an Adonis. However, I suspect that he preferred never to spoil a good story by too much accuracy of detail.

On one occasion, CC and another member of staff had been carrying out the audit work on one of my sisal estate clients in Tanganyika. I was contacted and informed that the detail work was virtually complete and ready for my review and a final meeting with the general manager of the estate. I instructed that one of our staff should return to Mombasa, but that the other (which turned out to be CC) should remain for my visit in case there were any additional matters which needed to be dealt with.

All went well on my review and final meeting, and we were invited, as was customary, to dine with the general manager and his estate manager (the bwana shamba) before returning to Mombasa by air the next day.

The estate manager, Swiss by nationality, formal by nature, but a good host, provided an excellent dinner accompanied by pleasant wines and, finally, coffee and liqueur brandy. Eventually I heard CC utter the words "I will top up my own glass – old Kenya custom" and decided it was time for us to retire.

CC and I were accommodated in the two-bedroomed guesthouse of the estate and I soon fell asleep, only to be rudely awakened by the deafening noise of a siren after an hour or so. I was aware that the houses of the European managers had emergency warning systems, but I soon realised that the noise was coming from the guesthouse where we were staying. I found that CC had needed to get up in order to seek the bathroom and had pressed or pulled the wrong switch!

It took a little time for me to gather my senses and stop the noise. Thereafter, one look at CC was enough for me to tell him to get back to bed and feign illness.

As I feared (but expected), within a few minutes the general manager arrived, followed in due course by an open Land Rover bearing the bwana shamba, whose house was on the estate but about half a mile away. Finally, a second Land Rover driven by the manager of an adjacent farm turned up. The last two arrivals were carrying shotguns! I apologised as best I could but felt that the incident was hardly a success in strengthening client relations.

CC received my tongue lashing the next morning, but I suspected that it would have little effect on him. I never reported the matter up the line as his service contract with Coopers was coming up for renewal, and I decided that his entertainment value outweighed my other concerns.

Some months later, I was in Tanga dealing with a different client at the time when CC's service contract had expired. The firm encouraged European staff to get away from tropical Africa between tours and CC was, somewhat reluctantly, proceeding to the UK for the first time in about 30 years. He had chosen to journey by the Union Castle Line, travelling down the east coast of Africa, round the Cape, and north up through the Atlantic to the UK with the numerous ports of call that this journey entailed. I think he eventually spent only about eight days in the UK, most of which was in bed with a bad cold!

CC's first stop after leaving Mombasa was Tanga and he asked if I could join him on board the ship for drinks. Of course, this was before the present-day security restrictions when only crewmembers and passengers are allowed on board.

Tanga harbour was not deep enough for the liner to dock and I had to go out to the ship by lighter. CC was waiting for me, in holiday mode, and soon giving me his impressions of fellow passengers. He had been delighted with his companions at the dinner table and particularly a very attractive young woman seated next to him. Apparently, she came from Nairobi and was travelling down to Cape Town. CC said that she had been "utterly charming", and he gained the impression that (in his words) "she rather cared for me". CC had responded to the encouraging situation by saying, "Of course, I'm an old Nairobi man myself, you know." This had brought the reply, "Oh, you must know my grandmother." CC said, "And dammit, Barrie, do you know, I did."

After a few months of gaining a feel for Mombasa, Kath and I moved from the former Winnings' abode. Our new home was the ground-floor apartment in a block of two, which stood on its own site. It was larger and more secluded than our previous apartment and had a largish garden (although quite steep and rough in nature), which ran down to Tudor Creek, the stretch of sea separating Mombasa from the mainland. We were happy to remain there for the rest of our three-year tour.

Most Europeans in East Africa employed one or more domestic servants, usually a cook/houseboy and possibly a shamba boy (gardener). However, the European population tended to change quite rapidly as service contracts ended and, even if renewed, were often punctuated by longish periods of home leave. Consequently, there were usually plenty of Africans looking for domestic positions and often proudly bearing their testimonials from previous employers. Such testimonials were worth reading as they sometimes contained messages, which were apparent to other Europeans but not to the bearers – for example, I recollect one which included the comment "this boy would probably make a good pastry cook as we found him to be very light fingered".

We were fortunate. Our cook/houseboy (Henry) was recommended to us by people returning to the UK. We found him very satisfactory – although he did have idiosyncrasies. Henry's duties included the washing and pressing of my clothing. The first part of this chore was no problem, but Henry appeared to have a fear of electric irons. If we returned when ironing was in progress, we would find him standing on two or three mats or towels. On several occasions, he left the iron heating for too long until it fused or became blackened. In the latter event, he would scrub the iron bare, to try and cover the mishap. I bought three new replacement irons in the three years of Henry's employment with us.

The laundry which Henry dealt with included my white knee-length stockings, which were part of the office uniform at the coast. After washing, Henry would hang out the laundry to dry, but I found that every few days a pair of my stockings would "go missing". I tackled Henry on this, but the problem continued, until I finally told him that, on the next occasion, the cost of a pair of stockings would be deducted from his wages.

Henry was clearly upset, subsequently, when I carried out this threat. He said that he had not taken my stockings and would not steal from "his bwana". He explained that if he wanted stockings,

78

he would take them from the clothesline of the bwana next door! I replied that this might also be the approach adopted by the houseboy next door and that it was Henry's responsibility to see that this did not happen. I lost no more stockings.

We had made friends with an English couple, Arthur and Pam Merrick and their four-year-old daughter, Petra. The Merricks were nearing the end of their tour and had decided to spend a few days over the August bank holiday visiting Tsavo National Park, about 120 miles north of Mombasa. We were invited to join them and were delighted to accept. Accommodation was booked at Macs Inn, Mtito Andei, located just outside the park.

I have heard it said in recent times that one cannot drive in Tsavo for more than a few hundred yards without meeting a vehicle load of tourists. This was not the case in 1958. The tracks were narrow and rough in places and the vegetation lush and sometimes dense, but opening up, from time to time, into grasslands or where water holes existed. The animals were difficult to find but this added to the excitement. We were fortunate to see elephant, hippos, buffalo, crocodiles, gazelle, baboons (which were difficult to remove from the outside of our cars) and many other types of wildlife. We occasionally met park rangers, but I cannot recollect seeing any other visitors. No doubt there were some in the park but, with 8,000 square miles to explore, there was plenty of room for everyone. We were starting to appreciate the variety and sheer vastness of Kenya.

Shortly after we returned to Mombasa, Petra was due to celebrate her fifth birthday at a party with her friends to be held at the swimming club. We had become fond of Petra, and Kath volunteered to provide the birthday cake. We were slightly late arriving, and Kath hurried on ahead, while I recovered the plastic box containing the cake from our car boot and carried it horizontally, with care, using both hands.

The path from car park to the club house at sea level was down quite a steep grassy bank. The children had come out of the club house on hearing our arrival, and I heard Petra leading the shouts, "Uncle Barrie has got the cake." I think that I involuntarily tightened my grip on the plastic box, with the result that it cracked and the lid on the side away from my body flew open. I dropped to my knees to try and restore equilibrium but, too late, the cake had "jumped out" and started to roll down the bank.

The children's shouts had frozen on their lips, but Kath was amazing. She flew up the bank, scooped up the cake and, within seconds, had disappeared in the club house kitchen where she removed all traces of grass, twigs and other foreign bodies. She emerged with the cake, wrapped (and probably held together) by a fancy frill, complete with candles and appearing as good as new (well almost). "Uncle Barrie" could breathe again.

The closest friend of Kath and myself in Mombasa was David Ferrell, a Londoner, who was deputy manager of the local branch of the Ottoman Bank. David was a regular visitor to our apartment and, now that we had direct access to Tudor Creek, he and I discussed the possibility of acquiring a small boat. David was aware of a rowing boat, with oars, etc., for sale at £20 (this would be over £400 on current values – which sounds expensive). It seemed a fun idea and so we purchased the boat as partners – £10 each.

Over the next couple of weeks, we tried out the boat, but neither David nor I were great oarsmen. The creek was very deep, and the tides could be quite strong. However, probably the worst aspect was that we had no mooring point and felt it necessary to pull the heavy boat well up the garden when not in use to ensure that it could not drift away on a high tide or be easily stolen.

George McLarnon, a mutual friend (whose work was in Kilindini Harbour) hearing of our problem, mentioned that there was an outboard motor at the harbour which had not been used for some time and did not appear to have an owner. George said that we might as well have it for our use – an offer we accepted with alacrity.

As David was not available the following weekend, I decided to try out the outboard by travelling the two or three miles down the creek to the swimming club. I got the engine to start without difficulty and chugged away, travelling fairly quickly with the tide in my favour. I noticed a loose screw on top of the outboard motor, which I tightened; otherwise it seemed to be in excellent condition.

After refreshments and a little time socialising with friends at the club, I set off on the return journey. However, after only a few hundred yards, the outboard stopped and none of my efforts to restart it were of avail. Furthermore, the tide had changed direction and was taking the boat away from my intended destination. There was nothing for it but to take to the oars. Against the tide and with the extra weight of the outboard, progress was not easy, and I finished the day tired, with blistered hands and in bad temper. I still had the chore of pulling the boat up the garden and carrying the heavy outboard to a storage room under the apartment. My demeanour was not improved when I discovered that the problem with the outboard was my entire fault. By tightening the "loose screw" I had created a vacuum, which prevented the flow of fuel to the engine.

I spoke to David the next day. We decided that we were not seafarers and the boat was sold a few days later for what we had paid. As the outboard was of no use to us, this was included free of charge. Some weeks later, George McLarnon got in touch. He said that someone had turned up at the port looking for their outboard motor!

If asked for my overall memories of East Africa 60 years ago, they would be of a beautiful, contrasting and unique territory, where one could find the two highest mountains in Africa (Mounts Kilimanjaro and Kenya), the second largest lake in the world (Lake Victoria) and the magnificent Great Rift Valley. However, these memories would be matched with recollections of numerous and close friendships with people of many different nationalities which were often nurtured in timescales which would be rare in a European environment.

Good friendships were easily made in Mombasa. With a European population of less than 2% of the total and a high proportion of younger people within this group, one felt an urgency to seek out those of similar cultural backgrounds and interests. Of course, with many people subject to periodic transfer to other areas of East Africa or on contracts for limited periods, relationships could be transient and if enjoyable needed to be grasped when available.

Our closest friends over the three-year period were:

David Ferrell (previously mentioned).

Roger Caulton from New Zealand, an accomplished amateur boxer (holding the middleweight championships of both Rift Valley and Coast Provinces) and a good rugby player.

Pat Holding and her brother Robin, both Kenya born (we attended Pat's marriage to John Russell, a New Zealander, while in Mombasa).

Ann Milchem, born in Kenya and a pharmacist by profession.

Keith Traynor, my companion on a climb of Kilimanjaro, which I discuss in Chapter VI; and Maurice and Mina Mauro, Italians who had settled in Kenya.

In addition to the above, we had a further dozen or so good friends whose company we enjoyed. In some cases, Kath would be closer to these than me and in others vice versa, often depending upon shared interests.

In my case, involvements in soccer and rugby (to which I refer later) were an important opportunity for establishing links with people. However, of a more social nature, membership of Mombasa Sub Aqua Club (more of a friendship group of about 20 people than a club) was of great value. Excluding the rainy seasons, the group would decide upon a venue to meet each Sunday. This would usually be one of the wonderful beaches to the north and south of Mombasa or, occasionally somewhere such as Mtwapa Creek (about 15 miles away) where we could swim and water ski.

Swimming is not one of my best abilities but, armed with flippers, snorkel and spear gun, I would join my colleagues and go out beyond the reef to seek our prey. Eventually, we would return to the beach with the day's catch, where our "experts" (some of the Kenya-born members) would gut and prepare the fish for a subsequent barbecue. This would take place late afternoon, after sunbathing or kicking a rugby ball around the beach.

These were happy occasions, although I can recollect a couple of near mishaps – one much more serious than the other. The first concerned Roger Caulton. After our exertions beyond the reef, Roger decided to relax on the beach. For fun, he dug a deep hole in the sand where he took refuge from the sun and his exuberant colleagues. Fooling around, we filled in the hole around him with sand, leaving only his head, complete with hat, above the ground. We then amused ourselves by kicking a ball on the beach, drifting away from where Roger was "entombed".

No one noticed that Roger had dozed off, but he was awakened by the incoming tide which engulfed him, filling his mouth and eyes and creating such a weight of wet sand that he could not escape from the hole. Fortunately, one of the group noticed the problem, but by the time we had dragged Roger to safety, he was unconscious. We tried first aid and removed sand from his mouth and eyes as best we could. Meanwhile, one of the group had brought his car as near to the beach as possible. Roger was rushed to the hospital, where he remained for several days. It was a close call and a sobering experience for all of us.

The second incident occurred on a bank holiday, when we had arranged to have a full-scale barbecue with drinks on the beach, meeting in the afternoon and continuing festivities until after dusk. Roger Caulton, having thankfully re-joined us, had acquired an inflatable commando canoe, which he had brought along. Ann Cloté, an athletic young woman from South Africa, and I decided to borrow the canoe and paddle out to sea. Roger warned us that he had accidentally punctured one of the main side panels, but this did not seem to give any problems as we paddled out with the tide for a mile or so before turning south down the coast. When we decided to return, we found a different situation. The tide had turned, and with the defective panel, it was impossible to travel directly towards the coast. I started to feel very concerned and tried not to show this to Ann. The best we could do with much energetic paddling was move diagonally, gradually edging closer to land but eventually beaching more than a mile farther down the coast than we were aiming for.

We trekked back in the dark to the barbecue, feeling quite exhausted by the time we arrived. However, everyone was still talking, laughing and drinking. No one had felt any concern by our longish absence. This was Kenya, and we were expected to be capable of looking after ourselves.

Another of our circle was Ivy Horton, a very pretty South African girl with a stunning figure and a dress sense which enabled it to be seen to best advantage. I was driving up Kilindini Road in the centre of Mombasa in David Ferrell's Volkswagen Beetle (which I had borrowed while my Morris Minor was being serviced) when I noticed Ivy walking on the pavement in the same direction. She was looking very attractive, wearing a blue skirt which fitted tightly around her bottom and flared out at the knees. I was brought to a stop by traffic lights just before drawing level with Ivy. I gave a toot on the horn, but she appeared not to hear, so I decided that when the lights changed, I would zoom forward in a sort of racing start and give another toot.

The lights changed – amber, green, I slipped the car into gear and hit the accelerator. The Volkswagen crashed backwards into the car behind. I think my mind had been on other things! I had forgotten that the gear stick movement for engaging first in my car (a Morris Minor) was for reverse in a Volkswagen.

I paid for the repairs to both vehicles. Of course, in my view, it was all Ivy's fault. However, when tendering my apologies to David for denting his car, I decided it was wise not to go into too much detail as to the reasons for the mishap!

Despite the relatively small size of the European community in Mombasa, there was plenty of scope for leisure activities. These included clubs for golf, rowing and swimming and societies for amateur dramatics and Scottish country dancing (of which Kath was an enthusiastic participant). However, the main centre for sporting activities was the Mombasa Sports Club (MSC) with its facilities, including playing fields and tennis and squash courts. The club fielded the only European teams in Mombasa for football (soccer), rugby and hockey and the best of the town's two European cricket elevens (I played for the other one – Coast Stragglers). I had been proposed for membership of MSC shortly after arrival in Mombasa and was soon selected for the soccer first XI. A few months later I was appointed Football Captain (a role I held for the remainder of my years in Kenya). This entailed skippering the first XI and selecting both first and second teams. Because of the hot coastal climate, games usually took place after work and before dusk, the time when it was cooler. Football training was held on Monday evenings, first XI matches played on Wednesdays and second XI games on Fridays. I always selected myself as one of the reserves for the second XI which, in practice, meant that I would play in about 50 percent of their fixtures. Football activity two or three times a week plus an occasional game of squash was my idea of Utopia.

Except for a few occasions each season, when MSC played in a knock-out competition against other European teams (usually from Nairobi) and were drawn to play away, all games were played on our ground. Opponents included local sides from African, Arab and Asian clubs. (The Goans, in particular, usually had a good side, which included two of Kenya's Olympic athletes.) There were also fixtures against visiting ships mainly of the Royal Navy, and these contacts might include other sports and the exchange of hospitality.

All games against local sides were "friendlies" but strongly contested. There was a small stand with seating to accommodate club members and Kath was a regular attender. In addition, there would often be quite a few visiting supporters standing around the touchlines. My aggressive style of tackling seemed to be appreciated by the Arab spectators in particular and, if I ventured into the Arab town to purchase fruit or vegetables, I would usually be greeted by some of the stallholders with shouts of "Jambo, Bwana Captain". Fame indeed.

However, one should not think that work and sport were the only aspects of life in Mombasa. The Sports Club itself had a strong social side. Kath would attend as a spectator at most football games and usually be in the company of friends, having a sundowner drink, by the time I had showered and changed. Often this might be followed by a party of us remaining in town for dinner at one of the several good restaurants available in Mombasa.

Also over the course of a year, there would be many cocktail parties, receptions or other functions such as "At home" invites from the officers of visiting Royal Naval or other vessels, receptions given by the consuls of foreign countries represented in the town and visits from celebrities or sporting heroes. Of course, there were also the constant introductions to new arrivals and goodbye parties on departures of friends and business contacts on their transfers or tour completions.

Because of the small size of Coopers office staff, in place of the traditional annual party, we would try to do something different. One year this was the hire of two boats (*Sansum K* and *Bridget K*) for a big game fishing trip. We were all quite successful with catches of tunny, fellusi and two sailfish weighing 87lb and 58lb, respectively. We gave the fish to the boat boys to take to the African market, but I have the photographic evidence to prove our success.

Overall, life in Mombasa and the coast could not have been better. Workwise, I felt that I was obtaining good and varied experience. I was able to enjoy a range of sporting activities several days a week. There seemed to be limitless places of interest to visit and functions to attend, and Kath and I had quickly established a group of good friends. Nevertheless, I could not help feeling that I was experiencing the end of an era – and so it proved.

VI

Kenya – Kilimanjaro

August 1960

In August 1960, in company with Keith Traynor (a footballing colleague and good friend), I took a few days holiday to climb Kibo, the higher (but much less difficult) of the two peaks of Kilimanjaro, Africa's highest mountain.

Shortly after completing the climb, I prepared a diary/ scrapbook of the "adventure", which I subsequently gave to my son, Nigel, but have recently borrowed back.

One should appreciate that 60 years ago journeying up Kilimanjaro was very different and, I believe, much more challenging and exciting than today, when climbers huts and facilities have been extended, mountain paths and tracks improved and travel companies provide guides and sometimes transport for parties of tourists to "enjoy" the experience. However, one thing which cannot be changed is the altitude of Kibo, with a summit of over 19,340 feet. I understand that despite the help and facilities now available, a good proportion of those undertaking the climb do not succeed.

Having recently reread the account of our days on the mountain in my diary/scrapbook, I have decided to include it in this separate chapter without editing. Although it lacks some interest from the absence of relevant photographs, letters and cartoons, which are contained in the original document, I think it gives an indication of life in East Africa 60 years ago and the reason I still have happy memories of those days.

Kilimanjaro – Diary of the climb written in August 1960

Introduction

"Ngaje Nga", the House of God, so the Masai tribesmen call Kibo, western summit of Kilimanjaro, the highest mountain in Africa. First seen by German explorers Rebmann and Krapf in 1848, this extinct volcano remained unconquered for over 40 years until in 1889 Professor Hans Mayer and Ludwig Purtscheller reached the highest point, Kaiser Wilhelm Spitze of Kibo, 19,340 feet. On the 29 August 1960, seventy-one years and hundreds of ascents later, another expedition set out for Kibo summit. Keith Trayner and I had commenced our holiday, if holiday be the correct description.

At this juncture, I hasten to add for the benefit of the unenlightened, that climbing Kilimanjaro in these modern times is no epoch-making event. The ascent requires no mountaineering skill or experience. However, in the words of the guidebook, "It calls for great physical endurance". Reasonably strong and fit, and hopeful that the guidebook had exaggerated, Keith and I felt quite confident. Our only doubt was our own ability to bear the altitude, this proved to be well founded.

Derbyshire born, Derbyshire bred, strong in arm, thick in 'ead. Only the first part applies in Keith's case. Born in Derby, good natured, cheerful, resourceful and intelligent, Keith proved an ideal companion. A master mariner by profession, Keith, like myself, had lived all his life little above sea level; 19,340 feet sounded frightfully high.

It had been my ambition to climb Kilimanjaro ever since arriving in Kenya over two years earlier (or maybe even earlier still, since the time I had seen a film starring Ava Gardener in which, while scaling Kilimanjaro's snowy slopes, she had, with varying degrees of success, fought off the attentions of ferocious animals, frenzied natives and fractious lovers). Keith, being similarly inclined, we had decided to team up, take a week's holiday and have a go.

Immediately our decision was known, we were bombarded with stories from previous climbers, or, more often, the friends and acquaintances of climbers, telling of frostbite, damaged lungs and mountain sickness. These stories, of course, deterred us none but merely increased our conviction that this was just the thing for a couple of tough, rugged characters like ourselves. It must be admitted however that Keith did mention that if it was a choice of him bursting his lungs or reaching the summit, he had very little doubt as to which it would be. My sentiments were substantially the same.

One of the problems confronting us was equipment. We had little idea of what to expect and what gear was necessary. In addition, neither of us had brought much in the way of heavy clothing when coming to tropical Africa. Our climb was to start from Marangu Hotel, one of the two hotels standing at the base of the mountain, and we discovered that certain essential items of equipment could be borrowed from the hotel. By begging, borrowing and (only as a last resort) buying, we managed to acquire the remainder.

We eventually arrived at Marangu in time for tea on 27 August after an uneventful journey from Mombasa, having seen elephant, water buffalo and buck on the way. On Sunday, 28 August, at the suggestion of the hotel proprietor, we walked to the first hut and back (Bismark Hut – 9,000 feet) with the object of getting acclimatised. Twenty-six miles in all, we found it rather strenuous and hard on the feet, particularly as the only walking we were accustomed to was from car to office and back. The prospect of having to make the same journey again the following day, as the first stage of the climb, was depressing, although it must be admitted that the walk seemed much easier and our breathing more even at the second go.

Diary of the climb

29 August

10.35	Depart Marangu Hotel
12.20	Enter forest

12.45 to 13.30	Lunch
16.00	Arrive at Bismark Hut
18.00	Supper in style
20.15	Lights out

The lower slopes of the mountain are extremely fertile and African coffee and banana "shambas"[1] cover the area from the hotel until the start of the rain forest. The Africans, Chaggas, we found very friendly and always ready with a greeting. As Keith remarked, the higher up the mountain you climb, the higher they raise their hats. The 29th being a Sunday most Africans were dressed in their "Sunday best" ready for attendance at one or other of the Lutheran missions which abounded. Keith and I appeared to be the only ones not heading for church.

Once in the rainforest it was like being in England again. Singing birds, lush vegetation and the scent of flowers. All very pleasant and relaxing.

We eventually arrived at Bismark Hut, with our retinue of guide and porters, feeling like Livingstone and Stanley blazing new trails. Our feeling was short lived; the hut already had occupants, Helmut Schwarz and Wolfgang Heiduk, two Germans who were doing the climb the hard way, without guide or porters and carrying all their own food and equipment.

While we sat down at an immaculate white tablecloth, complete with napkins, to an excellent three-course dinner prepared by our very own "pishi"[2], our companions opened a tin of bully beef, cut a loaf in half and commenced their evening meal. So much for our own daydreams of roughing it. We eventually insisted that they share our food, thereby salvaging our injured pride.

After dark, our new-made friends built a bonfire and attempted to take photographs by its light. It was not a great success, it turned quite cold, and we were all glad to turn in by 8.15pm.

---

[1] Shamba – farm or garden
[2] Pishi - cook

30 August

7.00	Arose and breakfasted
8.40	Depart from Bismark Hut
12.20 to 13.10	Lunch
14.35	Arrive at Peters Hut

For half an hour after leaving Bismark Hut, we toiled up a steep forest path eventually emerging into moorland. Now above the cloud, I had my first view of the twin peaks of Kilimanjaro, an impressive sight.

To Peters Hut is a steady climb across rather rough country. Our German friends, having no guide, asked if they may accompany us; we had no objections, carrying their packs they appeared to have difficulty in keeping up with us, however. At this stage neither Keith nor I noticed the altitude greatly. It was a pleasant day's walk reminiscent of the Peak District of Derbyshire.

Peters Hut was quite adequate except that the stove smoked badly and created a fug. Owing to a combination of this, the cold and the altitude, none of us slept very well. By this time, I was experiencing a severe cold.

31 August

9.00	Depart from Peters Hut
12.15 to 12.50	Lunch
14.30	Arrive at Kibo Hut

A few miles from Peters Hut is the last spring, from there on all water must be carried. We made the most of it and drank deeply. Two or three miles further on we reached "the saddle".

The saddle is nothing more than desert. Flat, barren and rocky, the wind blows bitingly across and the sun beats mercilessly down. We were lucky, the weather was good. Nevertheless, this stage of the journey could not by any stretch of imagination be described as pleasant.

At the start of crossing the saddle, Keith and I led the way, Helmut and Wolfgang still lagging under their packs. By the time we reached Kibo Hut, the Germans had overtaken us and still appeared reasonably fresh when Keith and I staggered in. The altitude was taking effect; we had found it a gruelling day. Both Helmut and Wolfgang were veteran mountaineers and had lived for the last few years in Switzerland, where they climbed regularly. The altitude appeared to have little effect upon them.

The climb from Kibo Hut to the crater edge is made at night when the scree is frozen and more solid than in daytime. We planned to take an early supper and have a few hours' sleep before starting on the final climb about 1am. We discovered that sleeping was much easier said than done. It was one of the most unpleasant evenings of my life.

I was unable to eat very much food owing to a permanent feeling of nausea, which had persisted since our arrival at Kibo. I also suffered from mountain sickness and on two occasions, I was compelled to make hasty excursions from the hut. In addition, I found the cold almost unbearable. I had no sleep and my companions fared little better. 1am, zero hour, it could not come quickly enough. It eventually came after what seemed an age.

1 September

1.15	Set off from Kibo Hut.
4.30	Keith gave up and returned to Kibo Hut, Cottingham continued.
6.50	Cottingham arrived at Gilmans Point.
8.00	Keith arrived back at the Hut, after resting in the Hans Meyer cave.
10.30	Cottingham arrived Kaiser Wilhem Spitze, 19,340 feet.

92

12.45	Keith wakened to be informed that Cottingham's head "haribika"[3]. Set off up the mountain armed with a first aid kit.
13.45	Cottingham arrived Kibo Hut.
14.45	Departed from Kibo Hut.
18.30	Arrived back at Peters Hut.
20.00	And so to bed.

The first stage of the final ascent went well. Aleapende, the guide, leading, carrying a lantern, Keith, myself and the two Germans following in single file. The scree at this stage was not too loose and progress was good. Stopping frequently for short rests, we reached the Hans Meyer cave without mishap, although by this time it was noticeable that Keith needed slightly longer rests than the remainder of us. At the cave, Keith insisted on lying down to rest, apparently oblivious of the cold which the rest of us were feeling. With difficulty, we persuaded Keith to resume.

We now found progress extremely difficult, for every step forward we seemed to slide back two. Rather demoralising and very tiring, Keith seemed to suffer most. We found it necessary to stop and rest after every 10 or so paces. To make matters worse, the lantern went out and in the pitch darkness, allied by a gusty wind, we were unable to relight it. The going was now really difficult, we staggered and stumbled in the darkness. After a further attempt to light the lantern, we gave up the task as hopeless. Keith decided that he had had enough; taking the useless lantern, he returned on his own to Kibo Hut.

The ascent now became increasingly difficult, every few paces I found it necessary to lie down and rest; face down and rest describes it better. My exhaustion was so great that even the cold was not noticeable. I appreciated how Keith had felt. The Germans, being much more accustomed to high altitudes, were not affected to nearly the same degree. I was obviously delaying

---

[3] Haribika – destroyed or spoilt, unusable.

93

them. Eventually, I persuaded them to go on ahead, while I struggled slowly onwards accompanied by the guide.

Little by little, a few paces at a time, we climbed with frequent rests. Aleapende was wonderfully patient and apparently scarcely affected by the altitude. Dawn broke, and still we climbed steadily upwards. Shortly afterwards, Aleapende pointed skywards and told me we were almost there. I still needed several rests before I finally made it.

Gilmans Point, the lowest summit, a little less than 19,000 feet. The Germans were there waiting, taking photographs and admiring the views. After a short rest, I suggested that we attempt the real summit, Kaiser Wilhelm Spitze, we were all in agreement.

KWS is two miles farther round the crater rim. From Gilmans Point it is necessary first to descend a little way into the crater and then climb back onto the rim; it is then a steady walk round the rim of the crater, gently climbing to 19,340 feet. Once again, no climbing skill is necessary. It sounds so very simple; I found it extremely difficult. By this time, the sun had risen and, in this rarefied atmosphere, was very hot. The combination of heat and altitude was trying, progress was very slow. Laboriously we trudged, with numerous stops, for two miles, which seemed like twenty. We eventually arrived; the roof of Africa, Kaiser Wilhelm Spitze.

The view from Kaiser Wilhelm Spitze is breathtakingly beautiful. Nature in all her glory. To the south the magnificent southern glacier glides majestically downwards in indescribable grandeur, while on a clear day mighty Mount Kenya is visible to the north-west. We were unfortunate, cloud prevented us from seeing any great distance.

Amidst all this beauty, I am ashamed to admit that the thought uppermost in my mind was to get back down again. Down to an altitude where my head would cease to pound, where my chest would cease to heave. Aleapende and I started the descent leaving the Germans madly photographing everything in sight like a pair of American tourists.

The descent to Kibo Hut is very hazy in my mind. The combined effect of sun and altitude sent me temporarily crazy (I hope it was only temporarily). I remember reaching Gilmans

Point, from there on, all is very indistinct. I suffered the delusion of an African revolt much to the dismay of my guide, who I regarded as one of the leading insurrectees and attempted to spear with my pointed climbing stick. The guide eventually yodelled down the mountain for assistance and Keith was roused from his slumbers to be informed that the other bwana's head was haribika. Armed with a first-aid kit he set out to meet me fearing the worst, only to be greeted with the words, "Did you manage to escape too?" Keith makes an excellent nurse, he humoured me, put me to bed for a short sleep and got me back to Peters Hut, by which time my delirium had passed. Keith tells the story much better than I do, even though he only witnessed the latter part of the incident. Rumour has it that the guides now demand increased pay in the form of danger money.

2 September

7.40	Left Peters Hut
10.35	Arrived Bismark Hut
10.35 to 11.30	Early lunch
11.30	Left Bismark Hut
14.35	Arrived back at Marangu Hotel

Our wish at this stage was to get back to the hotel and civilisation as quickly as possible. The journey was uneventful, and we made good time, leading the Germans, much to our pride, by several hours. Never before has a hot bath given me so much pleasure. Back to a normal altitude, my nose started to bleed and kept it up all evening. Apart from that, slight sunburn and a few blisters, I felt fine. The following day, after a brief visit to Moshi, we returned to Mombasa. The drive back was uneventful except for a close-up view of elephant.

Conclusion

Was it worth it? My answer in retrospect is "yes", whether or not Keith feels the same after the disappointment of not reaching the

95

summit, I do not know. Our holiday could certainly not be described as restful, nor even, after the first couple of days, as pleasant. It was, however, in my case at least, satisfying. I regard it as time and money well spent.

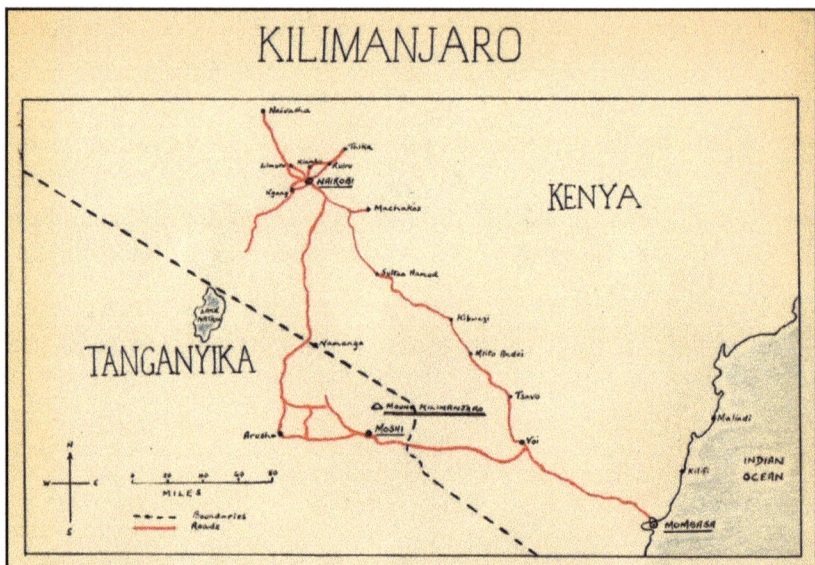

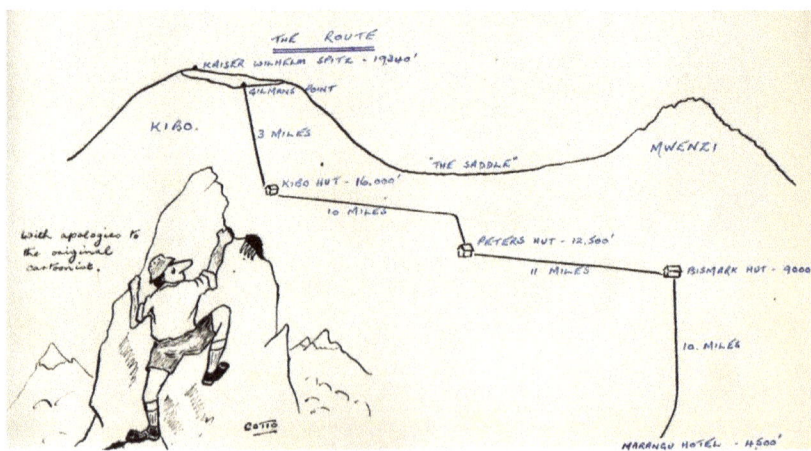

SCHWYZ, in Switzerland, 2I. 9. 60

Dear Mr. Cottingham!

You will wonder yourself, to get a letter from me. I don't know, if you understand german, and so I will me to my some words, which I did learn in our school, remember.

At first, I wish to send to you many good wishes to your climbing of the Kilimandjaro. This is a thing, what is n o t done from most people of the world.

I am sorry, that, how my friends have written to me, on the top of this mountain your camera was not allright. I have now order, to send these four pictures to you.

Number I. 2. and 3. show the glacier from Kibo.

Number 4. show Helmut Schwanz and Wolfgang Heiduk on the top, on Kaiser- Wilhelm- Point.

If you come in next time (or next years), what in your vitality easy may be, to Switzerland, than I would be glad, if you would come for a few days to visite me.

Good luck and

many salutes

97

VII

Kenya – The Winds of Change

April 1958 to April 1961

As a British colony and protectorate, apartheid did not apply in Kenya but, in practice and subject to a few exceptions, there was little social mixing between the races. I believe that at this point in time, this was largely due to differences in the size of population, wealth, education, customs and religions of the various communities.

It would not be appropriate in these jottings to review in detail the differences referred to above, but an indication of the different size of the communities with some analysis of their membership might help to give an understanding of the situation.

Based upon estimates of the East African Statistical Department, the population of Kenya in 1959 was made up as follows:

RACE	NUMBER	% OF TOTAL
European	66,400	1.0
Indian	169,900	2.6
Arab	37,100	0.6
Others	5,900	0.1
Ethnic African	6,171,000	95.7
Total	6,450,300	100.0

In the above table, the description "European" includes all Caucasians wherever born. The figure for "Indian" is made up of Hindus, Muslims, Sikhs and Goans, even though each of these groups has their own religion and customs.

Although "Ethnic African" represented almost 96% of the population, to consider this as one homogeneous group would be a mistake. At this time, although the population census stated that the lingua franca of Kenya was Swahili, there were four main language groups, embracing 87 main tribes of which 19 each accounted for more than 1% of the population of Kenya.

These main tribes had their own traditions, social customs, superstitions and, sometimes, Gods, although the mission schools were converting increasing numbers of Africans to Christianity. The government was also spending substantial amounts on improved educational facilities, but attendance at school for African and Arab children was not compulsory.

A further hindrance towards tribal integration was the topography of Kenya with its wide variation of physical features from coastal beaches to high lands (with a mountain of over 17,000 feet), areas of grassy steppes and the second largest lake in the world. The tribes occupying the different areas of Kenya had different interests, ways of life and occupations.

The Mau Mau: In October 1952 (and, therefore, before my time in Kenya) a state of emergency had been declared in response to the Mau Mau rebellion against the colonial government. Mainly involving members of the Kikuyu tribe in the highlands of Central Province and Great Rift Valley, this rapidly developed into a civil war with as many Kikuyu fighting with the government as those against.

In course of the emergency, which continued until November 1956, there were 25,000 African lives lost, the vast majority real or suspected Mau Mau activists. Sixty-three European combatants died, and 32 European settlers were murdered.

For a period of almost two years prior to the state of emergency, the administering of oaths (oathing) by militants had been taking place on an extensive scale across the Kikuyu community. A vile practice in the eyes of most Europeans, oathing appeared to have some similarity to the traditional Kikuyu circumcision ceremonies and involved the eating of thorax and other body parts of animals, the raw meat of goats, soil and banana leaves. Witch doctors were often involved in the ceremonies with acts of prayer towards Mount Kenya (where the Kikuyu God, Ngai was deemed to reside) which concluded that should the participant fail "may this oath kill me".

Many Kikuyu were taken to oathing ceremonies, which were normally held in secret and at night, under false pretences. The oaths were administered under duress, with violence, coercion and merciless beatings (sometimes to death) being part of the process.

There seem to be differing views of the extent to which the colonial government were aware of oathing, and certainly of its purpose as a method of mobilisation of fighters for the violence to follow, and an attempt to gain support of the local population and their silence as to the identities, operations and whereabouts of the rebels.

Many accounts have been written about the Mau Mau activities, the complex nature of its cause and the reasons for the division in loyalties of the Kikuyu tribe. Ownership of and access to land, a breakdown in the traditional tribal structure, unemployment in the towns and trade union involvement all appear to have been factors. However, my impression is that the barbarism of the Mau Mau against both settlers and its own Kikuyu community made its downfall inevitable and guaranteed that the strongest possible action would be taken by the colonial government for its eradication.

Possibly the defining event for many loyalists and the one which gave greatest focus to the evil nature of Mau Mau, and marked the start of its decline, was the massacre in the village of Lari in March 1953. The local home guard had been called away on pretence of investigating a murder, leaving the undefended village free to be attacked by 600 Mau Mau fighters. Between 74 and 100 Kikuyu loyalists, of which two-thirds were women and children, died from panga wounds or were burned to death in huts set on fire.

Although the events referred to in the preceding paragraphs had occurred before my period in Kenya, they are mentioned in these memoirs because of their relevance to me before I decided to take up an appointment in the territory. However, even after my arrival in 1958, I felt that there was still an atmosphere and air of hostility upcountry and in "Kikuyu Nairobi", which I was pleased to find did not exist on the coast. The Arabs and ethnic Africans on the coast always proved to be helpful and friendly. I can recollect two occasions when my car skidded off the road in sand in remote locations and, within a short time, Africans appeared from the bush as if by magic and, with much laughter and chatter, pushed the vehicle back onto the road.

Although soccer was my first-choice sport, in my last year in Mombasa, I started to play rugby again. This was possible because only Europeans played rugby in Kenya at this time and the games took place on a Saturday to allow necessary time to travel for away fixtures or for visiting teams from other towns in East Africa to get to Mombasa. As soccer games were usually on weekday evenings, there was no clash in timing between the two sports.

In the Easter holiday break of 1961, I toured with the Mombasa Sports Club rugby team. We played three games in three days against Nakuru, Eldoret and Kericho, which involved travelling a total distance of 1,200 miles. All these venues stood at 6,000 feet or more and I had found from playing soccer upcountry that living at sea level and playing at high altitude was difficult. If one adds to this the cumulative effect of the generous hospitality of our hosts in post-match celebrations, it is easy to understand why our results were disappointing. Nevertheless, a good time was had by all and, in my case, it was also a wonderful opportunity to visit parts of Kenya which I had not previously seen.

Our tour commenced with the usual overnight train journey to Nairobi, where we were met by cars which provided our transport for the next three days. From Nairobi, the distance to Nakuru is approximately 100 miles, but after only about 25 miles one reaches the escarpment and commences the descent into the Great Rift Valley, a 6,000-mile long fissure in the earth's crust down Africa, which runs for the whole length of Kenya, effectively cutting the country into two. An early landmark on the escarpment (which I had seen before) was a tiny white church, which had been erected by Italian prisoners of war in World War II.

Nakuru, the fourth largest town in Kenya and regarded as the farming centre of the Highlands, stands almost on the shore of a lake (one of the chain of lakes, which run through the Great Rift Valley) which appeared pink from the presence of an estimated one million lesser flamingos.

The next day we were on the road again travelling about 90 miles north-west to Eldoret. On crossing the equator, we stopped for photographs. Eldoret was founded by Boer farmers from South Africa and was the most northerly point reached in their Great Trek to get away from the British in Victorian times. Several names on the Eldoret team sheet were Afrikaans, reflecting descendancy from the pioneers, but the friendliness and after-match hospitality of everyone was excellent. I did not mention my grandfather's service in the Boer War!

Our final game was against Kericho, about 80 miles south of Eldoret in a beautiful, green tea-growing area. One could have been in England on a summer's day. We played quite well but lost 9–8, nevertheless.

This was to be the last time Roger Caulton (who we had nicknamed Kiwi) would turn out for the club as he was returning home to New Zealand. Some friends from the Coast, but working upcountry, had arrived to support us and brought along a banner with the legend "Kiwi go home", which had been attached to the car in which Roger was travelling. While waiting for us in Londiani, a few miles from Nakuru, the poor unsuspecting African driver (together with the banner) had been arrested as a Mau Mau suspect. The police thought that Kiwi was a Kikuyu word for Europeans. Fortunately, he was released by the time he was required to drive back to Nairobi. Hopefully, he was given a good tip.

The Masai: Although not strictly in sequence in these memoirs, I recollect having travelled on the Nairobi/Nakuru road prior to the previously mentioned rugby tour. However, on that earlier occasion, after dropping down the escarpment into the Great Rift Valley, I turned south before the extinct volcano of Longonot on the road towards the Narok and Mara Reserve. My objective was to see something of the Masai people, the most famous warrior tribe in Kenya and the traditional enemies of the Kikuyu, who they would have readily killed on sight 50 years or so earlier.

Unlike the Kikuyu, who are basically farmers by nature, the Masai are nomads, wandering the grass steppes of Kenya with their cattle, strong in the belief (at least at that time) that God had given them ownership of all the cattle in the world – a possible justification, in their eyes, for instances of rustling which occurred from time to time.

After travelling along the road for some miles, I could see Masai manyattas (villages) in the surrounding hills, but it was several more miles before I came across the first young tribesmen herding the cattle, which provided their staple diet of curdled blood and milk.

Descriptions of the Masai warriors were always the same – cold, aloof and proud, tall and slender in stature, hair plastered with red ochre and dressed in the traditional loose sheet of material, knotted at the shoulder and hanging in front to cover their manhood. Even these young men seemed fierce and impressive.

In the past (and probably still at that time) the Masai tribesmen were famed for their need to fight a lion, armed only with a spear, in order to become a warrior and earn the privilege of wearing the traditional lion head-dress.

Times change and I feel privileged to have seen the Masai at this point in their history. With Kenya's commendable policies for wildlife conservation, the killing of lions is no longer permissible. Less justifiable (in my view) are requirements introduced which affect the traditional dress of the Masai – the need to wear trousers to avoid accusations of nudity!

Changing times: By 1960 the "winds of change" had started to blow across Africa, and Britain's reluctance to continue to pursue colonial ambitions but accept African majority rule in the countries which it controlled or influenced had become clear. Understandably, colonial governments sometimes lacked enthusiasm for the speed with which these changes were taking place. As regards Kenya, a conference was held in London to discuss the future in 1960, and the first general election to include participation of the African political parties was held in 1961. Against the above background, there was a feeling of unease and uncertainty in the mind of many Europeans (both expats and locally born settlers) as to whether they would have an acceptable future under an African controlled government. In East Africa generally, the concern and worry was much greater for the large Asian population, mainly descendants of the Indians who came to Kenya in 1890 to help build the railways from Mombasa into Uganda.

In my case, I was enjoying life in Kenya and had many good friends. I felt that my longer-term career would be in the United Kingdom, but there was a temptation to remain for one more tour. However, several friends were moving on (or had already done so). David Ferrell was back in London, Roger Caulton had returned to New Zealand, John and Pat Russell had been transferred to the London office of John's insurance company employers, but would move to New Zealand in due course, Pat's brother Robin was going to Australia. My world was changing. I decided to return to the UK, but the possibility of moving overseas again remained in my mind for several months.

The first of the East African countries to gain independence was Tanganyika in 1961, when it became Tanzania. Kenya followed, being granted independence in 1963 (by which time I had returned to the UK). The first President of the Republic was Jomo Kenyatta, who had been arrested on the first night of the Emergency in 1952 for his alleged leadership of Mau Mau and remained in prison until released in 1962. He served as President for 15 years until his death in 1978. While a popular figure, his "reign" would be characterised by a strong hold on power which was often used to benefit family or allies.

In January 1985, Kath and I together with Michelle (aged 22) and Nigel (20 years) returned to Kenya for a holiday almost 24 years on since our departure. Our base was the Bamburi Beach Hotel, north of Mombasa and only a mile or so from Nyali Beach Hotel where we had first stayed on arrival in Kenya. However, the miles of largely deserted white, sandy beaches which I remembered, were now well populated by tourists and frequented by Africans selling souvenirs and other wares. Most sadly (in my eyes) were the Masai, the great warriors of Kenya (who I had never before seen at the coast) walking the beaches in their traditional garb and hoping to find someone who would pay for a photograph in their presence.

Our hotel was secured by a steel-linked fence with entrances guarded by Askaris to keep out non-guests and vendors. However, Kenya still had its allure, and we had an enjoyable holiday. Nigel and I took a small boat to the reef, from where we could swim and snorkel in the clear waters. Later in the holiday, we left Kath and Michelle to sun themselves on the beach, while we made a trip by air in a six-seater Bretton Norman Islander plane with an African pilot and another family of three people. We visited a private game park in the Taita Hills close to Amboseli, before flying to a holiday lodge comprising rondels around a central facility in the shadow of Mount Kilimanjaro.

In the game park we had seen rhinoceros, lion, giraffe, buffalo and elephants by the score, including one which had been killed for its tusks by poachers. Engine problems had delayed our flight to the holiday lodge, and we did not arrive until early evening in low cloud, but, as darkness fell, we were able to observe various animals as they visited a nearby watering hole, which had been specially illuminated for the benefit of hotel residents. As we breakfasted the next morning, the sun gradually cleared the mist and low cloud to expose the peak of Kibo in all its glory. This was the highlight of the holiday for me.

Having re-joined Kath and Michelle, we visited the Old Port in Mombasa where a couple of dhows were moored before recommencing their journey down the east coast of Africa. However, no photographs were allowed in the harbour for "security reasons"! Tourists' cameras were being confiscated and films removed and destroyed.

The world seemed to be going mad, but I was pleased that, at the time, Nigel deemed the holiday as "the best ever" (maybe he doesn't remember this in view of all his subsequent travels). For myself, too many things had changed. It was not the Kenya I remembered and loved. I have never returned since.

Postscript: As I draft this paragraph on 29 November 2017, thirty-three years on from the aforementioned holiday and 54 years since I left Kenya and independence was granted, an article appears in the *Daily Telegraph* under the heading "Tear gas, chaos and killings as Kenyatta sworn in as president". This relates to Uhuru Kenyatta becoming president of Kenya for a second term after gaining victory in an election re-run following one held three months earlier, which had been overturned by the Supreme Court citing "illegalities in the count". Mr Raila Odinga, Kenyatta's main political opponent, had refused to participate in the re-run, arguing that it would be no fairer than the first and calling for electoral reforms. Clearly the political and ethnic divisions in Kenya, which had led to scores of people being killed between the two elections and further shootings (including the death of a seven-year-old boy) since the re-run, continue to exist. With little sign of compromise between the parties, violence appears to be escalating and Kenya's security forces taking an ever-tougher line.

I feel saddened (although not surprised) by the situation which has developed in Kenya, but thankful that I made the decision to leave at the end of my contract in 1961 and can still look back at the happy times and good friendships which I enjoyed in a beautiful country.

Mum and Dad – 1931

Family guests at Mum and Dad's wedding in 1931.

On holiday with my maternal grandparents about 1943.

In 1948 with my maternal cousins – John (aged 1 ¾ years), Ian (1 year) and Linda (2 ½ years).

Walter Price in Egypt during WWII.

Carfield School 1st XI in 1949. I am the last seated person at the end of the front row.

Blackpool, 1953, left to right – Gordon Dorling, Tony Worthington, Ted Machon, Myself, Bernard Gaffney and Frank Gunby.

At Royal Air Force, Leconfield, in 1956. Commissioned at last.

Sports Day at Leconfield, 1957. Sqn Ldr Harrison (on my right) joins
the athletes of the Accounts Section.

The ascent of Mount Kilimanjaro in 1960.

Crossing the "Saddle" between Kilimanjaro's twin peaks
of Kibo (19,340 feet) and M'wenzi (16,900 feet).

A brief respite with Helmut Schwarz and Wolfgang Heiduk,
Germans we met on the climb.

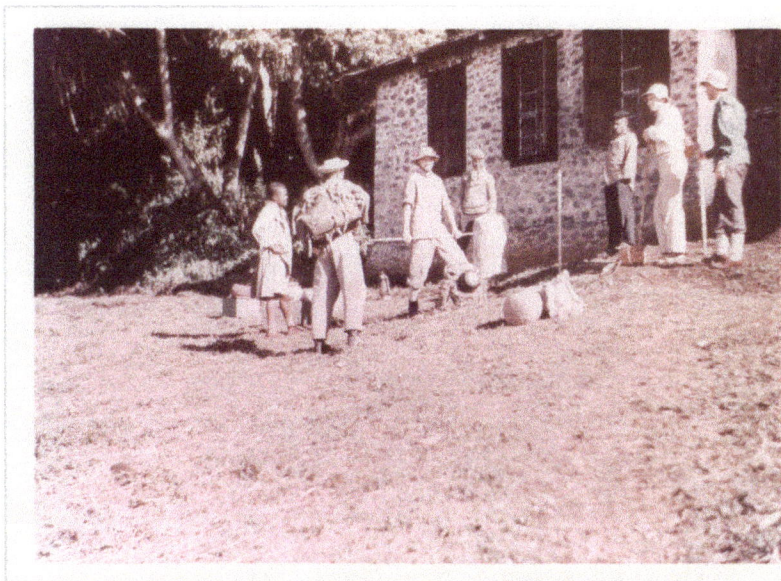

Bismark Hut with porters and our guide, Aleapende.

"Tossing the coin" – Mombasa Sports Club versus a
combined Kenya Schools XI in 1960.

C&L Mombasa Office Fishing Trip in 1960.

VIII

Return to the United Kingdom

June 1961 to March 1964

On return to the United Kingdom after three interesting and enjoyable years in Kenya, I was left feeling undecided on the next steps for my career. I had ruled out Kenya in view of the political situation following the granting of home rule, but not the possibility of one further overseas tour. However, I felt that my long-term future should be in the UK and wondered if this was the appropriate time to take steps in this direction and, if so, in which area of accountancy or finance – professional practise, industry or commerce.

There were several matters for consideration. These including Kath's health – she had been operated on for a toxic thyroid gland while in Kenya and, although this appeared to have been successful, she was still taking medication to balance the position. Furthermore, we both had friends and family in Sheffield, with whom it would be nice to re-establish contact and spend some time. There were no mobile phones at this time and working-class families (such as ours) did not have house phones. Therefore, contact in our period abroad had been only by the occasional exchange of letters.

A further issue for me was concern over my mother's health. While we were in Kenya, she had suffered breast cancer, which had resulted in a mastectomy. On her instructions, I had not been informed in case "it would worry me". She seemed to be making a good recovery, but I wondered if this was a time when I should at least remain nearby.

Around this time, I noticed an advertisement for a finance director to join Williamsons Diamonds Mining Company in Tanzania (formerly Tanganyika, in which country I had worked for several clients). This had been the first of the East African territories to be granted independence and Julius Nyerere, the first prime minister and subsequent president, was (at this stage) regarded as the ideal African leader. The salary and terms appeared exceptionally attractive and, although I had missed the stated date for final applications by a couple of weeks, I decided to send a letter expressing interest.

I was surprised to receive an immediate reply by telephone from Ian Livingstone, the finance director, who was creating the vacancy by taking over a similar position with the group parent company in South Africa. Ian had studied accountancy in Sheffield at about the same time as me, when his father (Doug) had been manager of Sheffield United FC.

Ian stated that there had been many applicants for the position, but these had been whittled down to two people for final interviews which were scheduled for the near future. However, it was considered that my qualifications and experience were ideal, and the board would like to also include me for consideration. I promised to phone back.

This development made me give immediate consideration to all the issues referred to in earlier paragraphs. On balance, I decided that my thoughts of a return to Africa were probably a case of "heart ruling head" and not a sensible course in all the circumstances.

A few days later, Ray Emmitt contacted me. Ray had been a senior manager during my initial period with Cooper Brothers & Co (CB&Co) in Sheffield, and I had established a good rapport with him at that time. David Corsan having returned to London; Ray had been brought into partnership and was now resident partner in charge of Sheffield office and its small branch in Leeds. Ray had heard that I would not be returning to Kenya and said that he would very much like me to re-join the office in Sheffield.

Although still undecided on my long-term future, I felt that I would enjoy working under Ray, at least for a period, and

I accepted the offer. Over the next 34 years, this proved to have been a very good decision.

I quickly settled into the Sheffield office, where the main senior staff supporting Ray (with their grades in CB&Co terms) were Bryan Enzor (senior manager) and Tony Wood (manager). Bryan had been in Sheffield at the time of my previous spell, but Tony had still been away completing national service. I soon established a good relationship with both of them.

There was more than enough work for all three of us and the office was expanding rapidly. We all had audit client responsibilities, but while Bryan tended to concentrate on serving some of the larger companies where long-standing relationships needed to be maintained, Tony and I tried to retain some spare capacity to take on new assignments, often of a one-off nature such as investigations, stock exchange documents, receiverships, etc. Over the next year or so, Tony and I became close work colleagues (consulting on problems and assisting each other whenever necessary) and also very good personal friends, which we remain to this day.

I found that there was an excellent camaraderie in the office, which extended into sporting and social activities outside business hours. There were also many incidents of humour, which helped to keep spirits high, although the funny side of such occurrences was not always apparent at the time – especially for those involved!

One such occasion was when I was in the process of taking over responsibility from Tony Wood for the audit of Staveley Iron and Chemical Company (Staveley), a major client engaged in the production of large iron pipes and castings used in the supply of water and other utilities. The Staveley offices, works buildings and structures, including two blast furnaces and a related chemical plant for producing by-products, were situated on a substantial, many-acre site on the outskirts of Chesterfield.

The message came from our London office that John Pears (SJP), who together with Henry Benson was one of the firm's two senior partners, was proposing to visit Staveley for discussions with senior management. I was instructed to meet SJP at Sheffield

Midland Railway Station on a specified day and time in order to transport him to Staveley.

After making a few tactful enquiries, I discovered that SJP had recently negotiated with the inland revenue (on behalf of a client engaged in heavy industry) and agreed that in certain cases the structures covering plant and machinery could be justified as being part of the cost thereof (rather than of buildings), with the consequence that much higher capital allowances were available for taxation purposes. He was keen to explore the situation with other clients of a similar type (such as Staveley) to see if they could also benefit from this decision.

I arrived at the station as instructed in good time on the appointed day and parked my second-hand, two-door Ford Prefect (the best car I could afford at the time) as convenient to the passenger exit as possible. Having purchased a platform ticket, I then awaited the arrival of SJP ("Sir" to me) with trepidation. He arrived accompanied by two other people, one of whom I recognised as Les Allchorne, the London office senior manager responsible for Staveley's tax affairs. The other person also proved to be a senior manager, name of Pollard (Denis, I think), who I believe had assisted SJP in his negotiations with the revenue.

All three were in London "city" attire – bowler hats, dark suits and carrying briefcases and rolled umbrellas (not a common sight in Sheffield). With the front seats in my car pushed well forward, Allchorne and Pollard climbed ("wriggled" may be a more appropriate word) into the back seats, briefcases and brollies spread across their knees (for some reason they had rejected an offer to make use of the car boot). SJP settled happily into the front passenger seat and seemed to be in affable mood (possibly amused at the discomfort of the other two!). He spent the next 30 minutes duration of the drive to Staveley firing a barrage of questions at me.

On arrival, I introduced the party to the finance director (name I forget) and company secretary (Mr Corker) – both appeared to be wearing their best suits. The enlarged party disappeared into the vastness of the works site to carry out their enquiries, and I was able to escape temporarily to the audit room.

In due course I was summoned to re-join the others for lunch in the directors dining room (a rare privilege for one of my meagre rank), which was presided over by Sam Martin, Chairman of Staveley. Whether or not the lunch was special in honour of SJP, or the normal fare of Staveley board members, I have no idea, but the excellent meal was accompanied by wine and concluded with coffee and liqueur brandy. Very conscious of the importance of my "cargo", I restricted myself to drinking water throughout.

Eventually, SJP thanked the Staveley directors for their hospitality and said it was time to leave for Sheffield station to catch his train. Sam Martin's response was, "No need, John. The train stops in Chesterfield and, in any case, the journey to Chesterfield station is much shorter. Have another brandy and I will arrange a car." John accepted the offer of a brandy but said, "Cottingham has a perfectly adequate vehicle, thank you, and he will take us to the station." (I felt quite flattered at the time.)

"Sheffielders" rarely needed to travel to Chesterfield and, in my case, with national service and time spent in Kenya, it was about six years since my previous visit to the town centre. Nevertheless, I had a reasonable idea of the location of the station and, noting what appeared to be the station approach, I pulled in and dropped off my passengers. However, there were few people around, which made me feel rather uneasy, and I decided to wait for a few minutes before driving off.

This proved to be a wise decision. Within seconds, three bowler-hatted figures came into view, waving umbrellas to indicate that I should not leave. I was out of my car and waiting when SJP arrived and I enquired, "Is there a problem, sir?" John said, "I asked when the next train to London would leave and the man replied, 'Don't know about the next one, guv. I think the last one left about 1950. This is only a goods station'."

My passengers reloaded and I drove off with some concern. Fortunately, after about 200 yards there was a sign indicating the railway station. The situation was saved. Otherwise these memoirs might have been very different!

Returning to more serious matters, I believe that the timing of my return to Sheffield and re-establishment of links with Ray Emmitt were advantageous from my viewpoint.

Son of a Yorkshire coal miner, grammar-school educated and having spent a few years' service as a guardsman with the Coldstreams, Ray was not a typical CB&Co partner of the time. However, he had a great deal of ability, not least in developing the practice and bringing in new clients.

Although we were very different in manner and personality, we had many things in common and Ray and I quickly established a good working relationship (Ray the senior participant of course) and close personal friendship. On one thing in particular, we both held strong views – the opportunity to grow and expand the firm on the eastern side of the Pennines. To achieve this objective, it was clear that more partners would be required.

The past approach of the firm had been to send to the north new young partners from London (or returning from overseas) to fill any vacancies, sometimes only to see them return to London after a period. This had not proved ideal for development of the north. I believe that Ray, with support of Alex More, Manchester-based and the senior partner in the north, believed that suitable local candidates needed to be identified and developed to fill future partnership positions becoming available.

Although it did not occur to me at the time, looking back and considering the assignments, opportunities and introductions which were made available to me over the next two and a half years (some of which I refer to below), I think that Ray had identified me as a potential future partner from the outset on my return to Sheffield. Of course, in these years, the spells away and disruptions to home life, which were necessary in gaining the required experience, were not always appreciated by me.

After a short period of settling back in Sheffield, Ray Emmitt sent for me. He said that he had been contacted by Wilfred Molyneux, head of CB&Co's National Investigation Department, based in London, to see if he (Ray) could recommend someone to assist on an investigation into Wm. Cory Group of companies (Cory's), which (amongst other activities) operated as wharfagers in the Thames Docklands and oil and fuel distributors in East Anglia and southern England. The object of the investigation would be to determine the reasons for Cory's unsatisfactory financial performance (and consequently poor share price) over several years and to make recommendations for actions to be taken and a possible group restructuring.

Ray held Wilfred in high esteem, having worked for him in London office, and he considered that this was an opportunity I should grasp and would benefit from. Consequently, a few days later, I booked into a London hotel and then reported to Wilfred for briefing.

My first task (which covered a period of two or three months) was to visit each of Cory's wharfs in order to review their activities and financial performance. Of course, these were the days when the "Docklands" as we now know it (with its forest of skyscrapers occupied by the head offices of banks and other financial organisations) was not even a dream.

CB&Co's London office, at the time, was in the City with the insalubrious address of Abacus House, Gutter Lane, Cheapside and this was where Wilfred was based. However, in the basement of the building (unrelated to CB&Co) was Balls Brothers public house, which Wilfred and many of the firm's staff would visit for "refreshments" after work. Therefore, on one or two evenings per week, I would break the journey from Docklands to my central London hotel and call at Balls Brothers in order to inform Wilfred of progress. I found Wilfred to be a charming man and a pleasure to work for, but I quickly discovered the wisdom of matching only glasses of ale to his pints if I wished my reports to be coherent!

Following my work in the Docklands, I carried out a similar exercise on Cory's oil and fuel distribution activities. For this task, which took a further few weeks, I based myself in Ipswich.

In due course, the report was finalised (after some input from Henry Benson) and submitted to Cory's board. Wilfred wrote thanking me for my contribution and sent a copy of the final document for my information. I found it difficult to see much evidence of my several months of endeavour, but Wilfred seemed pleased, and the contents of the report and recommendations had been well received by Cory's board.

I assumed that this concluded my involvement with National Investigation Department, but on return to Sheffield, Ray Emmitt informed me that Wilfred had been in touch to ask for my secondment to be extended for a few weeks. This time the work was in connection with a report to the bankers of the Rubery Owen Group, a major client of CB&Co's Birmingham office, with regard to a proposed debenture issue. My role was to review the records of two large subsidiary companies situated in Warrington. The contacts and knowledge gained at one of these companies (Electro Hydraulics) proved valuable a couple of years later when I became involved with its flotation on the London Stock Exchange.

Ray Emmitt's prediction that a spell of working for Wilfred Molyneux would be beneficial to me was correct, not only because of the experience gained in financial investigation work, but the useful contacts made with partners and senior staff in both London and Birmingham offices.

On return to Sheffield, life was quite hectic as I picked up the threads with clients with whom there had been limited opportunity for contact during my period in London. However, it was not all work. There was a good spirit in the office and frequent opportunities for get-togethers after work in local pubs to celebrate promotions, departures, etc.

During the cricket season, there were also regular games against teams selected from the accounting/administrative staff of larger clients. These usually took place on their sports grounds in the evenings and were followed by refreshments, and sometimes further contests at darts, snooker etc. in their sports pavilions. Although social in nature, these activities were always strongly contested, and my suspicion was that companies sometimes included a ringer from a works department to strengthen their playing resources.

This may have been the situation in a game, which springs to mind, against the previously mentioned client – Staveley. Having lost the toss, we were batting last in steadily deteriorating light against a demon fast bowler, who no one on our side had ever seen before! I had already completed my innings for only single figures and none of the other batsmen had fared much better. Coming in at number 7 was my good friend Tony Wood – an unlikely saviour, and the prospect of enjoying the after-match refreshments seemed very close!

Tony prodded forward but failed to connect with any of the first three balls. However, the last of these appeared to brush his thigh on its way to the wicketkeeper. A few seconds later, and much to everyone's surprise, Tony was dancing down the wicket slapping his thigh. The ball had exploded a box of matches in his pocket (he was a cigarette smoker at the time) and set his trousers on fire. I think the scoreboard recorded that Tony had "retired hurt" – or was it hot?

Client games were fun but our serious sporting contests, at this time, were the annual cricket and football matches between teams representing the offices on either side of the Pennines – Sheffield and Leeds on the east and Manchester and Liverpool on the west. Without a need to consider client contacts and relationships, the teams for these "Roses" encounters could be selected purely on merit and many of those chosen were still playing regularly for club sides. Our star (in both sports) was Bob Crossley, who had played cricket for Yorkshire Colts (effectively the County 2nd XI) and was also a useful centre-half. Fortunately, as I was captain and sole selector, my place in the teams was always assured!

For the cricket match, each of the contesting sides was expected to nominate an umpire. However, as the game was always held on the annual sports day of the northern offices, for which all staff (both male and female) were granted leave to attend, this was never an easy position to fill in view of the competing attractions of food, drink, sunbathing (sometimes) and fraternisation with attendees from other offices.

Consequently, I was delighted when Archie Gallon, a recently appointed cashier for Sheffield office, put himself forward as a volunteer for the role of umpire. After a brief discussion with Archie, I felt some doubt as to whether his enthusiasm was matched by his knowledge of the rules of cricket. However, as the saying goes "a volunteer is better than a pressed man" and I accepted his offer.

I was batsman at the crease on the first occasion when Archie officiated. The ball struck my pad and the Lancastrians, in unison (even those fielding on the boundary), screamed howzat in hope of a "leg before wicket" decision. In my view the ball would have missed the stumps by at least a couple of feet. However, after a few seconds hesitation, Archie's arm went up, with finger pointing skywards.

I stood my ground, glared at Archie and said, "Are you SURE, Gallon." Archie's finger began to waiver and, to the fury of the Lancastrians, his arm fell back to his side and he pronounced, "Not Out." This incident guaranteed Archie's nomination as the choice of umpire by the east Pennines side for the remainder of his service with the firm.

In addition to enjoying the office camaraderie and work experience in this period, I was fortunate to deal with several able and interesting clients. Two of these people, of very different nature and character are discussed below. Both became excellent clients of the firm, providing work opportunities well beyond the period referred to in this chapter.

One of the pleasures of life at CB&Co at this time was the opportunity to serve talented, ambitious and demanding people of very different personalities, outlooks and qualities. This was possible against the background of CB&Co's highly documented procedures and guidelines set out in a manual of seven parts dealing with most areas of professional work, but accepting the need for some flexibility of approach, with personal responsibility for actions and, importantly, evidence of sensible consultation with appropriate colleagues where necessary.

The first of the individuals I will refer to is Ronald Arthur Palfreyman (Ron), who had been introduced to Sheffield office about 1961 from CB&Co, London. The introduction was probably because Ron's base office was in Heanor, Derbyshire (the area where his home, with wife and family, was also located), which was considered to be within the Sheffield catchment area. However, as explained in later paragraphs, at this point in time, Ron normally spent only Friday nights in Heanor, followed by a Saturday morning of attendance at his local office before moving on.

A qualified chartered accountant of reserved manner, but with a good sense of humour and a quiet charm, Ron gave the impression of being somewhat laid-back. However, he proved to be imaginative, ambitious and very entrepreneurial – exactly the type of client that Ray Emmitt warmed to. Therefore, it was no surprise that the two quickly established a good rapport and personal friendship.

For clients which Ray considered were likely to require frequent and speedy attention, it was his custom to involve an appropriate second CB&Co contact to ensure that the necessary service was readily available. This became my role in the case of Ron and, consequently, over a period, I also became quite close to him. However, throughout my years in practise, I maintained an awareness that client relationships should never become so strong that they could influence professional judgements. In due course, this belief became important in this case.

Ron lived up to the impressions that Ray and I had formed, and over the next two years I was responsible for financial investigations, on his behalf, into seven companies – three operating in the hosiery industry and four involved in construction and related activities, all of which companies Ron acquired. These were appropriately formed into two groups, of which he became chairman, and floated on the London Stock Exchange as Contour Hosiery in 1964 and FPA Construction Group in 1965, respectively. After these listings, CB&Co continued to benefit from a flow of work as auditors and advisors of the companies concerned.

As regards my personal development, apart from the valuable work experience in connection with the above activities, I established excellent relationships with the joint managing directors of Singer & Friedlander, the sponsoring merchant bank, with two partners in Slaughter & May (one of the leading City law firms) and with Ted Vickers, the very able lawyer, providing advice to Ron personally. I had the pleasure of working with all these people at various times (on assignments unrelated to Ron) over following years.

Ron continued to be very active making other acquisitions, some of which became clients of CB&Co – notably the David Dixon Group, although I was not personally involved in this case. My impression was that Ron had a wide range of contacts, providing a constant flow of smallish investment opportunities which he made in equity or loans, but that CB&Co would be asked to become involved only if these grew to a certain size.

Outside business, Ron's interests (as a spectator) appeared to be in sport and attendance at venues such as Wembley, Lords, Ascot and York Races were regular events in his diary, often providing an opportunity to strengthen his circle of contacts by providing entertainment to appropriate people on such occasions.

I particularly remember the 1966 FA Cup Final when Everton met Sheffield Wednesday at the "old" Wembley. I was walking together with crowds of supporters from the railway station to the ground when a white Rolls Royce, bearing the registration RAP1, pulled alongside me and hooted. Ron's head appeared at the window and he said, "Get in." For the last few hundred yards, I enjoyed the envious glances of the crowds believing that I was someone of importance! Wednesday lost, but I was not too saddened – I'm a Blade.

Another aspect of my non-business relationship with Ron was the occasional opportunity to meet some of the many interesting people with whom he had contact. One of these was the Duke of Devonshire, when I attended (as Ron's representative) a luncheon party of about a dozen people at Chatsworth House. This was hosted by the Duke, as President of Derbyshire County Cricket Club in its centenary year of 1970, seeking support of the "Great and Good" of the county to a fundraising initiative. I reported back to Ron and presumably he or one of his companies made a contribution. However, Ron was greatly amused that, although a member and supporter of Derbyshire's competitor, Yorkshire County Cricket Club, I was personally persuaded by the Duke to purchase several limited edition "Duchess Dishes", produced by Royal Crown Derby in support of the appeal – I still have them!

As I became more closely acquainted with Ron and gained a knowledge of his private life, I found that he had a second home and "partner" based in Chesterfield. Although obviously not legally married to this lady, within the local community and by friends and neighbours in the area, she was clearly believed to be Ron's wife and he appeared to treat her as such. However, strangely (it seemed to me), after the previously mentioned brief visit to Heanor, Ron's normal routine was to travel to Chesterfield on Saturday afternoon, where he would spend the remainder of the weekend, but return to his suite at the Hyde Park Hotel, London, for Monday to Thursday! I felt it tactful not to enquire into the reason for this.

With the close proximity of Ron's second home to Sheffield, my wife, Kath, and I (often together with Ray Emmitt and his wife, Pat) would occasionally meet with Ron and his partner (who proved to be a very likeable person) for dinner or at some other social function. However, my rule throughout the years was not to discuss clients' affairs (business or private) with third parties, unless there was a clear requirement to do so. I also applied this rule to my wife and, consequently, to the best of Kath's belief, Ron's Chesterfield partner was his wife. Unfortunately, there was an occasion when application of this rule proved an embarrassment to both Kath and myself.

Each year in respect of the "main meeting" at York Races, Ron would reserve a hospitality suite for two consecutive days in the names of companies of which he was chairman. My recollection is that this would usually be FPA Construction Group (FPA) for the first day, to be followed by the David Dixon Group. Guests and business contacts, with their spouses, would be invited to attend for the company with which they had connections. Ron and the other directors of the company concerned, supported by their wives, would be present and act as hosts.

As my dealings were mainly with FPA, Kath and I would attend on the first day, when Ron, accompanied by his Chesterfield partner, would be the principal hosts. One year, having enjoyed attendance on the first day, Ron phoned me in the evening to say that there had been a cancellation of guests for day two and he wondered if Kath and I would like to attend in order to restore the numbers – an invitation which we were pleased to accept. However, I was unaware that on this "David Dixon day", it was the turn of Ron's wife (and not his Chesterfield partner) to be present. Consequently, when we arrived, Kath suffered the surprise and embarrassment of being greeted by Ron, accompanied by a wife she had not previously met or even heard of. To her credit, Kath coped with the situation quite well, but made me aware of her views on my approach to client confidentiality on the way home! I did not make the same mistake again.

In the next few paragraphs, I continue my comments relating to Ron to a conclusion, even though this means going into events which occurred many years beyond the dates stated as covered in this chapter.

Over a period of time, my contact with Ron declined. In part this was because he had business interests, dealt with by other firms of accountants, which seemed to be requiring an increased level of his involvement. In addition, as CB&Co expanded, with more offices being opened and new partners admitted, I had started to hand over some responsibilities in order to create time for commitments in London and overseas – although I always retained the lead partner role for the FPA Construction Group.

The opportunity to see Ron socially also diminished from about 1972, when he and his partner moved their home from Chesterfield to Abingdon, near Oxford, into a delightful house with substantial grounds and a detached lodge, which Ron converted into his office.

I visited this house on a couple of occasions and, because of my Royal Air Force connections, found it of special interest as the birthplace and boyhood home of Group Captain Leonard Cheshire, VC, OM, DSO and 2 bars, DFM and bar, the most highly decorated British Serviceman of WWII. Group Captain Cheshire became particularly famous when, after taking over command of 617 (Dambuster) Squadron, he added to its lustre by establishing it as the Pathfinders, marking targets for bombing raids with an error of not more than 10 yards by dangerous low-level flying using Mosquito aircraft. He was the British observer when the atom bomb was dropped on Nagasaki on 9 August 1945, an experience he would never forget and was probably relevant to his post-war actions in establishing the first Leonard Cheshire Home, and involvement in the Foundation which went on to operate 75 such homes in the UK and numerous others in 45 countries throughout the world.

As time moved on and because of my reduced contact with Ron, I was unaware that he was experiencing financial problems, mainly, I believe, in connection with certain of the private investments and loans to friends, particularly in relation to guarantees given to banks which were being called in. Under these financial pressures, Ron had borrowed money from FPA, a public company of which he was a director (and CB&Co were auditors) in breach of Companies Act regulations.

The above action left me with no choice other than to qualify the CB&Co audit report on the FPA accounts and I believe that this was one of the matters considered at a disciplinary hearing of the Institute of Chartered Accountants in England and Wales at which the decision was made for Ron to be excluded from membership. However, much more damaging to Ron at this time was his decline into personal insolvency.

I took no pleasure from the above situation. I liked Ron and had enjoyed my dealings and friendship with him. He had also generated a great deal of work for CB&Co over the years. Sadly, as sometimes occurs with entrepreneurs, he appears to have failed to adequately recognise some of the risks he was taking. My final contact with Ron was in 1998 at the memorial service for Ray Emmitt. We had limited opportunity for conversation, but he was friendly and still very charming. Ron passed away only two years later.

Following on from Ron Palfreyman, a second client of significance with whom I first became acquainted in this period (although most of the work he generated for the firm came some years later) was also referred to Sheffield office from CB&Co, London. On this occasion the contact came from Francis Shearer (JFS), a partner of quite high seniority in the firm, in a telephone

129

call in late autumn 1963. Ray Emmitt was out of the office and I took the call.

JFS informed me that we should expect to be contacted by Robert Atkinson, the chief executive (on secondment from the merchant bank, Kayser Ullman) of Butler Machine Tools of Halifax (Butlers). Apparently, Butlers were considering the acquisition of a privately owned engineering company based in Sheffield, subject to receiving a satisfactory investigation report from CB&Co.

JFS continued by saying that we would find Robert Atkinson to be a most interesting character – a marine engineer by profession who, as a Royal Naval lieutenant in WWII had commanded corvettes in the Battle of the Atlantic, winning three Distinguished Service Crosses, being mentioned in dispatches and reaching the rank of lieutenant commander by the time of demobilisation. JFS concluded that, against this background, it should not surprise me to hear that Robert Atkinson would be determined in his objectives and expect a high level of service.

I apprised Ray Emmitt of the conversation with JFS on his return to the office. He instructed that, when received, I should take the phone call from Robert Atkinson and carry out the required investigation. Consequently, when he got in touch, I visited him in Halifax for a detailed briefing. I found Robert to be likeable, direct and impatient for us to get on with the work without delay. He fully justified the image I had formed of him in my mind from the comments of JFS, except in one respect, although impressive in presence, Robert was quite small in physical stature.

I was aware from previous investigations that, when management has devoted time and energy in considering a possible acquisition, and steadily built up enthusiasm for its consummation, the last thing they wish to receive is a financial report which pours cold water on the proposal. Unfortunately, in this case, our work gave rise to a number of concerns at an early stage and, without going into detail, we formed the view that both fixed and current assets were overvalued and, probably of more importance, that the expected future maintainable profit, which formed the main basis for the required purchase consideration, was suspect.

I decided to see Robert Atkinson before submission of our report in order to explain our concerns, rather than for him to receive the bad news cold in the form of a written document. It was a long meeting, and I was subjected to a thorough cross-examination. In particular, Robert found it difficult to understand why these concerns had not been apparent to everyone from a review of the unqualified audited accounts of the company. However, in due course, and to my relief, he accepted our views and thanked me for the work, stating that he had decided not to proceed with the acquisition. We parted on very good terms.

This contact with Robert Atkinson had been interesting but proved to be of great value in the longer term when, in 1972, he left the City of London to become chairman of Aurora Gear and Engineering in Sheffield. From this base, with the active involvement of CB&Co, Sheffield office, he played a major role over the next six years in the rationalisation of the private sector of the steel industry. However, more about this in a later chapter.

December was the month for annual staff reviews at CB& Co, when reports were prepared on each individual by their line managers as a basis for an interview with a partner. These interviews were normally conducted by the resident partners in each office, who would usually have a good knowledge of the staff concerned. Discussions would cover the person's performance in the year, salary, grade and prospects. People would be informed if they were not expected to achieve promotion to the next grade in future, in case they wished to make a decision to pursue their careers elsewhere.

There was always a steady inflow of people coming up through articled clerkship and there was no wish to retain staff unless they were of high quality.

The current, rather softer, approach for dealing with human resources had not been developed at that time – and certainly not within CB&Co. The basic rule was that people should demonstrate their abilities by grasping any opportunity to take on the

131

responsibilities of the person above them (thus providing that person with the time to do likewise).

Against the above background, it came as a surprise to Tony Wood and myself to be informed in December 1963 that our interviews would not be held in Sheffield but take place in London office, with the firm's joint senior partners, John Pears (SJP) and Henry Benson (HAB). I phoned Ray Emmitt the evening before the London visit to enquire why we were being summoned. His reply – "You will find out when you get there – but behave yourself" was not very helpful.

Tony was first to go into the lion's den. He emerged a few minutes later, looking somewhat disappointed. He said that the good news was of his promotion to senior manager, but that he would need to relocate to Newcastle to become resident manager of a new branch office we had opened from Sheffield. This move would not have been Tony's choice.

It was then my turn to face the "great men". SJP conducted the interview and after a few trivial questions, for which I felt he must already know the answers, he said, "If we offered you a partnership, would you accept?" This was not a question I had expected and, although I was enjoying my role with CB&Co, I still had thoughts of a possible career in industry or commerce in the longer term. Therefore, I replied, "Do you require a reply now, sir?" SJP's response was, "I had hoped that you would accept with some enthusiasm."

After a few seconds, I said, "It is just that it was rather a shock, sir." SJP's reply to this was, "I hope you mean a surprise rather than a shock." By this stage, I had gathered my thoughts and composure and I said, "Yes, sir, I would be very pleased to accept."

At this point, HAB spoke for the first time to inform me that I would become a senior manager forthwith, but my admission to partnership would be in three months' time at the start of the firm's financial year of 1 April 1964. He added that I must not inform anyone of this decision before that date. I observed this requirement, even in the case of Tony, who was sitting outside the room waiting for me.

In my short meeting there had been no mention of remuneration or profit share, required capital injection or any other matters relating to partnership. This was the way the firm was conducted in these days. Everything I needed to know was obtained later in discussion with Ray Emmitt and various senior clerks in the firm's administrative departments in London.

Unlike the present day, when partners seem to come and go and retire or move to other external roles in their early fifties, the acceptance of partnership in CB&Co in the 1960s (and for many years subsequently) was regarded as a commitment for the remainder of one's working life up to the age of 60. As partners we fared quite well financially but not, I think, as well as current partners in the "Big Four" firms. However, I believe that we had the best of times and a great camaraderie existed – a view often express by former colleagues when we meet. The decision I made in 1963 to become a partner in CB&Co was one I have never regretted.

A few weeks after my above interview with the senior partners, Francis Shearer telephoned. He said that Robert Atkinson had been in touch to inform him "as a matter of courtesy" that he intended to contact me in order to offer the position of finance director at Butlers. Francis said that he was aware of my meeting with John and Henry and that I had already accepted the offer of partnership with the firm. He assumed that I would honour this decision. I confirmed that this was my intention.

Robert phoned a few days later and made the offer referred to. I did not mention that Francis had already spoken to me. I thanked Robert for the offer and said that I felt quite flattered to be considered for the position, but I had decided that my long-term future should be at CB&Co. I said that I had enjoyed working for Robert on the proposed Sheffield acquisition, even though it had come to nought, and that I hoped there would be other opportunities for us to work together. As our conversation terminated, I felt that a good rapport had been established between us.

IX

Michelle, Mum and Dad

The Saddest of Times

Chapter VIII covered my return from Kenya and readjustment, over a three-year period, to a professional working life in the UK, which culminated in my admission to partnership with CB&Co on 1 April 1964. However, it was also in this period that one of the most significant events in the private lives of my wife, Kathleen (Kath) and myself took place, in the birth of our daughter, Michelle Jayne, on 5 August 1962. This was followed, approximately two years and four months later, with an equally important event, when our son, Nigel David, came into the world on 13 December 1964.

In the case of Michelle, she was a full-term breech birth, weighing only 4lb 2oz. She was, however, 21 inches long but very floppy and appeared to have little muscular strength. After birth, Michelle was kept in hospital for almost three months. Kath visited every day and I called at the hospital each evening after leaving the office (unless working away from Sheffield). However, as Michelle was kept in an incubator for the first two months, and still apparently not capable of making much movement, these visits were merely an opportunity to see her with no chance of physical contact. None of the medical staff seemed able to give any reason for Michelle's condition or make a prognosis for the longer term.

Kath and I (and not least my parents) were delighted when we were eventually allowed to take Michelle home. She had gained some weight but still showed little sign of movement. The instructions were to give Michelle a 3oz bottle every three hours throughout the day and night. Kath dedicated herself to this task, getting up once or twice during the night as necessary. However, Michelle seemed to have problems in sucking, and feeding her was not easy. Each session could take up to one hour, with Michelle frequently having to be kept awake in order to make sure that she received the required food.

Throughout these early months of her life, Michelle continued to show little strength or to give an indication of interest in anything. Even for her to grasp our fingers seemed a major step forward, and she was about 18 months old before she could sit up without support. Progress was very slow.

However, to our delight and surprise, Michelle tottered to her feet and walked a few steps at two and a half years. This followed many hours when we had placed her in a baby bouncer (which experience she enjoyed) hoping to strengthen her legs. She had never crawled but had shuffled along on her bottom for some months. Michelle's gaining of confidence and starting to walk coincided with Nigel appearing on the scene. As a normal but very active child, Nigel was probably good for Michelle's development – although, on occasions, we used to put Michelle in the playpen in order to give protection against Nigel's marauding nature.

From an early age, Nigel seemed to show an understanding of Michelle's problems and an appreciation of the frustrations, which sometimes gave rise to her tantrums. As a result, and as they grew up, he could often achieve more in cooling these outbursts than either Kath or myself.

We were still unaware of the reasons for Michelle's problems but, around this time, we were informed by the paediatrician that he believed she was suffering from a rare syndrome, although no name was given and on which condition there appeared to be very little knowledge. However, as Michelle had started to walk without difficulty, seemed to be getting stronger and was taking more interest in things generally, we believed (wrongly, as it proved) that the major problems were behind us and that it was just a matter of time for everything to be resolved.

At the age of about four years, a new problem arose. Michelle started to gain weight, and from being petite, she became quite roly-poly. Unfortunately, no one seemed able to give any reason or real advice, but Kath started to pay particular attention to Michelle's diet and to make regular hospital visits for checks on her weight and general progress. There was still no suggestion from the medical advisors that her problems were anything more than weight gain or that more complex cognitive and behavioural issues may need to be considered.

Michelle had attended a local playgroup from about three and a half years and transferred to a small private school approximately one year later. In some respects, she seemed quite intelligent, particularly considering her difficult start in life. She could read words before she was five and by the time Nigel joined the same school, she was quite proficient at reading and enjoyed trying to teach him – despite his occasional lack of enthusiasm!

After a year or so, Michelle moved to a large private school, where we hoped she would be able to take the GCE examinations. She had seemed to be developing into a normal child, but when about 10 years old more problems emerged. She was caught stealing food, not only at home but at school. It also became obvious that Michelle had to struggle in order to keep pace with the other children in her studies, particularly in anything involving figures. Furthermore, because of a lack of coordination, she could not take part in certain activities, for example needlework and physical training. Michelle seemed to have no close friends at school and was becoming isolated from the other children.

We tried to compensate at home by encouraging Michelle in the things that she could do – her reading of books and poetry, jigsaw puzzles, word games, etc. She also attended a dancing school, joined the Brownies and became a member of a local Sunday school. She was enthusiastic to be involved in any events arranged by these organisations, but often became upset or displayed tantrums at home from the frustrations of being unable to prepare properly for activities which required dexterity or physical strength. In some of these cases, Kath or I tried to help by becoming involved, but Michelle's anguish would continue until the very last second when she could see that everything had been completed.

In the end and at the age of 13, we found it necessary to take Michelle away from the private school she had been attending, as she seemed to be on the brink of a nervous breakdown. We managed to get her a place in a special school for "delicate children" at Bents Green in Sheffield. However, to achieve this, we had to move house from Derbyshire (where we had become happily settled) back into Sheffield. The staff at the new school (and particularly the headmaster) were understanding and helpful in dealing with Michelle's problems in connection with both diet and tantrums and she seemed much happier. She eventually obtained low-grade GCEs in English and History.

On leaving school, Michelle attended a two-year "general course for the handicapped" at a local college. She then had a year of Youth Opportunity Training at a NCH family centre, which she seemed to enjoy. This was followed by a period at a rehabilitation centre, but as the training was mainly for assembly line work, because of Michelle's poor coordination and control of her hands, this was of negligible benefit. Michelle subsequently worked on a voluntary, unpaid basis, assisting in a local playgroup. She clearly enjoyed helping the children but, because of physical and behavioural problems (including a further incident of stealing food), the position lasted less than a year.

Kath and I continued to seek an explanation for Michelle's problems and any possible way in which her condition could be improved. At the age of 13 years, the hospital doctor, whom we regularly consulted, recommended a course of growth hormone treatment. After consideration and partly, I think, in desperation, we agreed to this.

The course required injections three times per week for two years. Michelle bravely endured all this with little protest. However, the treatment was unpleasant, unsuccessful and left the legacy of future danger from Creutzfeldt-Jacob Disease (CJD), although no one had been aware of this risk at the time. The experience left Kath and myself feeling that we would need much more evidence of likely success before agreeing to any future proposals of this nature.

It was also during this post-school period, about 17 years after Michelle's birth, that we were eventually given the name of the condition from which she was suffering – the Prader-Willi Syndrome (PWS). There still appeared to be little information available on the syndrome, but we were told that those suffering usually have a compulsion to eat and, if uncontrolled, they could literally eat themselves to death. It was also suggested to us that Michelle's lifespan may not extend much beyond her late teens.

Although this news was devastating, in some ways it helped. We were able to start making enquiries into the syndrome and understand what to expect. We also realised that many of Michelle's actions – her tantrums, the obsession for food, etc., were part of her condition and not because she was being difficult or naughty. Despite the comments on possible lifespan, we resolved to make sure that Michelle lived for as long as possible and that we enjoyed our time with her.

Having lost her position with the playgroup, Michelle (at the age of about 22 years) was without any employment or daily commitments, with no realistic possibility of the situation changing. This was an immediate problem for Kath and me. Although Michelle seemed quite content to spend her time reading, completing jigsaw or word puzzles and watching certain programmes on TV, Kath had her own responsibilities and commitments and could not be tied down at home every hour of the day. On the other hand, we did not consider Michelle to be sufficiently mature or capable to be left at home alone – particularly as the Croft (where we now lived in Sheffield) was a very large house.

Fortunately, the answer came in arranging for Pat (Kath's help/cleaner) who attended several mornings each week (and got on quite well with Michelle) to remain in the afternoons as Michelle's companion. The arrangement worked well, and the pair would sometimes go out for walks or visit places of interest. Pat's presence also made it possible for Michelle to make use of our heated outdoor pool, situated in a courtyard next to the house. When in the water, Michelle enjoyed the feeling of weightlessness and would often spend 40 minutes or so swimming up and down the pool. This was useful exercise for Michelle, and we would not have allowed her to use the pool without another person being present.

The battle to control Michelle's weight continued over the years. Outwardly, Michelle gave the impression of co-operation and would meticulously weigh and check the items for her diet. However, in practice, she seemed more concerned with obtaining every morsel of her entitlement rather than in controlling the calorie intake. We were also aware that, given the opportunity, Michelle would cheat by buying extra food, or stealing from the larder if left unlocked. As we had been warned, eating was a compulsion which she was unable to resist no matter how unappetising the item.

In 1983, we were put in touch with the newly formed National Association for Prader-Willi Sufferers. This provided an opportunity to meet other families with similar problems as ourselves, although most of the sufferers were children and, therefore, much younger than Michelle. My suspicion was that, in the past, there would have been many PWS sufferers who had not been diagnosed but simply regarded as being obese and possibly unruly.

The objectives of the new association included:

- increasing public awareness and interest in the syndrome,
- providing finance for research; and
- in the longer term, assisting toward the financing of suitable sheltered accommodation for PWS sufferers.

The last objective was of particular interest to Kath and myself. We had long been concerned as to what would happen to Michelle if she outlived us.

Kath took an immediate interest in becoming involved with the association, often including Michelle in her activities. Together, over the next 10 years they:

- helped to raise funds,
- were the subject of an article giving details of the syndrome in *Woman's Realm* magazine,

- appeared on television (the presenters, camera crew and recording staff all coming to the Croft).

Kath also acted as a point of contact and source of advice for families of newly identified sufferers of PWS in the Sheffield and North Derbyshire areas. In addition, she gave a talk and answered questions on our experiences with Michelle to an audience including a doctor, care workers and parents.

A major hiccup during the above 10-year period was in 1986, when Michelle started to gain weight rapidly and, despite all our efforts, reached nearly 16 stone. Michelle was only 4ft 7in tall and the above weight was her highest ever. With the doctors' agreement, Michelle was hospitalised at Claremont Private Hospital (quite close to where we lived) to be placed on a monitored diet. Eventually, a diet was found which suited her and in 5 months she lost three stone (and raised £200 for the PWS Association).

Once back at home, Michelle continued life much as before, although as the years passed, she seemed increasingly inflexible in her attitudes and with regard to any change in circumstances or routines. Nevertheless, despite the periodic tantrums, she joined Kath and myself (and, in the earlier days, Nigel) on holidays in several parts of the world (to which I refer later). She also demonstrated that, in some respects, she was quite capable. She prepared many of her own meals, could bathe and dress herself and, for accustomed journeys, could travel alone by bus to meet her friend (whom she had originally been with at Bents Green School).

However, as we moved into the mid-1990s, Michelle's weight started to increase again, and she also seemed weaker and slower in her actions. Even getting into and out of the bath became a problem and required help. Stupidly, I assumed that the problem was simply weight and diet related, as in the past. However, after consulting our doctor and being referred to a specialist, tests showed that (probably as a result of Michelle's condition over many years) her kidneys were beginning to fail and would not be effective for much longer.

Fortunately, Nigel, who had spent several years living and working in Australia, was in Britain on a year's sabbatical. Much of the year had already passed and we had seen Nigel on several occasions, including a visit he had made to the Croft when he had taken Michelle to see a film of her choice followed by a meal out.

In the new and tragic circumstances, Nigel delayed his return arrangements for Australia to provide help and support to Kath in dealing with Michelle as she steadily declined. His presence, patience and influence with Michelle were of immense value as she became increasingly less mobile and difficult to care for. Kath would have been unable to cope by herself.

However, after a few weeks, Michelle required more medical treatment and attention than could be provided at home and she was re-admitted to the private hospital where her weight reduction program had taken place in 1986. Kath and Nigel visited Michelle at different times each day, and I attended straight from the office in the evening. This was the time when the medical specialist usually made his visit and I was able to check on the latest position, which sadly was rarely good news. These visits were shortly before Michelle's evening meal was due, and she would usually be fretting in anticipation that food shown in the menu may not be available. Whatever I said to try and calm her, Michelle would become upset and I would return home depressed.

In the early hours of 6 February 1998, we were awakened by the telephone to be informed that Michelle had very little time left. We quickly threw on clothing and were at the hospital within about 20 minutes but were too late. Michelle had already passed away at the age of 35 years. We returned home grieving – it was still night, and everything seemed unreal.

The few weeks up to the date of Michelle's death were the most difficult and unhappy period of my life and, I am sure, in the lives of Kath and Nigel.

Fifty-seven years on since Michelle's birth (at the time of writing) and with much water gone under the bridge, it is interesting to read the information on PWS which is now available on the internet. In particular, I found the opening summary (part of which I paraphrase below) to a 20-page report by the National

Organisation for Rare Disorders of relevance to the case of Michelle – "PWS is a genetic multisystem disorder characterised during infancy by lethargy, diminished muscle tone, a weak suck and feeding difficulties with poor weight gain and growth and other hormone deficiency. In childhood, features of the disorder include short stature... and an excessive appetite. Affected individuals do not feel satisfied after completing a meal. Without intervention, overeating can lead to onset of life-threatening obesity. The food compulsion requires constant supervision. Individuals with severe obesity may have an increased risk of cardiac insufficiency, sleep apnea, diabetes, respiratory problems and other serious conditions that can cause life-threatening complications. All individuals with PWS have some cognitive impairment ... behavioural problems are common and can include temper tantrums, obsessive/compulsive behaviour."

In the body of the report, mention is made of people with the disorder, if left unsupervised, endangering themselves by "eating harmful food... and in excessive quantities". Reference is also made of unusual behaviours such as "hoarding of food".

Wikipedia provides similar information to that contained in the above report. It also confirms that PWS (which, it states, affects between 10,000 and 30,000 people) has no cure, but stresses that a program of treatment from birth may "improve outcomes". If this information had been available at the time of Michelle's birth, we may have been able to take more actions to help her. However, as will be explained in Chapter X, despite the problems and concerns we experienced, Michelle gave us a great deal of happiness.

It is also worth recording that, looking back, I feel great appreciation for the care, patience and understanding of the doctors and medical staff, with whom Kath and I dealt over Michelle's life. They appreciated and recognised our concerns and did their best to help. The problem was a lack of knowledge of the syndrome and, therefore, how to respond in the critical first half of Michelle's existence.

The 35 years span of Michelle's life substantially coincided with the period I served as a partner with CB&Co/Coopers &

Lybrand – starting shortly before my admission into partnership and extending about two years after my retirement. During this period, my role in the firm steadily progressed, with a need to spend a good deal of time in London and other UK offices and also make regular visits to Scandinavia.

I discuss my professional life during these years in later chapters. Suffice to say, at this stage, that for reasons mentioned below, I was fortunate to be able to keep my home and a base office in Sheffield. Most importantly, in this connection, Michelle always reacted badly to change, unfamiliarity and uncertainty. A move to a different area and the loss of support from family and friends, particularly my parents, would have upset Michelle and made life for Kath and myself much more difficult.

In his book *Goodbye to Yorkshire*, Roy Hattersley, the former Under-Secretary of State at the Department of Employment and Minister of Defence (Administration) in the Labour government of 1966, Sheffield born and often (in my experience) to be found in the stands watching Sheffield Wednesday on match days, quotes Oscar Wilde, who believed that "when good Americans die, they go to Paris." Roy then expresses his view that "There is no doubt where good Sheffielders go. They go to Sheffield."

This is a sentiment which I can appreciate. The opportunity to be in Sheffield on most weekends, with chance for a round of golf at Sickleholme GC on Saturday morning (with my usual partners – Tony Wood and Matt Sheppard), followed by attendance at Bramall Lane in the afternoon on days when the Blades were at home, and a game of squash before lunch on Sunday morning against my regular opponent, John Swynnerton, were the greatest of pleasures.

Add, to the above, a visit to the Lyceum Theatre following a meal at one of our favourite local restaurants to obtain the perfect antidote to the pressures and long working hours of the weekdays.

I have previously mentioned my parents – Eleanor and Jack – I could not have wished for better. They were quietly supportive to Kath and myself throughout their lives and unfailingly loving towards Michelle and Nigel.

Around 1972, as Dad moved towards retirement at the age of 65 years, he had not been very well, and my parents moved from their council house with a garden to a council flat. The move was primarily instigated by Mum, partly I believe to be nearer to the home of her sister Connie. However, it proved to be a mistake. The accommodation was cramped, the outlook poor and my parents missed the friendliness of their previous neighbours.

Mum and Dad never complained, but Kath quickly recognised the situation and suggested that we should try to help. Having been a CB&Co partner for seven or eight years, and with my profit share steadily increasing, I was beginning to accumulate a little cash. Therefore, the following Sunday we picked up my parents and drove around the Intake area (which they did not wish to leave) in order to check on properties available.

We quickly identified a modest but suitable apartment to which my parents were immediately attracted. This was within walking distance of the homes of both Connie and Mum's brother Walter and family. We were allowed to view the apartment, and this confirmed my parents' delight.

The next day I spoke to the estate agents dealing with the property and agreed a price. The purchase was completed within weeks and my parents took up residence and lived happily in the apartment for the remainder of their lives. It was one of the best investments I ever made.

An added bonus for Kath and myself, to the pleasure of seeing Mum and Dad happy and settled in their new home, was that they had room to accommodate Michelle whenever she wished to visit and on the numerous occasions over following years when we attended events and functions which would sometimes continue until late in the evening or even require being away from Sheffield.

One of the bedrooms in my parents' new home was nominated as "Michelle's room" and always kept available. Grandma and Granddad were pleased to see Michelle at every opportunity and, of course, were aware of and able to cope with her problems and needs – although I know that her occasional tantrums were always upsetting to them.

I suspect that, on Michelle's visits, "dietary requirements" may not have been as strictly enforced as at home. We accepted this as being a privilege for soft-hearted grandparents. Of course, Michelle never admitted to any breach of the rules.

In retirement, Dad seemed to have a new lease of life. For many years after the major operation for duodenal ulcers in his twenties, there had been a need to closely control his diet, otherwise his constitution could be easily upset. Consequently, he had rarely been prepared to risk going on holidays, and Mum had sometimes joined up with her sisters.

Over the years, these dietary problems had become less severe and Mum and Dad started to take annual breaks, usually accompanied by Connie. Their favourite holidays seemed to be with organised coach tours to various areas of interest in the British Isles, with stopovers for a couple of days each at pre-arranged hotels, where evening entertainment would usually be provided. I understand that on some of these occasions, Dad was even tempted onto the dance floor, but I am not sure that he ever admitted it!

Very sadly, on 19 December 1988, at the age of 81 years, and about 16 years after retirement, Dad passed away. He had laboured in manual occupations all his working life at a time when the regulations on health and safety were much less stringent than the present day. The cause of death was shown as "respiratory failure" and "chronic bronchitis" but, no doubt, 10 years of breathing in coal dust from the age of 14 years and about 20 years in later life at J B Duckett & Co mixing powders for export as a base for making inks and watercolour paints, would have contributed to these causes. In common with most working-class men of his day, Dad also smoked cigarettes throughout his adult life, which would not have helped.

I felt some satisfaction in the impression that Dad had enjoyed his later years and the feeling that I may have made at least a small contribution towards this. He had also gained much pleasure from being able to see his grandchildren, Michelle and Nigel, grow up.

Dad had been ill for some weeks before he passed away and Mum was tired and emotionally drained from taking care of him.

However, although gentle in manner, she had a strong personality and had always played the main role in running the home.

As the months passed and Mum adjusted to life alone, with more time available for herself and greater freedom, she seemed to flourish. Connie would visit her two or three days during the week, and they would be company for each other and often go out shopping together.

Kath and I established the routine (to include Michelle, of course) of visiting Mum and staying for tea on alternate Sundays. On the Sundays in between, I would collect Mum and Connie about mid-day and take them back to the Croft for lunch. They would usually stay until early evening, when I would run them home or (if I had partaken in a couple of glasses of wine) organise a taxi.

Michelle would always insist on coming along on these journeys to take Grandma and Connie home. Once I had dropped off my passengers, I would play discs on the return and, for fun, question Michelle on the artist or musical pieces. After a few weeks, Michelle could remember all the names, from Freddie Mercury (a favourite of hers) to *Finlandia* by Sibelius. Despite her problems, Michelle had an amazing memory.

During these years, Nigel having obtained his degree was working away from Sheffield, first in Oxford and subsequently in the London area. If one of his occasional weekend visits coincided with Mum coming for lunch, this was a special pleasure for her.

I recollect one of these occasions when, out of the blue, Nigel received a telephone call from two former college friends (with whom he had been involved in amateur theatricals), who happened to be visiting Sheffield. We invited them to join us for lunch and afterwards, having adjourned to the sitting room for coffee, one of them started to play the piano and his colleague joined in as vocalist. We had a wonderful session of Noel Coward style entertainment. Mum and Connie were absolutely delighted.

No doubt Nigel will be able to remember the names of his friends. I can recollect the second name of only one of them – Benson, the same as Sir Henry, my former senior partner. How could I forget?

In 1997, after enjoying nine good years following Dad's death, Mum started to experience medical problems. My understanding is that some of the lymph nodes on the left side of her body were not working properly and this was giving rise to paralysis and also affecting her ability to swallow food. Surprisingly (to me at least) the problem appeared to be a legacy of damage caused about 35 years earlier when she had undergone a mastectomy and radiation treatment.

As Mum's condition steadily worsened, she was unable to properly take care of herself and became dependant on visits by carers. Always proud and strongly independent, she hated this intrusion into her privacy. Of course, she could have come to live with us at the Croft, but she loved her apartment and wished to remain in the area where she had easy contact with Connie and many friends.

Mum's condition continued to deteriorate, and in due course, she was admitted to Northern General Hospital. This is situated in the north-west of Sheffield and was rather inconvenient for visits by any friends or neighbours relying on public transport. However, she was not short of people going to see her, including of course Kath, Nigel and myself. I tried to attend on weekday lunchtimes and at weekends.

Although Mum never complained, I felt that she was steadily declining and (out of character) had decided that it was time to give up and leave this world.

On the morning of Saturday, 24 January 1998, I travelled to the hospital to visit Mum and, with some difficulty as always, found a space in one of the several car parks. I had then started the trek up the stairs and along corridors towards the separate room where Mum was located, when my mobile phone rang. It was my cousin, John Strafford, who was visiting Mum accompanied by his wife, Jenny.

I could tell from John's voice that he was upset. He said that "Aunty Eleanor is in a coma" and the doctor had informed him that "she has not long to live". I sprinted down the remaining corridors but to no avail, Mum had passed away.

147

In an earlier paragraph, I state that the few weeks prior to Michelle's death were the most difficult and unhappy period of my life and, I am sure, the lives of Kath and Nigel. It will now be appreciated from these later paragraphs that the tragedy of Michelle's death was not the only depressing occurrence in this period. The weeks in which Michelle and Mum declined overlapped, both of them passing away within 13 days of each other. Neither was aware that the other was in hospital and moving towards the end of their life. Mum enquired about Michelle every time I visited her. I always said, "She is alright." Had I told her the truth, Mum would have been distraught.

X

Michelle and Nigel

Happier Days

The sombre nature of the events referred to in the previous chapter, leading up to the deaths of Dad, Mum and Michelle should not be allowed to obscure the pleasure that each of them provided to our whole family during their lives. In particular, I think it is important, in the case of Michelle, to try to explain the balance between the concerns we experienced from her PWS condition and the happiness we enjoyed from her existence in so many other respects.

Michelle had many good qualities, amongst which were her determination and enthusiasm to take part in everything. This would include such activities as school or church outings, Girl Guide camps, pilgrimages and competitions of various types. During the build-up to these events (and as more information became available), Michelle would become increasingly tense and wound-up, and it would often be clear to the rest of the family that because of a lack of physical strength, knowledge or dexterity, she would probably be frustrated and upset by the outcome. However, Michelle could never be deterred.

I remember a family holiday to Rhodes in 1980 when, after a hot and dusty visit to some historic monument (the highlight of which had been a donkey ride for part of the journey!), Nigel and I decided to hire a pedalo to cool off in the quite choppy sea. We had assumed that Michelle would remain on the beach with Kath but found her tagging along with the comment, "I want to come with you."

The first requirement was to lift Michelle onto the pedalo, which was rising or falling several feet with every wave. We managed to get her half-aboard and clinging on, despite her shouts of "help me", but at this stage we had a new challenge when her straw hat and beach shoes were washed into the sea. By the time Nigel and I had recovered them, we were almost helpless with laughter, while Michelle was still squawking, "help me" as she went up and down. We chuckle about the incident whenever it is recollected all these years later – although I always have a tear in my eye.

In contrast to the above happy occasion was a time in Scotland when Mum (still quite fragile following Dad's death) had accompanied Kath, Michelle and me for a few days break. We were staying at the apartment which we owned in the grounds of Gleneagles Hotel. However, as a change from the rather formal hotel environment, a table for dinner had been reserved at a restaurant about 20 minutes' drive away.

We were all in a relaxed and happy mood on arrival and made our selections from the impressive menu. However, the waiter returned a few minutes later to say that Michelle's choice of main course was no longer available. As will be apparent from earlier paragraphs, food is an obsession for people suffering from PWS, and we could tell that Michelle was struggling to control her emotions with this disappointment. Unfortunately, she failed to do so and burst into tears, followed by noisy tantrums, completely oblivious of the feelings of the rest of us, and, more importantly, the enjoyment of other diners at nearby tables.

On embarrassing occasions of this nature, when Michelle had been a child, one could have picked her up and left. However, this was no longer possible for an adult weighing more than myself! The only option was for the rest of us to depart from the restaurant, leaving Michelle weeping at the table but with no one to rant at.

Mum was very upset by Michelle's distress and I drove her back to Gleneagles, leaving Kath sitting in the bar outside the restaurant waiting for the storm to pass and for Michelle to cool down. None of us had dinner that evening – we had lost our appetites. The way in which Michelle's moods and behaviour could change so quickly over relatively trivial (to us) matters was one of the most difficult aspects of life with her.

When at her best, Michelle could be charming, especially with people she liked. However, she was something of a maverick. For example, in our family of Sheffield United supporters, she glorified in being an "Owl". This may have resulted from the influence of two of her favourite people, my close friends – Matt Sheppard (also a chartered accountant but more importantly, in Michelle's eyes, Chairman of Sheffield Wednesday) and my C&L partner and colleague, Sean Mahon. Sean never missed the opportunity to "feed" Michelle with some derogatory tale relating to the Blades, which, to her glee, she could repeat to her father!

Towards the end of the 1983 football season, and with Michelle's 21st birthday rapidly approaching, our family (Kath, Nigel and myself), together with a few close friends were invited to MICHELLE'S VIP DAY, a celebration in the director's area, before a home game at Sheffield Wednesday's Hillsborough Stadium. Michelle was presented with a birthday cake (in blue and white stripes) by Bob Grierson, a member of the Wednesday board. We were then allowed to go down the tunnel to the pitch and sit in the player's dugout for photographs. At this point, several of the Wednesday team, in their playing strip and ready for action, also came running down the tunnel to congratulate Michelle.

Presumably, Matt Sheppard had been the instigator of the celebration. Michelle was so happy and excited that she was close to tears. It was a day she would never forget.

One of Michelle's other attributes was an excellent memory, which ability never ceased to amaze me. She could relate details of events which had occurred many years before and, in relation to food, could quote the items which had appeared on restaurant menus – and the choices she had made! She loved puzzle books and jigsaws and would always select those with the largest number of pieces. With only an occasional glance at the picture on the box, she would pour-out all the pieces into one pile and set about completion of the jigsaw without any apparent system.

151

Although Michelle's moods could change quickly, she had quite a good sense of humour, which I would describe as of the "slip on a banana skin" type. Her favourite people as mentioned above (Matt Sheppard and Sean Mahon), together with Nigel and two more of our good friends – Fred Webster and Bryan Hancock – could make Michelle giggle within seconds of their arrival. She loved to be present at parties (of which we had many over the years) and at family gatherings – especially if Grandma and Granddad were there. At mealtimes on these occasions she would always insist on being seated between them.

From being children, both Michelle and Nigel had been excellent travellers, whether by car, bus, ship or plane. This removed some of the concerns which can be felt when deciding upon family holidays. Nevertheless, in the children's earlier years (partly through financial considerations) we tended to holiday in the United Kingdom (Cornwall, Norfolk, Wales, Scotland), sometimes linking up with our friends Ted and Margaret Machon and/or Bryan and Rita Hancock. Each of these couples also had two children in a similar age range to ours. However, five out of the total of six children were boys. Adding to these the three fathers provided enough candidates for two four-a-side teams for beach football. This left Michelle happy to stay with the "mums", reading books and doing her puzzles. Of course, the picture would probably be different in the current more liberated times – everyone (except Michelle) would want to play football!

From about 1970 (with Michelle aged eight years and Nigel six) we started to go farther afield for holidays, but still within Europe or the Mediterranean areas – Italy, Spain, Crete, Corfu, etc. It was in this period that we visited Tunisia and the children experienced their first camel rides. I can still remember the camel driver's facial expression when he lifted Michelle down and sank ankle-deep into the sand before his knees buckled – her weight had started to increase.

In 1973, the decision was made by the Coopers & Lybrand International Accounting Organisation that, in order to establish a common identity, the 90 firms operating in countries throughout the world under various local names (including Cooper Brothers

& Co), should drop these and adopt the single name of Coopers & Lybrand (C&L). Therefore, I have used this name when referring to events in the years after 1973 in subsequent paragraphs.

In 1974 I became a member of the Executive Committee of C&L, UK, and, in addition to the responsibilities of this role came the privilege (usually every other year) of being one of the UK representatives attending the Annual International Partners' Meetings. These meetings took place over a period of two and a half to three days, in different countries each year, and usually in places where the firm was particularly strong and well established.

As there were dinners to attend and a social element to these occasions, partners were normally accompanied by their spouses, for whom a daytime programme of events would be arranged for the periods when partners were entombed in the meeting sessions.

In the times when Kath and I were attending these international gatherings, Michelle would happily stay at her grandparents and, because the venues were often quite distant and in countries which we had not previously visited, we would sometimes tack-on an extra few days holiday. For example, following the meeting in Sydney (our first ever visit to Australia), we took a plane north and a boat to Hayman Island on the Great Barrier Reef. When the International Meeting was held in Quebec, we travelled to Canada in advance and spent a couple of days in Banff in the Rockies, before flying west to visit Vancouver and Vancouver Island and eventually returning to the East Coast for the meeting.

On occasions such as the above, because Kath and I had been away, Michelle clearly considered that the annual family holiday should be "her choice" or at least that she should have a say in the decision. We were quite happy with this as Michelle was always easier to deal with when she felt involved, and Nigel was normally content to accept and enjoy whichever location was chosen. Furthermore, I could usually influence Michelle's suggestions by telling her about places I had visited. Maybe this was the reason that Michelle started to show a particular interest in visiting the Scandinavian countries to which she was aware I travelled regularly as C&L UK liaison partner. Consequently, we had several holidays in Scandinavia. These included Denmark (where we first visited Copenhagen and a few years later toured around Jutland) and Norway (where our time was spent mainly in Oslo). In each location (as for everywhere we travelled to with Michelle) she identified things she "must see".

For example, on our holiday to Copenhagen, Michelle's list included the bronze statue of *The Little Mermaid* (which was displayed on a rock by the waterside at Langelinie) and a statue of Hans Christian Anderson (HCA). *The Little Mermaid* was no problem, I had travelled past the statue many times on the way to one of my favourite restaurants. As regards HCA, I recollected seeing a statue in a park close to the hotel where we were staying. However, on arrival – disaster – this was not the statue that Michelle was expecting. According to Michelle "he should be wearing a top hat". I suggested that possibly a tourist had placed a hat on the statue before taking the photograph which Michelle had seen, but she was having none of it. To my relief, as we headed for Tivoli Gardens (another item on her wish list) later in the day, there in City Hall Square facing the Gardens was the required statue, with HCA wearing a hat and holding a book and cane. I must have passed a dozen times without noticing it before. All was well, but these incidents were typical of the way Michelle's mind worked as a Prader-Willi sufferer.

For the trip to Oslo, Michelle's "must see" items (selected from the travel brochures she had seen) included Thor Heyerdahl's Kon-Tiki raft, the Viking ships and Roald Amundsen's Polar Exploration Vessel, *Fran*. We took her to see all these at an early stage of the visit, after which we felt that we may be able to relax!

One aspect of Scandinavian life for which Michelle (unsurprisingly) displayed great enthusiasm was the food! For the first time, she experienced the many different styles of herrings which were available and gravlax, the dry-cured marinated salmon. These days I believe that these dishes can be obtained in any good supermarket, but that was not the case in the early 1980s. Michelle's joys were increased when she found that neither of the dishes mentioned were to Kath's taste. Michelle always enjoyed a little gloating in a semi-humorous way over either of her parent's chagrin.

Moving a few years forward, in 1983, with Nigel aged 19, we felt that, in order to encourage him to continue joining us from time to time on family holidays, we needed something which gave greater interest than was usually available at static resorts, but would also be suitable for Michelle. Therefore, we arranged our first cruise on the *Sea Princess*. At a time when cruise ships were generally much smaller than in the present day and the experience more intimate and traditional, the holiday was a great success. Consequently, we cruised on the same ship, but with a variety of destinations around the Mediterranean, Adriatic and Black Sea for the following three years. Nigel joined us for all but the final holiday in 1987, having provided me with a regular opponent for deck quoits over the earlier years. The sheltered environment of cruising proved particularly suitable for Michelle, who became a shadow to Sharon, the deputy entertainments director, a Rotherham "lass" and someone we continued to see occasionally for some years when back in Sheffield.

As mentioned in Chapter VII, in 1985 (in addition to a cruise), we had holidayed in Kenya, where Kath and I had lived for three interesting years. This holiday had been a success, particularly so far as Nigel and Michelle were concerned, and we decided that following the cruise of 1987 it was time for a change. Therefore, for the next nine years up to the time of Michelle's death, we enjoyed holidays with Michelle (and, in the earlier part of this period, also with Nigel) in many new and sometimes quite distant locations. These included two visits to the USA (Las Vegas, which included a flight over the Grand Canyon), and Orlando (experiencing the delights of Disney World – Epcot, The Magic Kingdom and Sea World, etc.). We also enjoyed holidays in Bali, Hong Kong (where my cousin Ian and family were living), Heidelberg (where another cousin, Linda, resided having spent several years working for the United States military forces in Germany), Barcelona and a return to Tunisia.

I believe that the last-mentioned holiday in Tunisia, in 1994, was the one before Nigel moved to live and work in Australia. So far as I was concerned, the holidays when Nigel joined us were always the best. We were both quite sporty and competitive and his presence provided me with an opponent for whatever contests were available at any resort, be it squash (where, sadly, he had started to give me a thrashing), golf, table tennis, our version of beach tennis and, in the evenings, the occasional game of chess.

In Tunisia, at Port el Kantaoui where we were staying there were two nearby golf clubs, one of which had three 9-hole courses. With permutation, this provided the opportunity to play three different courses of 18 holes and a fourth course at the other club. On the penultimate day of our holiday, Nigel and I were all square, having won two rounds each, and we were level after the 17th hole on the course selected for the decider.

To my annoyance, on this final hole, I "pulled" my drive but was pleased to see it finish on what appeared to be a small, sea-washed beach adjacent to the fairway. It was only when I jumped down onto this "beach" that I found the sand to be merely a crust covering several inches of sewage, into which I sank up to my ankles. Having suffered this indignity, I decided to try to play my ball back onto the fairway. This resulted in a cloud of filth, most of which seemed to descend upon me. Matters became even worse when I found that the golf club was producing a new publicity video and there were cameras on the 18th green. As Nigel marched smartly ahead, smiling sweetly, I slunk off down the rough, heading for the showers.

Over the course of her life, Kath experienced several medical problems, most of which she shrugged off and carried on with a minimum of fuss. Probably the most serious of these problems had occurred at the time we lived in Kenya, when Kath had an operation to remove a large part of her overactive thyroid gland. This was followed by many months of taking the appropriate drugs in order to rebalance the position.

Kath also endured several other operations arising from injuries caused by accidents (to which she was somewhat prone), including a knee replacement. However, two particular incidents during the period covered by this chapter, and which have some relevance to the actions and attitudes of Michelle (as influenced by her Prader-Willi condition) are referred to below.

The first of these occurred on a Saturday morning in the mid-90s. I returned from playing golf to find that there was no one at home, but a note from Kath Hallam (our next-door neighbour and good friend) to the effect that she had received a telephone call from Kath stating that she felt unwell. Kath Hallam had immediately gone round to the Croft but found that Kath had fainted and collapsed onto the floor. She had called a doctor, who, after examination, arranged for Kath to be admitted to the Northern General Hospital. Rather than accept a delay waiting for an ambulance, Kath Hallam had driven Kath to the hospital and remained with her.

Fortunately, Michelle was staying with her grandparents for the weekend and I was able to go straight to the hospital and release Kath Hallam for her to return home. My recollection is the diagnosis was that Kath was suffering from very high cholesterol and she was kept in the hospital for a few days. On returning home, she consulted Doctor Cullen (Derek, I think), who had previously provided her with treatments (and, I believe, also given advice in relation to Michelle). Kath had a good deal of trust in Dr Cullen and I believe he could see that, at this time, she would benefit from a break in dealing with Michelle and her various problems on a daily basis.

Consequently, Dr Cullen mentioned that the Catholic Church in Sheffield arranged a pilgrimage to Lourdes, St Bernadette, each year which took water from the spring in the Grotto of Massabielle. He said that the pilgrimage (which, including travel by coach and ship, lasted for about five days) was not restricted to Catholics and he wondered if Michelle would be interested. He continued by saying that he would be accompanying the party in case there were any medical problems and, therefore, would be able to keep an eye on Michelle. Also in the group, he informed us, would be two nurses from Claremont Private Hospital, who Michelle would know from her periods of treatment there.

I have stated previously that Michelle was always eager to take part in any function or event – even though she usually became nervous and wound-up as the date approached. Therefore, it was no surprise that, when mentioned to her, she jumped at the opportunity to join the pilgrimage. In fact, she enjoyed the experience so much that she attended subsequent pilgrimages for the next two or three years, although by the last occasion she had physically slowed down and had to be taken through the grotto by wheelchair.

Many of those on the pilgrimages attended each year, and Michelle would recall their names and become increasingly excited at the prospect of seeing them again as the dates approached. Of course, as one might expect in the case of Michelle, she always had to be at the rendezvous 30 minutes or so before the necessary time, during which periods she would fret that "we must have got the wrong date" or "the pilgrimage must have been cancelled". However, when a few people had arrived and particularly any of her friends from earlier years, she would be happy, and we would become redundant and free to leave.

By the time that Michelle was attending these annual pilgrimages, we had disposed of our apartment at Gleneagles and, shortly afterwards, had replaced it with a holiday lodge at Overstone Park in Northamptonshire (on a site we had purchased from the World Motorcycle Racing Champion, Barry Sheene). This overlooked a lake on one side and an 18-hole golf course on another and also included access to other facilities, including an indoor swimming pool and gym. As it was only about a two-hour drive from our home in Sheffield, the lodge provided an ideal opportunity for short family breaks and we also made use of it on the occasions when Michelle was away on the pilgrimages.

One reason for acquiring the lodge had been that Nigel, who was working in the London area, may have been able to drive there in a couple hours in order to join us for the occasional weekend. However, in practice, traffic from London travelling northwards on Friday afternoons/evenings was so slow and congested that this hope was rarely achieved. Nevertheless, it provided a useful hideaway for the occasional weekend break with several nearby places of interest of the type which Michelle enjoyed visiting.

The second medical incident I would mention as an example of the way in which Michelle's mind worked was in 1996 when, during a holiday on the Isle of Wight, we were on our way by car to visit Osborne House, the favourite summer residence of Queen Victoria and Prince Albert, situated high above the Solent on the North Shore. This was an important item on Michelle's agenda. However, Kath suddenly informed us that she felt very unwell. By chance, we had travelled past a doctor's surgery only a few minutes earlier and I turned the car round and returned. After a brief examination, the doctor decided that Kath needed to go to St. Mary's Hospital in Newport for tests and specialist advice. Arrangements were made for her to be taken to hospital by ambulance without delay.

In fact, Kath's problem proved to be quite serious (an embolism of the lungs) and she was kept in hospital undergoing treatment for the remainder of our holiday period (about another five or six days) before she was considered well enough to be taken back to Sheffield.

This situation, with its uncertainty and disruption to plans, was exactly the type that Michelle (with her Prader-Willi condition) was unable to deal with. The problem in Michelle's mind was not that her mum had been taken ill, but that her promised trip to Osborne House was in jeopardy. In the doctor's surgery she was becoming increasingly upset and on the brink of a major tantrum. Of course, Kath fully understood the position and we spoke briefly before she was transported away to hospital. We agreed that Michelle and I would carry on with the trip to Osborne House and the remainder of the holiday and that I would visit Kath at the hospital each evening. By the time Michelle and I arrived at Osborne House, there were only about 40 minutes remaining before closure. Nevertheless, the visit had taken place and Michelle was happy.

For the remainder of the holiday, I arranged for Michelle and myself to have dinner at the latest sitting available, which allowed time for me to visit the hospital beforehand. As regards the holiday itself, Michelle and I continued to see all the places that had been planned. Now that she had my undivided attention, she was as good as gold, taking over without asking the front passenger seat normally occupied by Kath and generally agreeing to everything I suggested without dispute!

The only minor blip was on a visit to the south-east of the island (Shanklin or Ventnor, I think). Matt Sheppard had jocularly asked Michelle to bring him back a jar showing layers of the different coloured sands which were to be found on the beaches of the island, but this casual request became an imperative to Michelle. We were informed that such jars were sold only at a stall on the beach, which was accessible by using a constantly moving chain of hanging chairs. Getting tubby, short-legged Michelle aboard a moving chair, with time for me to take my place on the seat next to her was a challenge which I almost failed to meet when the safety bar came down across Michelle's lower chest rather than her waist! There was no danger, but to my embarrassment, she proceeded to squawk "hold me, hold me", to the alarm of those sitting on the beach below for the whole of the journey. Such was life on holiday with Michelle.

I think it worth stressing that, despite her Prader-Willi condition, Michelle's enjoyable life experiences were not confined only to holidays. In 1987, Kath and I received an invitation to attend a Buckingham Palace Garden Party. My recollection is that, at this point in time, the rule was that one could also take along an unmarried daughter (sons, whether or not married, were not acceptable). Of course, we chose to take Michelle.

The night before the event, we stayed at the Berkeley Hotel and I arranged for John Fisher, the senior C&L chauffeur, to pick us up the next day and transport us for the relatively short distance to the Palace. Michelle was clearly excited and looking gorgeous in her new dress and hat, chosen specially for the occasion. She was full of questions, and I told her that we would wave to any onlookers and drive through the courtyard to the Palace front door.

Travelling from the Berkeley, we arrived at the entrance on Buckingham Gate to be informed by a polite and smiling duty policeman that, as the main traffic flow was down the Mall, that was the entrance for vehicles with a one-way system to exit from the gate we had chosen. However, the policeman said it was quite permissible for us to get out of the car and walk through the courtyard to the Palace entrance.

This seemed a sensible suggestion, but I had reckoned without Michelle's reaction to the change of arrangements – "you said we would drive to the front door" – she refused to move. By this time traffic was building up behind us and the nice policeman seemed to be losing his smile. I told John Fisher to drive on and continue up the Mall until he could find a way to join the traffic travelling down to the Palace. He was a proficient driver, and all ended well.

Michelle enjoyed the close-up view of the Queen and other dignitaries as they strolled down the lines of people attending. This was followed by cake (a special concession for the occasion) and a glass of fresh orange juice in the marquee. It was a day for her to tell Grandma and Granddad about.

I have previously mentioned Michelle's 21st birthday celebrations at Hillsborough Football Stadium and, in May 1993, she joined me in a coachload of friends (comprising both Blades and Owls supporters) travelling to the "old" Wembley on another footballing occasion – the FA Cup Semi-final between the two Sheffield teams.

Four years later, Michelle, Kath, Nigel and myself (and I believe Pauline and Sean Mahon) made another visit to Wembley for the play-off between Sheffield United and Crystal Palace. Unfortunately, the Blades lost both the above-mentioned games, but at least Michelle and Sean were happy.

I have my doubts as to whether Michelle ever really understood the proceedings on these footballing occasions, but she remembered the names of players taking part and clearly enjoyed the atmosphere and excitement.

In 1996, Michelle joined Kath and me for a holiday in Sydney where Nigel was based. For anyone not familiar with Sydney, it is probably one of the most attractive and exciting cities in the world, with numerous places of interest to visit and things to do. Nigel had arranged several outings and also gave Michelle some one-to-one time, which she always enjoyed. Apart from Sydney itself, we visited several adjacent areas, including a few days spent with Nigel and some of his friends in the Blue Mountains, where we rented a large house with sufficient accommodation for everyone.

One minor incident which sticks in my memory was an evening when Nigel and his friends, accompanied by Michelle, brought back a take-away supper from a nearby restaurant. Everyone had selected their own dishes and Michelle had chosen the special "jungle curry" (which I suspect was something of an advertising gimmick). Unusually, Michelle appeared to be slow in consuming her food but, when I tried a spoonful, it was so hot that it almost blew my head off. She finished the meal, nevertheless. Fortunately, she had her own bedroom!

I think that this visit to see Nigel in Australia would rank as Michelle's best ever holiday and, although we were not to know at the time, it would also prove to be the final one at which both our children were present.

In 1997 our annual holiday, with Michelle, was in Jersey. We stayed at a very pleasant hotel – Longueville Manor, quite close to St. Helier, and rented a car to provide us with access around the island. This was particularly important as Michelle had gained weight and become less mobile.

One day we travelled by boat to another member of the Channel Islands, Sark, where motor vehicles were not allowed, except in a few special cases, including an open pick-up bus to transport visitors up the steep pathway from the jetty to the village, and a strange sightseeing vehicle, where seating was on a platform on top and accessible only by a sort of built-in ladder of about eight foot in length.

Most people of Michelle's bulk and physique would have been deterred from taking a trip on this contraption, but not her. With my help from behind, we managed to get Michelle up the ladder and comfortably seated. There she remained for the next hour or so, although there were a couple of stops at places of interest, where some people alighted, to take photographs etc.

However, the problem for Michelle occurred at the end of the tour, when it became necessary for everyone to exit the vehicle. When stretching down backwards on the ladder, Michelle, with her short legs, was always a few inches away from reaching the next rung. At this point she would panic and pull up her leg – having to start again but with the same result. She became quite frustrated and the next batch of trippers, waiting rather impatiently to board the vehicle, tended to create even more pressure on her.

Eventually I found two strong-ish looking volunteers, who were prepared to catch Michelle if necessary. I returned to the platform and, while kneeling, held Michelle's hands to give her confidence as she stretched her leg downwards. At the crucial point, I shouted ready to the volunteers and released my grasp of Michelle's hands. This left her to fall a couple of feet into their arms. Once on terra firma, I was forgiven, and Michelle was happy again.

In Chapter IX, I have referred to Michelle's final days, and I have no wish to return to this subject. However, I feel it appropriate, these 20 plus years later, to briefly reflect upon her life and the way this impacted upon our family, even though this may involve some repetition of matters previously mentioned.

Michelle suffered from Prader-Willi Syndrome from birth, a condition from which there is no cure and of which (at the time of her early life) there appeared to be no awareness. We were first informed of Michelle's condition when she was 17 years old and, while this knowledge explained some of her actions, particularly where these related to food, it was little help in knowing how to deal with them.

From appearing to be happy and contented, Michelle could erupt into tantrums, with negligible warning, for what seemed (to us) the most trivial of reasons. On these occasions, which could occur in private or public, she would seem entirely selfish with no regard for the feelings, wellbeing or enjoyment of anyone around her. This situation was particularly embarrassing and difficult to deal with in, for example, shops, restaurants, and on public transport, etc. However, in one respect at least, Michelle was fortunate, she was well loved by her close family. We recognised that many of her actions were not within her control and that she would need our support.

In contrast to the above, when Michelle was in a happy mood and everything was going according to plan, she could be charming and show the widest of smiles. On these occasions, her pleasure could be contagious, and one could forget for a time the rapid change in her personality which could take place.

As the person dealing with Michelle and her problems on a daily basis, the main burden of providing support fell upon Kath. She devoted herself to this task and was Michelle's guardian and protector throughout her life. Nigel, only a couple of years younger than Michelle and brought up alongside her from childhood, was probably the person with the best understanding of her moods and behaviour and could sometimes provide a calming influence, while Michelle's grandparents, although possibly having the least knowledge of her condition, accepted her unconditionally and were loving and available to her throughout their lives.

Despite the problems experienced by Michelle from her Prader-Willi condition, there were many enjoyable aspects to her life. She loved living at home, with her own room, full of books, pictures and souvenirs of places and events she had visited or attended, and she could sometimes be found sitting in there contentedly reading aloud to herself. In clement weather, Michelle made good use of the pool and was quite a proficient swimmer, if somewhat unconventional in style. Food was important to Michelle and, within the restrictions of her diet, Kath produced the sort of meals she enjoyed and always ensured that a wide choice of fruit was available.

Michelle greatly enjoyed holidays and travel and we always included her in our plans. As evidenced by the information in earlier paragraphs, despite her shortish life, she was probably privileged to see more of the world and to participate in more rewarding experiences than the majority of people with a normal span of years.

However, despite all the efforts of her close family, it was never possible to eliminate the problems and disadvantages of the Prader-Willi Syndrome. The mood changes, displays of anger, and uncontrollable tantrums continued throughout Michelle's life, and her physical problems from lack of growth, obesity and poor dexterity remained and steadily increased. Michelle never achieved puberty, never had a boyfriend or even a close friendship with someone of her own age. The people Michelle described as "my friends" were usually her family's friends, who showed her understanding, kindness and consideration.

To the question "did Michelle have a happy life?" I could not give an answer – I was never sure what thoughts were in her mind. However, I feel that we (her close family) did our best to make her life as full and happy as possible. We still think about her and miss her.

XI

Partnership in CB&Co

The Early Years

In the previous two chapters, I covered certain aspects of life during the 35 years we were fortunate to have Michelle. We lived in Sheffield (or a few miles over the border in North Derbyshire) throughout this period, but for various reasons had several moves of home. In part, these reflected my progression in the firm (and the increasing funds which became available), but they were also influenced by Michelle's schooling requirements.

Initially, on return from Kenya, I had been undecided as to the direction of my future career, and we purchased (with the help of a mortgage) a smallish, but quite pleasant, detached house in the Meersbrook district of Sheffield. This was our home at the time Michelle was born in Nether Edge Hospital on 5 August 1962, as referred to in Chapter IX.

On admission to partnership in April 1964 and recognition that, at least for the foreseeable future, my base with the firm would be Sheffield, we acquired (again with the help of a mortgage) a rather larger but semi-detached house in Totley (which we considered to be a more pleasant area of Sheffield in which to reside and bring up children) at a purchase price of £5,300. It was in this house that Nigel was born on 13 December 1964, and it was still our place of residence some years later when both children first attended nursery/playgroup and, subsequently, a small locally situated private school.

We had excellent next-door neighbours at Totley in Doctor David Linfoot and family (David became our GP) and, through Kath's contacts with other mothers in course of taking the children to and from school etc., we formed good friendships with several other families including, in particular, Rita and Fred Webster (previously mentioned) and Fay and Dennis Branon. These friendships continued well beyond the time we lived at Totley but, very sadly, Fay, Dennis and Fred have all passed away from various illnesses or medical conditions at ages well before their expected span of years.

As regards life at CB&Co, I thrived on the increased opportunities, responsibilities and variety of work, which became available following admission to partnership. However, my elevation was not an immediate case of rags to riches. I found that, in accordance with the normal arrangement for new partners, I would be salaried for the first three years before being admitted to profit-sharing if I proved to be satisfactory.

Nevertheless, I was more than satisfied with my initial salary as a partner of £3,000 per annum which, dependent upon the index used, was equivalent to about £55,000 in 2019 terms. Furthermore, I was fortunate to be brought into the profit-sharing pool after only two years at "one and a half old points" giving an income of £7,500 in 1966/67 (equivalent, if adjusted for inflation, to approximately £130,000). However, this sum was diminished under the partnership agreement, which required partners to fund their own pensions by paying 10% of annual income (which, fortunately, could be deducted from income free of tax) into a pension scheme.

Thereafter, over the next 28 years, my income grew every year (sometimes quite substantially), partly because of the annual improvement (except, I think, for one year) in the firm's profits, but also as my pointage in the profit pool increased as I progressed within the firm.

Apart from the financial aspects of partnership, I was privileged over the years to enjoy the support and camaraderie of many very talented colleagues, to serve a wide range of interesting and entrepreneurial clients and to establish several good friendships with people from both these groups.

I consider myself to have been very fortunate to have been given these opportunities, but to review the years in any detail would take several volumes. However, there are some assignments, events and individuals, which stand out in my memory for various reasons (both good and bad), and I mention certain of these in subsequent paragraphs in the hope that they may be found interesting or even amusing.

Starting on a depressing note, one of my worst experiences occurred shortly after I became a partner and related to Sheepbridge Engineering (Sheepbridge), a publicly listed group of companies which was based on the outskirts of Chesterfield. Having been audit manager for two or three years, thereby gaining a good knowledge of the group, it was considered that this was a suitable client for me to take partner responsibility.

However, most of my dealings in the past had been with Teddy Derbyshire, the financial director, who was a reasonable man to deal with, although I was sometimes surprised that he seemed reluctant to make decisions on quite straightforward matters without first clearing these up the line with Tom Brown, the group managing director. As a mere audit manager, my contact with Brown in these early days had been minimal, but my impression was that he was quite dictatorial and feared by his management team.

An issue on the Sheepbridge financial statements, which had been unresolved over several years, related to a dispute between the company and the inland revenue (as it was then called) in connection with expenses of directors' entertaining and the maintenance of an apartment in London, which was used by directors (and most frequently Tom Brown). The issue concerned the extent to which these expenses were an allowable charge against the company's revenue for taxation purposes.

From an audit viewpoint, there was an additional issue in relation to the above expenses arising from the Companies Act requirements for disclosure in financial statements of details of directors' remuneration and emoluments. Pending settlement of the dispute, the company had made its own estimates of the sums which it believed should be included in this respect. CB&Co had accepted the company's estimates on the basis (or so I believed) that when the dispute with the inland revenue was resolved, any differences between the figures agreed and the estimates included in the financial statements of past years would be included in the statements of the year in which this agreement was reached.

It was my misfortune that the resolution of the above matter occurred in the year for which I took on partner responsibility for Sheepbridge and (unsurprisingly in my view) the outcome had been that the agreed figures for past years were much closer to those claimed to be appropriate by the inland revenue than the company's estimates. Consequently, these several years of understatements, when added to the current years charge for directors' remuneration and emoluments, produced a total figure which was several times greater than any amount shown in the past.

It was against this background that I had my first (and, as it proved, last) meeting with Tom Brown, which had been arranged to discuss finalisation of the financial statements – a draft of which had previously been sent to him. On entering his office, but even before I was seated, Tom Brown said, "These figures for directors' remuneration and emoluments cannot be shown."

This was probably the point at which I should have made an excuse and retreated for consultation with a more senior partner. I doubt if there could have been any change to the figures, but there may have been a more palatable form of presentation, which might have satisfied Tom Brown.

However, with the confidence of youth (and possibly because I disliked Tom Brown's manner towards me), I replied (calling him sir) that while he could clearly decide upon the information to appear in the financial statements, the Report of the Auditors was a CB&Co document and if the statements were not in compliance with statutory requirements (which appeared likely in view of his comments), it would be necessary to qualify our report and disclose such information as we deemed appropriate.

At this response, Tom Brown seemed to turn puce in colour and, so far as I can remember, made no reply. However, he stood up from his chair and stormed out of the room, slamming the door behind him. I waited a few minutes to see if he would return (maybe he had gone to the toilet) but then concluded that the meeting had been terminated.

Inevitably this was not the end of the matter. The next I heard was of a meeting between John Pears (as previously mentioned, one of CB&Co's senior partners) and Lord Aberconway, the chairman of Sheepbridge and several other listed companies. I believe that this meeting was followed by a letter to John from Aberconway stating that "his managing director was insistent that CB&Co should resign as auditors of Sheepbridge and, failing this a motion would be presented at the Annual General Meeting for their removal and replacement by another firm".

John Pears was not a man to be intimidated and he apparently made it clear that the firm would not resign and that if a motion were to be proposed for a change of auditors, we would exercise our rights to speak at the AGM and write to shareholders. This was enough to repel Brown's threats and we were duly reappointed. However, we were powerless to resist the Sheepbridge Board's decision to remove the firm from the audits of the wholly owned subsidiaries, which carried out much of the group's activities and, consequently, provided most of the audit fees.

Sensibly, I handed over responsibility for Sheepbridge to another partner. However, although I felt disappointed with my part in the loss of fee income, I did not consider that I had been in the wrong and it was some comfort that I never experienced any criticism from my partners, although I heard that Henry Benson had commented to John: "If only Cottingham had a few grey hairs."

Ten years later, as President of the Sheffield & District Society of Chartered Accountants, I was pleased to welcome Sir Henry as an honoured guest at our annual dinner in the Cutlers' Hall. In my speech, I expressed my pleasure at his attendance but said I must apologise that "I had still not acquired any grey hairs". I suspect that no one but Henry understood this "in-house" joke.

Many more years later and as a sequel to the above events, Sheepbridge was acquired by CB&Co's important client, GKN. In accordance with that group's normal policy, we were immediately appointed as auditors of all Sheepbridge companies. Ironically, the senior GKN executive, who moved north in order to manage this Sheepbridge sub-group, was Gilbert Jones, a good friend of mine since we had first met about 30 years earlier when, as young managers at CB&Co, we attended a conference at Churchill College, Cambridge. I felt that justice had been done by this Sheepbridge "home-coming" under the control of a Coopers trained man!

In complete contrast to the aforementioned tribulations was an experience in 1965 when I was contacted on the telephone by "a Mr Kevin McDonald (Kevin)". This proved to be the start of a most enjoyable and rewarding professional and personal relationship, from which a good friendship developed and still continues these 54 years later.

Kevin informed me that he was owner of Bartol Plastics Limited (Bartol), a small manufacturing company based in Swinton, South Yorkshire. He said that he had reached a stage where some financial advice was required in connection with his business and had been recommended to contact me by the manager of the National Provincial Bank in Mexborough. Many years later I discovered that this bank manager was brother of Tony Wood, my close friend and colleague at CB&Co.

A few days after this conversation, I visited Kevin at his small office. Also present was Brian Leesing, his auditor, a partner in a local accountancy practice. My immediate impression was that Kevin, a plumber by trade, was a very intelligent person. However, he was also down to earth, amusing in conversation and clearly full of energy and enthusiasm. We got on well and established a good rapport immediately.

Kevin explained that he had designed and patented a domestic waste system, including the U-bend, which could sometimes be a troublesome area, to be produced in polypropylene, as compared with the traditional systems in copper or other metals that were in use at the time. Apart from lightness of weight, an advantage of Kevin's polypropylene products was that they could be produced at a fraction of the cost of their metal counterparts. Consequently, operating for only a few months from a small workshop using two extruding machines, Bartol had achieved rapidly increasing sales with high margins of profitability and growing demand for its products. However, the company was approaching a point of maximum capacity from its production facilities and decisions needed to be made for the future.

Not surprisingly, Bartol's products were creating a good deal of interest in the industry and Kevin had been contacted by Hepworth Iron (Hepworth), a locally listed group of companies based in Penistone, which would like to acquire Bartol, including its designs and patents. Faced with the requirements for increased working capital and additional premises and machinery if Bartol were to continue expansion on its own, against the alternative of disposing of his investment in the company with an immediate benefit to his personal wealth, Kevin was seeking help to assess the situation.

Although it is now many years since our meeting, I can still recollect some of the areas we discussed. Bartol's results covered only a few months and it seemed appropriate that at least a few more months of operations should be completed to provide greater evidence of the increasing demand and profitability. It would then be desirable for the figures to be audited to give them more authority in any sale discussions. These additional months would also provide time for longer-term projections to be prepared, backed by detailed and realistic assumptions covering important areas such as additional premises and machinery required, the costs thereof and sources of funding, etc.

Taxation implications needed to be considered, including in particular Kevin's personal position. I believe that, at this time, a capital gain on disposal of a controlling interest in a company could incur taxation of up to 90%. Therefore, the structure of any deal needed careful consideration.

I advised Kevin that the terms of any sale contract for Bartol would need careful drafting by an able and experienced lawyer. As Kevin had no one in mind, I said that I would introduce him to Ted Vickers (the solicitor used by Ron Palfreyman, as mentioned in an earlier chapter). Subsequently, Ted became involved and proved to be an excellent choice for the job, establishing a good relationship with Kevin from the outset.

Having established at the meeting the way to move forward in general terms, I cannot remember in detail the timing of all events.

I think that, at an early stage, Brian Leesing resigned as auditor of Bartol and became financial director. CB&Co became auditors and financial advisors, reporting on the current accounts and assisting with the preparation of future projections, which subsequently became important in sale negotiations with Hepworth.

Kevin and I (I think Brian Leesing may also have been present) eventually met with Messrs Booth and Hinchcliffe, chairman and managing director respectively of Hepworth. The meeting was quite friendly and relaxed, and Kevin had instructed me in advance to negotiate on his behalf. After a little thrust and parry on the figures, Booth made an offer of a price and terms for acquisition of Bartol which I considered to be very acceptable and I passed a note to Kevin recommending that we accept. Kevin confirmed his agreement and we all adjourned for drinks and lunch in the Hepworth directors' dining room.

Following discussions on Kevin's tax position, Ted Vickers had prepared a draft contract for the disposal of Bartol on the basis of an immediate sale of a 40% interest, followed by annual sales of 10%, based on profits of each of these years, until Hepworth acquired the full 100% ownership, and this had been accepted by Hepworth. However, they had insisted that the contract should contain a seven-year restrictive covenant, which would prevent Kevin from producing or dealing in the type of items made by Bartol. This was a normal requirement in contracts of this type.

The above arrangements proved to be very beneficial to Kevin. Not only did they minimise his tax liability but, because the profits of Bartol (which formed a basis for calculating the price of the annual sale of shares) steadily increased, so did the sum paid to Kevin.

Although I think it was not part of the sale contract, it was agreed that Kevin would join the main Hepworth Board and continue to manage and develop the Bartol activities. I was also pleased that CB&Co would continue as auditors of Bartol, even though Hepworth group had two of the "Big Five" firms of accountants as joint auditors.

Kevin was not a man to waste time and, away from his business activities, he was equally energetic and decisive in his actions. The consideration monies for the initial 40% interest in Bartol had made him a relatively wealthy man and, with the prospect of substantial annual sums to come over the years, it was no surprise to me that one of his first acts following the sale was to acquire an impressive Ferrari motorcar. This put my MGB GT (the best vehicle I could afford) very much in the shade.

Some weeks after conclusion of the above events, I visited Kevin to agree the fee for all work carried out by CB&Co, which included audit, tax advice, preparation of projections, meeting with Hepworth, etc. I explained to Kevin that, although our scale rate costs amounted to about £3,500, I felt we had done a particularly good job in helping negotiate the sale of Bartol. Therefore, with his agreement, I proposed to bill a total of £5,000 (equivalent to about £90,000 in current values). Kevin gave his agreement and reached for a cheque book, but I said, "No need to write a cheque now, Kevin, I will send you a bill."

Unexpectedly, Kevin said, "OK, but this £5,000 is for you." Once I had overcome my surprise, I replied, "I can't accept a private payment, Kevin, it would not be permitted under my partnership agreement." After a few seconds pause, Kevin replied to the effect that he believed I liked his Ferrari but, as he had the later model on order, when this was available in a month or so, he would give me his existing vehicle.

Such temptation! Maybe if I had been more senior in the firm, I could have informed my partners that "we now own a Ferrari, which I will take care of on behalf of all of us". Wishful thinking – instead I suggested to Kevin that, rather than sending a bill for £5,000, I would make this £10,000 and Kevin should leave me to sort out with my partners how I might benefit. Very generously, Kevin agreed to this.

In fact, as I was still a salaried partner at the time, I did not gain any immediate financial benefit. However, I was well satisfied to have obtained an attractive new client and a substantial surplus over scale rate costs on my billings to date.

Although I have owned several interesting motorcars since these days, it was another 30 years before I acquired a Ferrari – a 328 GTS. However, I believe that the one offered to me by Kevin was a 275 GTB/4 Daytona. If correct, I believe that in 2013 a surviving model became the most expensive road-going car ever sold at auction!

Over the next few years, Kevin continued to expand Bartol under the Hepworth umbrella. However, he also made good use of his newly gained wealth, purchasing an excellent house, complete with helicopter pad, and he generously entertained his friends and colleagues at several parties. I recollect one of these which was attended by Babs Lord, possibly the best known member of the glamorous dance troupe Pan's People (so named after Pan, the Greek God of dance, music and debauchery), which troupe appeared weekly on TV in *Top of the Pops* at the time. In course of the evening, Babs was hoisted (by several willing hands) onto the roof of Kevin's Ferrari in order to be photographed. Clearly, such classic vehicles are not designed to withstand indignities of this nature and an indentation was left on the roof in the shape of Babs' bottom! I believe that Kevin decided to leave this on the grounds that it might increase the value of the vehicle!

In referring to Babs, it is only fair to mention that she was not just a pretty face and accomplished dancer. After leaving the dance group in 1975 to marry the actor Robert Powell, she became quite well known as an amateur yachtswoman and explorer, making trips (amongst other places) to the Himalayas and both of the Poles, and being the subject of a BBC *This Is Your Life* programme.

Returning to business matters, Kevin was probably too much of an entrepreneur to be comfortable on a traditional PLC board such as Hepworth and after a few years, when several more tranches of Bartol shares had been acquired by Hepworth, he decided that he wished to leave the group and go his own way. He contacted me and I assisted in negotiating the price for sale to Hepworth of the remaining balance of shares.

Although freed of the shackles of being part of a public group, Kevin was still subject to the restrictive covenant, which prevented his involvement in the activities where his knowledge and interest was greatest. I kept in touch with Kevin during this period but felt that he was not enjoying the business aspects of life to the same extent as in the past. Therefore, I was delighted to hear from Kevin (in enthusiastic mood) around the time that the restrictive covenant was due to expire with the request that I should arrange to see him.

It transpired that Kevin had acquired a site at Edlington, near Doncaster, with the factory and plant of a company which had gone into liquidation but had previously been engaged in the manufacture of similar products to those of Bartol. He intended to commence such operations again and had formed a company (with the name of Polypipe) to take over these activities. He had already identified several experienced individuals to join his management team and was ready and poised to commence operations as soon as permitted.

Under Kevin's management, Polypipe was an immediate success, rapidly expanding its products, with systems for a wide range of applications for use in both residential and commercial markets. Understandably, the emergence of this new player in the market with its very competitive prices was not welcomed by everyone (not least Hepworth), but such opposition was of no deterrence to Kevin.

Commencing business about 1972 as a private limited company, Polypipe soon obtained over-the-counter status for its shares, followed after a few years by membership of AIM and in 1986 (beyond the period stated to be covered by this chapter), a full listing on the London Stock Exchange. Kevin benefitted financially from disposal of shares in Polypipe at this stage, but he still retained a substantial stake in the company.

During the above years, my role within CB&Co had steadily expanded, with a need to spend time in London and Scandinavia. Consequently, while I was determined to maintain an active involvement with my main clients, not least Polypipe, it was important to ensure that high-quality partner input was always available when required. This was consistent with the CB&Co "Two Partner Principle". In my case, and especially for Polypipe, I decided that the perfect person to provide the necessary support was Sean Mahon (about whom more in later chapters).

I had recruited Sean at the time of his qualification as an accountant with a small Sheffield firm in 1968 and seen his development through the years with CB&Co until admission into partnership in 1977. He was competent technically, and a glutton for work, but with an excellent personality and charming manner – exactly the sort of person that I believed Kevin would warm to.

Therefore, I arranged for Sean to take on first partner responsibility for Polypipe, while I would continue my involvement in the role of review/consultant partner. This arrangement worked well, and Sean quickly established a close working relationship and good friendship with Kevin.

The Polypipe Board contained some interesting and likeable characters, including two non-executive directors. One of these, Geoffrey Harrison, I had known for several years, having provided advice to his family business. The other, Kevin's good friend, Mikey Strathmore, 18th Earl of Strathmore and Kinghorne, head of the Bowes-Lyon family and first cousin once removed of the Queen, had helped John Major to put the Maastricht Bill into law. With such individuals complementing the executive directors on the Polypipe Board, meetings (and the luncheons which usually followed) were always interesting and enjoyable events.

To complete the Polypipe story, in March 1999, with Kevin in his mid-sixties and other challenges attracting his attention (some of which I refer to in later paragraphs), he accepted an offer for Polypipe to be acquired by IMI at a value of £337 million. It is on record that Kevin's share of this was £70 million, with Geoff Harrison making £10 million from the deal. It was a far cry from the days when we first met in Kevin's single room at Bartol 34 years earlier.

1964 was an excellent time to be admitted into partnership with CB&Co. Since the end of World War II, the firm, which had been established in 1854, had grown rapidly under the leadership of John Pears and Henry Benson, reaching over 7,500 partners and staff internationally, but with still only about 1,000 people in the UK. Of this latter number, only 36 were partners, of which 21 were based in London, 8 in Birmingham (mainly admitted in 1960 on a merger with Carter & Co) and the remaining 7 spread throughout the other five offices in the provinces. To me, admission to partnership at this time felt like becoming a member of an exclusive club.

Both John and Henry were descended from families which had been significant in the establishment and early development of the firm. Henry was the son of Sir F. Darcy Cooper and a grandson of Francis Cooper, one of the four original founding brothers. John was the son of Sydney Pears, only the fourth non-Cooper family member to be admitted into partnership in 1896.

The UK partners included two other descendants of the aforementioned families – Vivian Rupert Vaughan Cooper (quite senior in the partnership rankings) and Sidney John David Corsan, admitted only in 1955 and the partner I had first served under when joining the firm in Sheffield on leaving the RAF.

Vivian Cooper was a larger than life character and reminded me in appearance and manner of Rex Harrison, the actor who played Professor Higgins in the film version of *My Fair Lady*. Several of the more senior members of the partnership addressed him by the nickname "Chim". I remember enquiring of Ray Emmitt when it would be permissible for me to use this name rather than calling him Vivian. His rather unhelpful (but as it proved, accurate) reply was "you will know when". I did; and found Chim friendly and always helpful.

At this period of time, partners were known and referred to (at least by more senior staff) throughout the firm by their initials of up to four letters. For example, the aforementioned David Corsan was SJDC, while having only two names, I was known as BC. I remember a client, on hearing me so addressed by one of my staff commenting, "BC! Before Christ," and after a pause, "But after Henry Benson."

With only 36 partners, we were still small enough (just) for monthly meetings to be held in London office. These were chaired by Henry and commenced promptly at 9.30am. Consequently, most partners from the provinces would travel to London the previous evening and stay at the Waldorf Hotel in Aldwych. We would congregate in the bar and join together in small groups for dinner in the restaurant. It was an excellent opportunity for partners from the provinces to get to know each other and exchange views and information. Although a "new boy" and the youngest partner, I was quickly made to feel comfortable within the group.

Over following years, as the firm grew in size and reputation, establishing itself as one of the Big Five accounting organisations in the UK, it was inevitable that changes would have to take place. In the three years after my admission, the number of CB& Co partners more than doubled (partly through mergers with smaller firms in the provinces). It was no longer practicable for all partners to meet monthly in one place and, instead, the offices were grouped into a few geographic locations, and the partners within these would meet under the chairmanship of the local senior partner. In addition, there would be an annual gathering of all partners at a hotel or other venue which had the necessary facilities.

With the increase in partner numbers, the use of initials when addressing or making reference to partners, also became inappropriate and was discontinued (although sometimes persisted unofficially at a local level).

These changes were necessary and a reflection of the firm's growth and progress. However, on a personal basis, I was grateful to have experienced and enjoyed a couple of years as a partner in a more traditional and intimate environment.

At this time, with the exception of Birmingham, the provincial offices were few in number and small in size and no formal regional structure or lines of command had been established by the firm or appeared necessary. However, Ray Emmitt and I were clear in our minds with regard to the geographic target area on the eastern side of the Pennines, which we should attempt to develop. This stretched from Newcastle in the north down to (and including) Derbyshire. Consequently, in late 1965, we sat down and gave consideration to the actions required for further growth.

Sheffield office, with its strong base of steel and heavy engineering clients and a growing reputation for carrying out special assignments, seemed to be moving in the right direction and, we felt, needed no special attention. As regards Newcastle, we had opened the office only the previous year, with Tony Wood (who we considered to be next in line for partnership) as resident manager. Although we had several clients in the Tyneside and Teesside areas, we recognised that it would take time to build upon this base.

This left Leeds, where we had opened an office in 1963, following several years of servicing the area with staff on the Sheffield office payroll. In a city where several of the banks had their regional headquarters, a merchant bank was already established and a number of large legal firms had their main northern offices, we felt there must be excellent scope for further development. Consequently, we decided that Ray, with his strong practice development skills, should relocate to Leeds office and leave me to run Sheffield.

Our analysis of the situation proved correct and over the next eight years to 1973, all three offices in the North East achieved excellent growth. In the case of Leeds and Newcastle, this was helped by mergers with smallish but well-respected local firms. In order to cope with our increase in size and range of services provided, seven new partners were admitted (three joining as a result of the mergers referred to).

In 1973 I became senior partner for the North East when Ray moved to London office as one of three possible candidates to succeed Henry Benson on his planned retirement. This was also the year when all firms throughout our international organisation discontinued the use of any local names (such as Cooper Brothers & Co in the UK) and adopted the one common name of Coopers & Lybrand (C&L).

Over a period, we had obtained several clients to the south of our initial target area and established a good relationship with the regional head office of Barclays Bank in Nottingham for whom we had carried out several receiverships. Consequently, in 1974 we opened an office in Nottingham and transferred a partner from Sheffield to take charge.

As a little light relief to the above summary of progress, I describe below the proceedings leading up to our first merger following the previously mentioned review carried out by Ray

Emmitt and myself in 1965. These commenced with a meeting at the Grand Hotel in Sheffield (now demolished) between Ray Emmitt and myself, and Stanley and Trevor Middleton, cousins and the sole partners in a smallish but well-respected firm in Newcastle. Stanley was a member of the Council of the Institute of Chartered Accountants and it was in course of this role that the initial contact had been made with Henry Benson.

Ray and I liked the Middletons straight away and a good rapport was quickly established. Consequently, after a couple of hours discussion (and numerous drinks) we had thrashed out a basis for merger. As Stanley had a meeting in London the next day, it was agreed that Trevor would come into Sheffield office for me to brief him on the procedures, reports and other requirements which would be necessary after merger with CB&Co.

After a couple of hours of "instruction", I could see that Trevor was flagging. Therefore, as Yorkshire CC were playing cricket at Bramall Lane in a County Championship game, I suggested that we should adjourn to the Members Pavilion to watch a little cricket over a drink and sandwich – a proposal which Trevor agreed to with some alacrity.

Unfortunately, we found the stage of play to be rather slow and an elderly gentleman (probably much younger than I am now!) seated next to me, seeing an opportunity to break the monotony with conversation, introduced himself. After a few minutes he passed to me a rather dog-eared photograph of a pre-war Yorkshire team with the comment, "I bet you haven't seen many of those players." After I had admitted that I had seen only Len Hutton and Bill Bowes, he replied, "I thought that you wouldn't have." Then, passing the photograph to Trevor (about eight years my senior in age, but bald as a coot) he said, "But I'll bet your dad has." Trevor managed to keep a straight face, but I sometimes called him Dad thereafter.

An event taking place in 1967 had proved to be of great benefit to the firm and the North East region in particular. This was the second nationalisation of the steel industry (comprising the 14 largest UK-based producers) under the Labour government which was in power at that time.

CB&Co already acted for several of the 14 companies, with Sheffield office dealing with Parkgate Iron & Steel Company in Rotherham and Lysaughts (part of the GKN group) in Scunthorpe. However, the first chairman of the new British Steel Corporation (BSC), Julian, Lord Melchett, was aware of the major task he would face of merging 14 companies into one, including their accounting systems, policies, and lines of reporting and he sought advice from Henry Benson. One outcome of this was that Wilfred Molyneux (under whom I had worked prior to becoming a partner) left CB&Co to join BSC as director of finance.

Also, within a short period, the firm became sole auditors of BSC, resulting in Sheffield office taking responsibility for auditing the records of two more of the 14 nationalised companies – The United Steel Companies Ltd and English Steel Corporation – whose activities were concentrated mainly in our geographic area of Sheffield, Stocksbridge and Scunthorpe. However, the benefit to the firm was not merely from the additional audit work as, over the next 10 years or so, we provided assistance to BSC in the disposal of certain non-steelmaking activities (which had been carried on by the 14 acquired companies) and in the implementation of BSC's "Phoenix" schemes, which had been established to facilitate hive-offs and rationalisations of certain activities in conjunction with appropriate private sector steel companies.

I was fortunate to act as first partner on several of these schemes, but this role would not have been possible without the support of several able young men, each on different assignments, who had come through the firm's ranks into partnership in the region. In particular, the efforts of Sean Mahon, Paul Southern, Peter Croft and Peter Cummins were invaluable.

At some stage in this period, Tony Wood, who became a partner in 1966, had returned to Sheffield office. Although Tony's involvement in steel industry activities was limited, he was available to service other clients and deal with problems arising, to ensure that the office (and region) operated with maximum efficiency.

Apart from Tony's wish to return to Sheffield office, the cessation of his frequent car journeys up and down the M1/A1

182

was probably in his best interests and those of other road users! I believe that in one road accident he had tried to depart head-first through the windscreen of his car and, when released from hospital a few days later, needed to permanently change the side on which he parted his hair.

I also recollect him telling me of an incident when he felt he had been cut-up by a lorry. After Tony's long tirade at the driver, the poor man managed to get in a few words – "I would just like to say one thing, guvnor, I didn't do it on purpose." This apparently silenced Tony.

In 1972 (five years after nationalisation of the major steel producers) I received a telephone call out of the blue from Robert Atkinson, for whom I had carried out a financial investigation in 1963 (see Chapter VIII). Robert informed me that he was moving to Sheffield to become executive chairman of Aurora Gear and Engineering (Aurora), the parent of several operating companies engaged in the private sector of the steel industry.

Robert continued by explaining that, following the establishment of BSC, he believed that there was a great opportunity for rationalisation of the private steel sector and he would require the services of a good firm of accountants to assist him in this connection. Consequently, he would like CB&Co to become auditors and advisors to Aurora and for me to be personally involved.

In my previous dealings with Robert, I had been impressed by his drive and decisiveness, although he had been quite a demanding taskmaster. Therefore, I informed him that we would be delighted to become involved. However, I mentioned that we were always cautious in taking on the audit of a parent company, and therefore responsibility for reporting upon consolidated figures, where the main activities had been audited by other firms of accountants. Robert said that I should not be concerned with regard to this, we would be immediately appointed as auditors of any new acquisitions and, over a couple of years, he would ensure that we acted for all companies in the group. He proved to be as good as his word.

The next few years were exhilarating, with Robert making waves in Sheffield as Aurora obtained control of several long-established businesses for rationalisation or the closure of unprofitable activities. By 1980, the Aurora group had increased its workforce from 1,300 employees to 8,500 and were owners of four steelworks.

In addition to the new audits which CB&Co gained on these acquisitions, the firm had been involved in a number of investigations and in the work required on circulars and other documents needed by the stock exchange.

Although some other partners in the North East region became involved in the audits of certain Aurora subsidiaries as the group expanded, I continued to act as first partner (and the main contact with Robert), using Sean Mahon as my right-hand man until he came into partnership in 1977. Sean then took over as first partner of Aurora and I continued my involvement as review/consultant partner. However, I always attended and spoke on behalf of the firm at meetings when Robert Atkinson was present.

One such meeting took place on a winter's morning, when I awoke to find Sheffield (particularly the south-western outskirts where both Sean and I resided) under a heavy covering of snow. Nevertheless, we were both at Aurora, sitting outside Robert's office by 9am (the scheduled meeting time) dressed in typical Cooper's garb of dark suit, tie and shiny black leather shoes. Robert was slightly late but eventually arrived for the meeting resplendent in a pure white ski suit. We tried not to smile.

I commenced the meeting by stating the subjects to be covered but, after a few seconds, I was conscious that Robert was looking past me in the direction of Sean, who was seated slightly to my rear. It transpired that Sean (a cigarette smoker at the time) had absentmindedly (his explanation afterwards) taken a packet from his pocket and extracted a cigarette. Robert spoke, "I hope that you are not thinking of lighting that." Sean's response – "No, sir," as he stuffed the offending item into his pocket.

Sean disputes the accuracy of the above story. We were joined for part of the meeting by a solicitor in order to obtain advice on a legal matter, and Sean claims that he (the solicitor) was the person giving offence when 'fiddling with his pipe!' As both individuals were seated slightly to my rear, I will not argue – but think my account is the more likely one.

Although Robert was quite commanding in manner (as befitted a former senior Royal Naval officer), he could be charming, and I always enjoyed my dealings with him. I attended his marriage at Sheffield Cathedral in 1977 (his first wife having died in 1973) and the reception which followed at the Cutlers' Hall. This was a very pleasant occasion, and Robert endured much leg-pulling from his many guests from the Tyneside area where he was born.

From a professional viewpoint, one of my strongest recollections of these times was advice the firm gave to Aurora in connection with a debenture. At the time of our first involvement, Aurora had substantial bank borrowings, which were secured by the aforementioned debenture. However, as Aurora and its subsidiaries flourished and generated cash, the group moved into credit and we could see no justification for the continued existence of a bank charge against its assets. Consequently, at our suggestion, Aurora arranged for the debenture to be cancelled.

In the early 1980s, following a steelworkers' strike at BSC, the climate in the steel industry changed and the strike spread to the private sector, eventually bringing Aurora substantially into overdraft and close to insolvency. However, in the absence of a debenture, the bank was unable to appoint a receiver and after various consultations and negotiations (in which we took part) Aurora was provided with funding by a consortium of banks, which provided time for an orderly programme of selling off subsidiaries and the closure of unprofitable activities. It was sad to see the group fall into such decline after almost 10 years of success.

My commitments within the firm and periods away from Sheffield had become more demanding at this time and Sean would be the most appropriate person to report upon events, but I believe that Robert continued as chairman of Aurora in a non-executive capacity until 1984. However, in 1980 he had become chairman of British Shipbuilders (BS), which had been established by nationalisation under the Labour government in 1977 and was sustaining heavy losses.

SHEFFIELD FORGED AND TEMPERED

Other than exchanging Christmas cards, I had no contact with Robert at this time. However, my understanding is that – typical of his style and nature – he threw himself into the task of improving the situation, and by 1982 the BS loss (although still almost £20 million) was the lowest since nationalisation. At the end of the year, Robert was knighted.

Robert died in January 2015, only a few weeks before what would have been his 99th birthday. He had been a fighter all his life and I had greatly enjoyed my dealings with him.

XII

Partnership in CB&Co

The Second Phase

In Chapter VIII and XI, I mention in some detail certain client work assignments which are still clear in my memory all these years later, partly because of the interesting people involved. There were many other assignments which I could have included, but my intention is simply to provide sufficient information to give an indication of the type of work carried out by myself and other CB&Co partners these 50 or so years ago. Consequently, I will briefly relate just two more examples.

On one occasion I undertook an investigation for the Takeover Panel, reporting directly to Sir Hartley Shawcross (later Lord Shawcross), head of the panel, into a failed profits' forecast of a listed company. I found it impossible to determine the exact timing when certain information had been made available to directors of the company and, consequently, my report could provide only an opinion, rather than a factual statement. On this basis, the panel decided that no action could be taken.

This was a frustrating situation for me, but gave me a valuable insight into the workings and thought processes of the panel and an appreciation of the sort of reasons where, on occasions, the panel fail to take action in cases which an outsider may think would be justified.

A second interesting experience in my early years of partnership was on a receivership (under an appointment by the District Bank – subsequently to become part of NatWest) in respect of a company involved in opencast mining activities in Derbyshire, but which also owned two coal mines in the Irish Republic. These were a drift mine situated close to Sligo in the north-west and an anthracite mine located in County Kilkenny in the south. Over a two-day visit commencing in Dublin it was necessary to cover almost 400 miles by car, often on poor quality roads, in order to assess the value of these assets.

I found that the mine near Sligo was not in operation and appeared to have negligible remaining coal deposits. However, much worse, there was a legal claim in process against the company, of which I was now receiver, in relation to a collapsed bridge, allegedly caused by crossings of heavy plant used at the mine. I wasted no more time and moved on to Kilkenny without delay. However, the problems there were just as great. The mine was flooded but, more worryingly, there was a dangerous uncapped shaft!

Abandoning my claim as receiver to these two "assets" was not a difficult decision, but the experience gave me a foretaste of the sort of problems to be encountered on assignments of this nature.

Despite the above disappointments, from a personal perspective, the trip to Ireland was not a complete waste of time. On the Saturday following the mine visits, the Irish Derby was taking place at the Curragh, and Ray Emmitt, Tony Wood and myself had planned to meet up and attend. Furthermore, as Ray was joint owner of a horse, which was in training at stables in Ireland and running at Roscommon on the following day, we intended to stay on for that event.

The name of the horse of which Ray was 50% owner was Scoopaland, a name derived from Coopers (I don't think Henry Benson would have been consulted!) and Singer & Friedlander, the merchant bank of which Brian Buckley, the co-owner, was a director.

At the Curragh, we were greeted by Ray's trainer, who managed to gain admission for all of us to enjoy the comforts of the owners and trainers enclosure. However, next day at Roscommon the facilities were rather more primitive. Furthermore, the betting odds on Scoopaland steadily declined when it became known that "the English had arrived to see their horse run". Out of loyalty to Ray, Tony and I joined him in betting on Scoopaland.

Our horse started well going into the lead and hopes were high. However, there was a slight dip in the course, which took the horses out of our sight. When they re-emerged, Scoopaland was second last! I believe that this remained the position to the end and we all lost our stake money. Nevertheless, it was a fun day.

In the following 20 or so paragraphs of this chapter, I deal mainly with the development of the firm and my personal progression therein over the next few years. I appreciate that this information may not be of interest to some readers, in which case they may wish to skip a few pages. However, in personal terms, my long career with CB&Co/C&L has been an important aspect of my life and I have, therefore, considered it appropriate to cover events of these years, at least in outline, for my own satisfaction – and while my memory still permits!

Throughout my 38 years with the firm, I regarded client work, carried out to the highest level and with strong personal involvement, to be the matter of greatest importance and, therefore, that the need for spending time with clients and gaining an understanding of their affairs and requirements to be essential. Consequently, I always ensured that a high percentage of a "standard" working week was devoted to clients, even though my actual time on the firm's affairs was usually well in excess of this standard. This was important to enable me to play a wider role in both the development and management of CB&Co/C&L.

From well before I joined the firm, an important factor in its development had been the establishment of "the Manual", the first edition of which had been prepared by Henry Benson and issued to partners and staff in 1946. Designed to grow with the firm and provide guidance on most areas of professional work and conduct, the pages were in loose-leaf form and held together in blue-backed binders with extendable brass screws so that new sections could be inserted as necessary.

To digress, briefly, from the main subject, I remember that shortly after I became a partner, several of the articled clerks in Sheffield office (fortunate enough to have wealthy parents) acquired Mini Minor cars all in the same blue colour, which, I found, they described as "Manual Blue". This created a sort of "club" and they would meet up at weekends, accompanied by their girlfriends, at various Derbyshire Peak District pubs, where, consequently, one could find the car parks containing several vehicles of identical make and colour. Good fun, but a far cry from my days as an impecunious student.

Development of the Manual continued over the years and, in due course, comprised seven sections relating primarily to the different areas of professional work undertaken by the firm. The responsibility for maintaining the appropriate sections of the Manual, together with the preparation and issue of technical circulars and other documents on current matters for the guidance of partners and staff, fell to the Technical Committees of the firm. Therefore, I was pleased a few years after becoming a partner to be appointed to the Audit Committee, dealing with Manual Sections V and VI relating to Contents of Accounts and the Approach to Auditing, respectively. I served on this committee, with involvement in the updating of several parts of the Manual and drafting of technical circulars, from 1968 to 1975. Subsequently, as my client responsibilities moved towards investigations and other special assignments, I joined the Investigation and Prospectus Committee, on which I remained for the next seven years to 1982. I felt that the experience gained in the above roles helped improve my knowledge and abilities to serve clients.

As the firm grew in size and complexity, by necessity the structure of the organisation and the approach to management of operations needed to change and become more formalised and the 27 offices outside London were grouped into eight geographic regions of Scotland, Wales, Northern Ireland and five separate areas of England. In 1985 a Regional Operations Committee was established comprised of the Regional Partners in Charge (RPICs). By this time, I was RPIC of the North East region and became the first chairman of this committee. However, subsequently in 1986, in accordance with the wishes of Brandon Gough and Peter Allen – chairman and managing director, respectively, of the UK firm (following the retirement of David Hobson, to whom I refer again later), I was appointed Executive Partner in Charge (EPIC) of the

UK Regional Practice comprising all the above regions and with an eventual total of over 4,500 partners and staff. I held this position for the next seven years until reaching the firm's normal retirement age of 60 in 1993.

In operational terms, this appointment effectively placed me as a joint number three in the firm's hierarchy, together with the EPIC of London General Practice and the Head of Management Consultancy. It was also the pinnacle of my operational ambitions as, for various reasons mentioned in earlier chapters (particularly the wellbeing of my daughter Michelle), I would never have wished or felt able to move my home from Sheffield to London. Furthermore, the regional practice was my pride and joy and, in my view, superior to those of the other major accountancy firms.

Going back several years in time, I had been pleased (but rather surprised) in 1974 to be one of two young partners (Tim Lawrence of London office was the other) to be added to the members of the firm's Executive Committee to form an Electoral College with the responsibility of selecting the next chairman on the retirement of Henry Benson.

Henry was clearly going to be a very difficult act to follow, and it was not easy to decide upon his successor from the three chosen candidates of David Hobson, Greville Gidley-Kitchin and Ray Emmitt, all with different personalities, skills and experience. The eventual choice was a triumvirate, with David as chairman and Ray and Greville as his two deputies. While this might have been seen as a compromise, I believe that it was the best decision. David proved to be an excellent operator and the firm continued to flourish under his control and management for the next nine years. A possible weakness (in my view), as compared with Henry, of public image and stature was (at least partly) offset by the efforts of his deputies.

Intellectually, David was a match for anyone (I believe he had taken first place in his accountancy examinations and won a record number of prizes in various subjects). However, although I always enjoyed a good relationship with David and found him to be a very kind man, he could be quick-tempered and impatient, particularly when dealing with certain partners in whom he seemed to lack confidence. He also had several unusual mannerisms, which could sometimes be found amusing by his partners – but not, fortunately, to David's knowledge.

I remember meeting David in his office at about 8.30 one morning to discuss matters concerning Newcastle office, before the start of an Executive Committee Meeting. As we were short of certain information, David decided that he would telephone Stanley Middleton. A male Geordie voice answered the phone. This sounded to me like an articled clerk trying to be helpful before the arrival of the receptionist – I feared the worst. David having asked to speak to "Mr Stanley" experienced a longish delay before the response "I think he hasn't arrived yet". David said, "When he arrives, tell him to phone Hobson in London office." A further short pause, then the reply, "How do you spell that name, sir?" David looked as though he was about to burst, but fortunately a female voice came on to the line – "I will speak to Mr Stanley as soon as he comes in, Mr Hobson." The receptionist had arrived, just in time to save the day.

A few weeks after the election of David as chairman in 1974, I had been delighted (and felt privileged) to be appointed to the firm's Executive Committee (the EC), effectively the fifteen-man Board of Directors. At the age of 40 years, I was the youngest member and joining a group containing many experienced partners for whom I had the greatest respect.

At this time, the Executive Committee was a self-perpetuating body, but with the understanding that members would serve for only a four-year term. However, well before I had been a member for that period, the firm became rather more democratic (Henry's retirement may have been a factor in this!) and it was decided that members of the EC should be elected. My recollection is that in London the committee members were to be elected by partners engaged in the various professional disciplines (audit, tax, insolvency, etc.) but in the regions, it would be on a geographic basis. In my case, the constituency for voting purposes comprised the partners in the two northern regions either side of the Pennines, which had always worked closely together.

This new electoral system for membership of the Executive Committee proved to be to my advantage as until 1988, when the firm's management arrangements were changed, I was chosen every four years by the northern partners to continue as their representative. The only occasion when my election was not unanimous was when a taxation partner in Manchester office, Alan Ravenscroft (a good friend of mine or so I had believed!), allowed his name to go forward as a candidate, to the great annoyance of Phil Livesey, PIC of the North West region. Alan claimed that his candidature was "accidental", but he did receive one vote – his own!

In 1988 the Executive Committee was replaced by two bodies: The Management Committee to which members were appointed by the chairman of the firm, and the Governing Board, for which members were elected in a similar way to that which had been used for appointing representatives to the Executive Committee. However, it was decided that no more than four members of the Management Committee could also serve on the Governing Board.

I was delighted to be immediately appointed by Brandon Gough, to serve on the Management Committee, and also pleased (and rather flattered) to be elected unopposed by my northern partners to the Governing Board. However, I was brought down to earth when someone informed me that my "friend" and partner Miles Middleton (based in Newcastle office but having spent some years in Sheffield) had expressed the view (in my support!) that "we already have enough with Cottingham telling us what to do. We don't need another one".

The new committee arrangements lasted until 1989 when the UK offices of Deloittes left their international partnership in order to merge with C&L, but I comment upon this in the next chapter.

The international firm of Coopers & Lybrand (C&L) had started to operate on 1 January 1957, with the three largest members of the organisation:

Cooper Brothers & Co in the UK,

Lybrand Ross Brothers & Montgomery (Lybrands) in the USA, and

McDonald Currie & Co in Canada,

SHEFFIELD FORGED AND TEMPERED

each becoming responsible for a defined area of the world in which they would take action to develop the firm. Geographically, the UK firm had the largest liaison area, comprising the British Commonwealth countries and Europe. UK liaison partners were appointed (usually in addition to their UK roles and duties) to the various overseas firms to assist with expansion, effectiveness and technical quality of work, particularly in relation to referred audits and assignments from C&L firms in other countries, which were to be carried out in the Coopers & Lybrand name.

I was pleased and felt fortunate to be appointed liaison partner for the four Scandinavian countries. All these liaison roles commenced in 1975 and continued until 1986 in respect of Sweden and Finland and until 1990 for Norway and Denmark.

I found the duties, which required a few days visit two or three times each year to each of these beautiful countries, most enjoyable and, over a period of time, I made several good friends in the Scandinavian firms as they became soundly established within the C&L network. It was also pleasing to witness the gradual strengthening of relationships between the partners in the four countries which (partly because of historic reasons) had not existed at the time I first became involved. However, as the Scandinavian firms developed, increasing in size and taking on additional referred work in the Coopers & Lybrand name, I felt that the technical quality control aspect of my liaison role was becoming too time-consuming and I arranged for Tony Wood to provide support as Technical Liaison Partner. I believe that Tony came to enjoy these trips to Scandinavia as much as I did.

One of the few downsides of visiting Scandinavia was the high cost of living, with certain foods and, especially, alcoholic beverages, being very expensive. Consequently, I always called at the airport duty-free store and purchased a bottle of wine or malt whisky as a gift for one or other of my partners. On one occasion, when catching an evening flight from Manchester to Copenhagen, Dennis Law, the famous Manchester United international inside-forward (an old description), was travelling on the same aircraft and also carrying an expensive-looking bottle of malt whisky. As we awaited our cases following arrival, Dennis accidentally dropped his bottle, which shattered on hitting the ground. As the "nectar" drained away, a voice from behind with a strong scouse accent, commented, "It's a good thing you don't play in goal."

I had one other international commitment during these years as one of four members of the C&L International Construction Industry Committee. The other three members coming from USA, Canada and Germany. An objective of the committee was to increase dialogue with and hopefully obtain assignments from major construction groups, but much of the committee's work related to establishing and documenting acceptable accounting policies, standards and controls for use in the industry, where turnover was often substantial, profit margins small and valuations of contracts in progress difficult. We held seminars in several countries, but progress was slow.

In foregoing paragraphs (and to some extent in earlier chapters), I have commented briefly on my role in the firm as it grew and developed from 1964 to 1988. However, on reflection, I feel that I may have devoted insufficient attention to the first 10 of these years when (initially in support of Ray Emmitt) I was privileged to play an active part in the establishment of the North East region.

To witness the emergence of successful offices in Leeds, Newcastle and Nottingham with the admission of 10 new partners in the period (the majority having served in Sheffield), with the knowledge that several others were coming through, gave me great satisfaction. We knew each other well and developed a great sense of camaraderie.

Importantly, it was not only the efforts of the partners and professional staff which made these times so special. The support people (secretaries, typist, etc.) all played their part. We prided ourselves that every document leaving the office should be perfect. Consequently, reports and financial statements were called over against the drafts and (in these days before word processors) a single keying error could mean the complete retyping of pages, often with those concerned remaining well after normal hours. However, no one complained.

This sort of commitment continued down to what might be regarded as the final level in Mrs Harvey our office cleaner (known to everyone as Mrs H), who eventually served the firm for 25 years before retiring at the age of sixty-seven in 1980. To describe Mrs H as "a character" would be an understatement. Although never on the permanent payroll, she clearly regarded herself as part of CB&Co, unofficially extending her duties over the years to become self-appointed security guard, car park attendant, mother confessor to anyone in need and, on occasions, disciplinarian when dealing with untidy articled clerks.

Our office in these days was in a converted terraced property in the university area of Sheffield. It had parking for five vehicles to the rear, which area was overlooked by a modern university block. However, a constant source of annoyance to us was finding unauthorised vehicles occupying our spaces.

I arrived one morning to see a shiny new Hillman car, bearing the latest registration plates, in our car park and was met by a very agitated Mrs H. She greeted me with, "I caught one of those students walking away from that car. I told him it was a private park, but he said it wasn't his car." Pointing to the second floor of the university building, she continued, "That's him next to the window near the back. Shall I go and tell him that you say he has got to move it?" Smiling, I replied, "If you wish, Mrs Harvey."

The first person I met on entering the office was Alan Young, head of our tax department. He enquired why I was smiling, and I told him of the errant vehicle and Mrs Harvey's mission to invade the university. Looking rather concerned, Alan said, "But that's my new car!" I am not sure what transpired but I kept my head down.

Another Mrs H incident which sticks in my mind occurred a few years later, by which time we had moved to larger, more centrally situated offices in Sheffield. I had been contacted by the Canadian parent company of a client based in Retford. Two of the Canadian directors were proposing to visit this subsidiary because of concerns relating to the performance of the managing director and certain comments made in our post audit letter. The wish of the Canadians was for a meeting at our offices early in the day in order to allow plenty of time for their subsequent visit to the subsidiary. I agreed 7.30am and also arranged for Paul Southern (still a manager at the time but responsible for the subsidiary company audit) to be present.

The meeting duly took place and, as none of the secretaries or typists had arrived by 7.30am, Mrs H was asked to take orders for tea. I had never met the Canadians before, and the atmosphere at the start of the meeting was quite sombre. I remember that the first question (after we had shaken hands) with regard to the local managing director, was, "Do you think we should sack this guy?" At this point, Mrs H arrived with the tray of tea. The requirements of Paul and myself were well known to Mrs H. However, for the Canadians, their tea requests ("black and no sugar" and "same but two spoons of sugar, ma'am") had already been poured by Mrs H into nice china cups with saucers.

All seemed well, but I noticed a look of concern appear on the face of Mrs H and she enquired of one of the Canadians, "Was yours with sugar?" After having obtained this confirmation, Mrs H picked up his cup and took a sip of the tea. She then pronounced, "That's right then," returned the cup to its saucer and left the room. Silence descended, but as the door closed, we all erupted into helpless laughter. The ice had been broken and the meeting became much more relaxed.

We continued as auditors of the UK subsidiary for many years and, even after it had been sold by the parent company, I received a Christmas card each year from the Canadians. It usually ended with a postscript – "Give our regards to Mrs Harvey."

Another incident in these years, which could have had very serious consequences, concerned Sean Mahon. While the building to which we had relocated provided more room, the construction and finish proved to be of poor quality. Amongst the irritations, the lift frequently broke down and the large, plate-glass, steel-framed windows proved difficult to open, especially on hot summer days when, presumably, the metal frames had expanded. This was a particular problem in the typing pool where several young women sometimes had to toil away in hot, stuffy conditions. Enter Sean – always obliging. "Could you please open the

197

windows and let in some fresh air?" He accepted the challenge, but succeeded only in the latter part, when he pushed out a 6x3-foot glass pane from its frame to go crashing down towards the pavement three stories below! The pane hit a lamp standard on the way down, turning it into a cascade of jagged glass pieces.

My recollection is that Sean sprinted down the three flights of stairs, fearing the worst. To his great relief there were no bodies on the pavement but a yellow Lotus Elan, which had just parked, had taken a battering from the shower of glass. A few seconds later the driver, a very pregnant young woman, would have been stepping out. She was obviously very shocked but Sean, apologising profusely, took her into an adjacent café to help settle her nerves, while assuring her that any damage to the car would be rectified and offering any other immediate assistance he could provide.

Eventually, Sean returned to the office, still looking shaken and deathly white. He telephoned the appropriate admin department in London office to report details so that they could inform the firm's insurers. The response was on the lines of, "I hope you didn't acknowledge that we had any liability!"

These many years later, if the incident is raised in course of reminiscing, one can pull Sean's leg and raise a smile, but no one was amused at the time.

A client engagement in 1975, which I think is worth mentioning because it resulted in the establishment of the legal precedent of "Marshall v Cottingham" in Chancery Law (which precedent, I assume, still remains to this day) related to a receivership appointment under a bank debenture. Unusually (although this did not occur to me at the time) the debenture incorporated certain provisions of Section 109 of the Law of Property Act of 1925, although its purpose was to secure the recent borrowings of a company called Spitalgate Ltd. This company had been established to acquire Spitalgate Mill (a property in Grantham, Lincolnshire) and to carry out the conversion of this property into a combination of hotel, restaurant, public house and discotheque.

In addition to (but ranking behind) the bank debenture, Spitalgate Ltd had executed a legal charge in favour of Mr

Marshall, a director, for monies which he had paid into the company.

Paul Southern was assisting me on this assignment, and it soon became clear to us that as we were incurring costs but receiving no revenue from the property (which was in its final stages of renovation), the most sensible course was for an early sale. However, the property consultants we spoke to were pessimistic as regards the number of potential purchasers and the likely sale proceeds.

In the above circumstances, I made the decision to dispose of the property by closed bids, to be submitted by a certain date at which time they would be opened, and we would accept the best offer. This proved to be a good decision. There was only ONE bid received but this was at a figure which I regarded as satisfactory – thus justifying the rather risky approach taken.

The sum obtained for sale of the property of £125,000 (equivalent to about £1.4 million in current day values) was sufficient to provide for our fees and certain remaining receivership expenses, pay all costs relating to the sale of the property, clear the sum due to the bank and provide a remaining balance of £10,000, which I paid to Mr Marshall on account of his legal charge. I was surprised, therefore, to receive a demand from Marshall to pay over to him any monies still remaining in my hands, which represented our fees and certain outstanding receivership costs. This led to an action between Marshall and myself in the High Court of Justice before the Rt Hon. the Vice-Chancellor (Sir Robert Megarry).

I will not attempt to set out in any detail the issues involved but, briefly, in relation to my position as receiver, there appeared to be two questions to be considered. These arose from the aforementioned extension of the bank's normal debenture document to incorporate certain provisions of the Law of Property Act of 1925:

- Firstly, was I entitled to retain a remuneration, to include all costs and charges incurred as receiver, of up to 5% on monies received, without making application to the court; and,

- Secondly, were agent's fees and expenses on sale of the property, conveyancing costs and the wages of a caretaker (employed for security reasons pending the sale) to be regarded as part of my above remuneration.

Fortunately, Sir Robert's judgment was yes to the first question and no to the second, clarifying that these latter items should be treated as costs of realisation of the property.

These decisions were obviously a great relief to me as otherwise we would have been working for nothing.

I will not attempt to précis Sir Robert's judgment, which covered 10 foolscap-sized pages, but one amusing response in relation to the "considerable reliance" which he considered Marshall's barrister was placing on the importance of a comma in the Conveyance Act of 1881 was made in the form of a jingle:

"Every lady in this land

Hath twenty nails upon each hand

Five and twenty on hands and feet

And this is true, without deceit."

Sir Robert commented: "Leave this unpunctuated, or with punctuation only at the end of the lines, and it seems plainly untrue. Insert a comma or semi-colon at the beginning and end of the phrase 'Upon each hand five', and nonsense becomes sense."

In conclusion, I was pleased to come out of this situation with such a satisfactory result, but it was another lesson for the future.

XIII

Partnership in C&L

The Final Years

In 1983, with David Hobson approaching retirement, discussions took place in the Executive Committee, and soundings made more widely within the firm with regard to a possible successor. In due course, three candidates emerged, all of whom were well known to me as fellow members of the Executive Committee.

These were:

- Ray Emmitt, my colleague, mentor and friend over many years, and the firm's deputy chairman throughout David's period of office,
- Sandy Gordon, an able, experienced and well-liked partner based in London office of roughly the same vintage as Ray; and
- Brandon Gough, at 44 years of age, younger than the other candidates but with a growing reputation.

Brandon had joined the firm only in 1964, after qualifying with a small firm of City accountants, taking top place in the Institute final exams and obtaining several prizes. I had first met him a few weeks after he joined the firm when he had assisted me at the London end of work on a prospectus.

During the nine years of David Hobson's chairmanship, the firm had grown substantially (both organically and from acquisitions). There had been a massive increase in the numbers of partners admitted and a consequent reduction in the average age. Consequently a small selection panel, such as that when David had been elected, was no longer appropriate and the committee established to appoint the new chairman was very much larger, including Executive Committee members, representatives from the practice areas and other selected partners from Operations and the UK regions.

Although I considered that the quality of those selected for the committee was not in doubt, a concern in my mind was that many of the members had little or nil experience of working with the candidates or of seeing them in action. Therefore, I felt that there could be a danger of too much importance being given to the performance of the candidates on the day of interview, rather than the abilities they had demonstrated over a long period.

The candidates were granted only a brief period of time to make their pitch to the committee – Sandy appearing first, followed by Ray. To my surprise, neither made any detailed presentation but relied mainly upon a few opening remarks (in Ray's case I remember these to this day) followed by the opportunity for members to ask questions. The impression given by both Sandy and Ray was that, as the firm was continuing to increase both billings and profits, we should leave well alone, except for "a touch on the tiller here and there" (Ray's actual words). This was hardly an inspiring message and I felt saddened that two excellent partners had performed so disappointingly.

In contrast to the above, Brandon grasped his opportunity to make an excellent and quite detailed presentation to the committee, identifying areas where he believed there were weaknesses in our approach but referring to potential future opportunities at a time when the profession was experiencing rapid change. He well exceeded his allotted time for appearing before the committee but, with no one to follow, the chairman allowed him to continue without interruption.

The candidates having had their say, the members of the selection committee were given the opportunity to express views and a few straw polls were taken. However, there was little doubt that Brandon had won the day, and on the formal vote, he was unanimously elected as chairman. Despite the comments I have expressed above in relation to the constitution of the committee, I was left with the strong belief that Brandon was the best man for the job and that he fully justified his selection to lead the firm for the foreseeable future.

Articulate, innovative and possessing great presence, whether appearing before his several hundred partners at an annual meeting or speaking to an external body, Brandon also had the ability to recognise his strengths and to delegate certain aspects of his role to others who were better qualified to carry them out. Consequently, his efforts appeared to concentrate on developing the firm's strategy both in the UK and internationally and enhancing its public image. His numerous external appointments, including serving as a government director of British Aerospace, chairman of the Higher Education Funding Council and the Doctors' and Dentists' Pay Review, membership of the council of Lloyd's insurance market and involvement with several professional bodies, including the council of the Institute of Chartered Accountants in England and Wales, not only lifted the firm's profile and reputation but frequently provided opportunities for fee earning assignments.

Furthermore, in less than two years after becoming chairman, Brandon (in my view, still playing to his strengths) appointed Peter Allen to the new role of managing partner of the firm. Peter, who had served at various times as staff partner, head of business services group and head of London office, had an excellent knowledge of the people and activities of the firm and of London office in particular and was the ideal person to take responsibility for operations, leaving Brandon to concentrate upon the areas in which he excelled.

I had enjoyed working with Peter in the past, particularly when he acted as lead partner for British Steel Corporation, with which client, Sheffield office (and myself in particular) had been heavily involved in connection with the Corporation's activities in South Yorkshire and Lincolnshire. Consequently, as EPIC of the UK Regional Practice, I found it easy to establish a close working relationship and, over time, a good personal friendship with Peter which remains to this day.

In 2015, many years after Peter's retirement from C&L (and over 20 years since mine) he was persuaded to write an article for

Reflections, a magazine for former partners. For convenience, Peter chose to draft a paragraph under each letter of the alphabet. I was touched and rather flattered to read his contribution under letter C, which I reproduce below:

Cottingham, Barrie

"When I was Managing Partner, I appointed Barrie to look after the regions. Barrie was the most effective operator I ever worked with. He quietly, without fuss, just got on with reorganising Coopers outside London. I had a great rapport with him."

For much of my career, the accountancy profession in the UK had been dominated by eight large firms (the Big Eight), of which C&L was one. However, during the 1950s, in response to changing demands from clients in commerce and industry and new opportunities becoming available, there was a recognition by these firms of a need to both grow in size and improve their international networks.

A further stimulus towards these actions was the emergence of several large hi-tech financial consultancies, which were capable of competing for several important areas of work previously regarded as the preserve of the accountancy firms.

Despite the above, C&L performed well in these years and by 1985 had grown from fourth to first place in the annual table of accountancy firms in terms of fee income. However, this position lasted for only a short time when we were overtaken by the newly merged KPMG. Other mergers were also taking place in this period and by 1989, the Big Eight firms had become the Big Six.

Brandon and Peter were well aware of the changing situation and held the view that six large firms in the accountancy marketplace was probably at least two firms too many. However, the problem for C&L was to find a suitable candidate to join with, taking into account international considerations as well as those in the UK.

In 1989, an opportunity arose when a proposed link-up internationally between Deloitte Haskins & Sells and Touche Ross ran into difficulties. The outcome was that the Deloitte offices in the UK (and also in several other parts of the world, including the Netherlands and Australia), deserted the Touche Ross organisation to join C&L. The new combined firm in the UK was comprised of 60% C&L and 40% Deloitte, and for a few years operated under the name Coopers & Lybrand Deloitte before reverting to the C&L name.

Following the merger, a new partnership board of 14 people was established comprising seven partners from each of the two firms. Brandon became chairman with Peter continuing as managing partner. John Bullock, the senior Deloitte partner, was appointed deputy chairman, but soon left the UK to become liaison partner to the C&L firms in Europe. I was pleased to be appointed a member of this new board and also to continue as EPIC of the (now much enlarged) Regional Practice.

It was found over the next few years that a smaller Management Group (and subsequently an even smaller Chairman's Group) was necessary within the partnership board in order to achieve the speedy implementation of actions required to obtain the full benefits of the merger. I was pleased to serve on both of the above groups until I reached the firm's normal retirement age of 60 years in 1993. Therefore, since joining the Executive Committee in 1974, I had been a member of the firm's main management team, by whatever name, for 19 years.

While, after the merger, I was delighted to lead the much larger number of partners and staff in the regions (approximately 4,500) and to welcome the many new clients, I had always believed (and preached to anyone prepared to listen) that C&L were the most innovative of the major accountancy firms and possessed the best and most dedicated people. However, one of the principles upon which the merger had been based was "best man for the job". With two offices in almost every city in the UK, each with its own management structure, I now had to consider proposals and make recommendations on the merging of these offices and the management positions therein in a way which

205

would show recognition of the "best man" principle. The task was made even more difficult when it emerged over a period that the cultures of the two firms were quite different.

A further and equally important issue following the merger was dealing with clients, particularly in cases where competitors in the same industry were now going to have a common firm of auditors/financial advisors, thereby giving rise to fears that there could be danger of leakages of confidential information. I had several difficult meetings, particularly with two important clients in South Wales, where this matter was of great concern.

Over a period, the office rationalisations and management opportunities were completed, the main problems with clients resolved and general concerns of partners and staff smoothed over. However, dealing with these matters, particularly as many of the people involved were personal friends or colleagues of many years standing, was not my happiest time with the firm.

Moving towards my official retirement date in 1993, I was honoured to be given several parties, although in some cases where clients were concerned, I think that there was a greater awareness of the practice development opportunities provided at these functions than of my departure.

The first "celebration" was for Sheffield office staff, and I was presented with a leaving gift of a watercolour painting by the Sheffield artist Thomas Bush Hardy. Sean insisted on this painting being on display at all subsequent retirement events, presumably to show that my services were not being dispensed with on the cheap!

The second function, in one of the banqueting rooms at the Cutlers' Hall, Sheffield was for South Yorkshire clients, many of whom I had dealt with over long periods. Kevin McDonald was present, and I was given a silver model of a Ferrari car to remind me of the real thing, which (as related in Chapter XI) I had declined to accept in 1965.

A much smaller event, which also took place at the Cutlers' Hall, was held in the Master's private suite. Sean and I entertained 12 guests, including the current Master Cutler and some of our most prestigious clients who were mainly involved in the steel and heavy engineering industries. My recollection is that five of these people had served as Master Cutler in prior years, so there was quite a "clubby" feeling at the event.

The final and largest function (and the one I enjoyed most) was for my C&L colleagues and their spouses. This included all the partners in the North East region and many other people in the firm with whom I had worked over the years and formed good friendships – in total an attendance of about 150.

As the banqueting room filled up with guests taking their places following the pre-dinner drinks, Sean (acting as master of ceremonies) announced that there were two other attendees, who had just arrived. These turned out to be my son Nigel, who had returned (at Sean's suggestion) from Australia, where he was working at the time, and his London-based girlfriend. They had travelled from London to Sheffield by train, arriving less than an hour before the dinner. Kath and I were completely surprised and very delighted.

After dinner, both Sean and I made speeches and used slides to show photographs and other documents, in order to facilitate some leg-pulling of each other and of certain northern colleagues. The changes in men's hairstyles over the years (from long to, in some cases, bald) was a particular source of amusement. After this, Miles Middleton made an impromptu "appearance", which came as no surprise to the Northerners. He reviewed my years with the firm, including the time spent in Kenya, producing certain items which he claimed I had used or worn. One of these, supposedly a pith helmet, proved to be a large, inverted chamber pot with the words Pith Helmet painted on the side. The last two letters in "Pith" appeared to have been painted over two original letters s!

Next day (a Saturday) was "open house" at the Croft, with drinks and lunch for any of the guests remaining in Sheffield. The weather was excellent, and we had a good turnout. It was a very enjoyable weekend, with the added bonus that Nigel was able to stay for a few days before returning to Australia.

At some stage in these events, Sean asked to have a few words with me. He mentioned that, although two new partners had been moved into Sheffield over the last year or so from other offices, he was concerned that with my retirement, following that of Tony Wood a year earlier, coupled with the increase in his responsibilities as office partner in charge and a member of the firm's Governing Board, both the quality of work and, particularly, relationships with clients could be endangered. He wondered, therefore, whether there was a possibility that I could return to Sheffield office for say, 12 months, to assist in connection with the above areas and provide time for the new partners to become established.

I replied that, while I would be happy to assist in the way suggested, it was a matter which would have to be agreed at a higher level in the firm, starting, I suggested, with the Governing Board of which Sean was a member. Sean accepted this and acted without delay and, while I believe there were initial concerns expressed on the danger of creating an undesirable precedent, Sean's proposal was accepted. Consequently, I was pleased to delay my retirement and take on the role suggested by Sean, with an appropriately reduced profit share in line with these responsibilities.

Following the hectic post-Deloitte merger period, this return to home territory provided a welcome time for me to readjust and give consideration to the next phase of my life. However, I had greatly enjoyed my 38 years with the firm and to have been granted the opportunity to establish a place in a team of talented and dedicated people, several of whom have become close personal friends.

1973 – Nigel and Michelle on holiday in Venice.

With Kath, Michelle and Nigel visiting my cousin Ian and wife, Renä, in Hong Kong in 1988.

1983 – Michelle's "VIP Day" at Sheffield Wednesday's Hillsborough Stadium to celebrate her 21st birthday. By kind permission of Steve Ellis, Photographer.

Michelle with "The Great Derek Dooley". Sheffield born Dooley scored 62 goals in 61 league games for the Owls between 1950 and 1953, powering their promotion to the top division in English football.

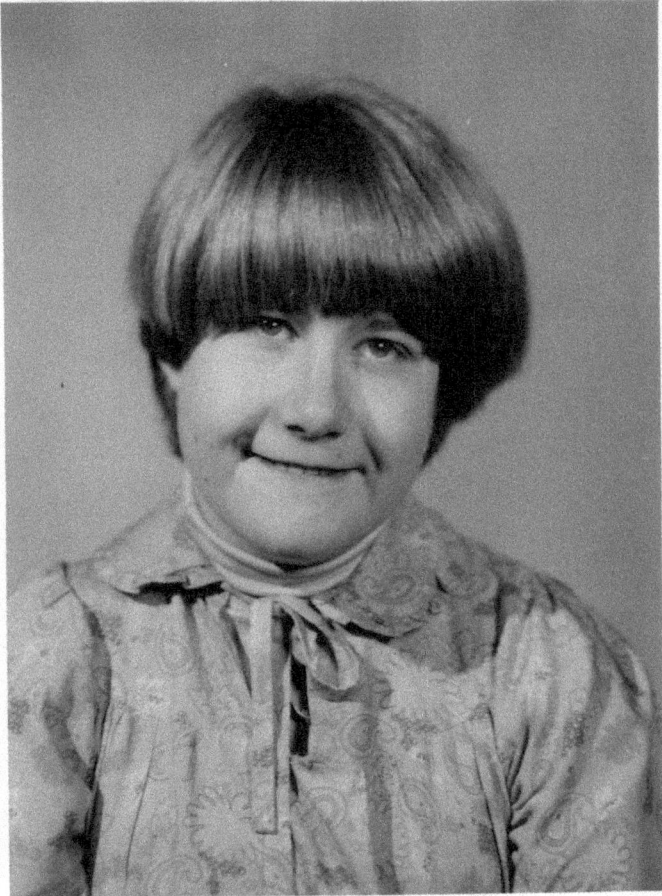

Michelle in 1979.

Visiting my cousin Linda in Heidelberg, where she resided for several years, in 1990.

My cousin John Strafford at Christmas in 1990.

The Croft, my home for 26 years until December 2002.

Aunt Connie and Mum in 1996 – "Will you drive, or shall I?"

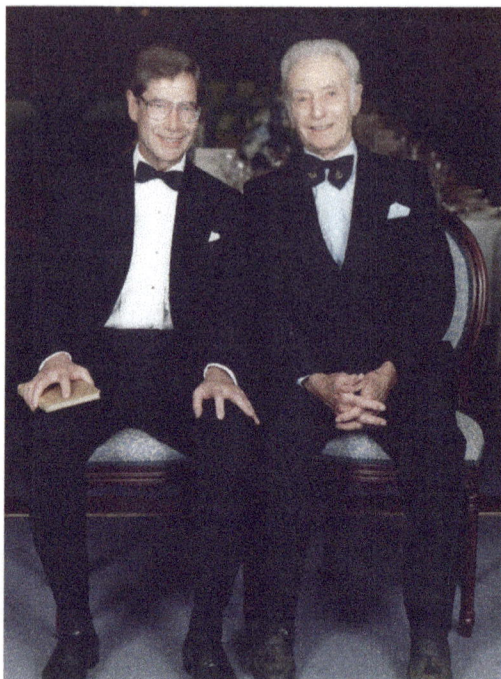

With Sir Stanley Matthews in 1998. Stanley was widely regarded as having been the greatest player in the British game. By kind permission of Steve Ellis, Photographer.

With Nigel and Lisa.

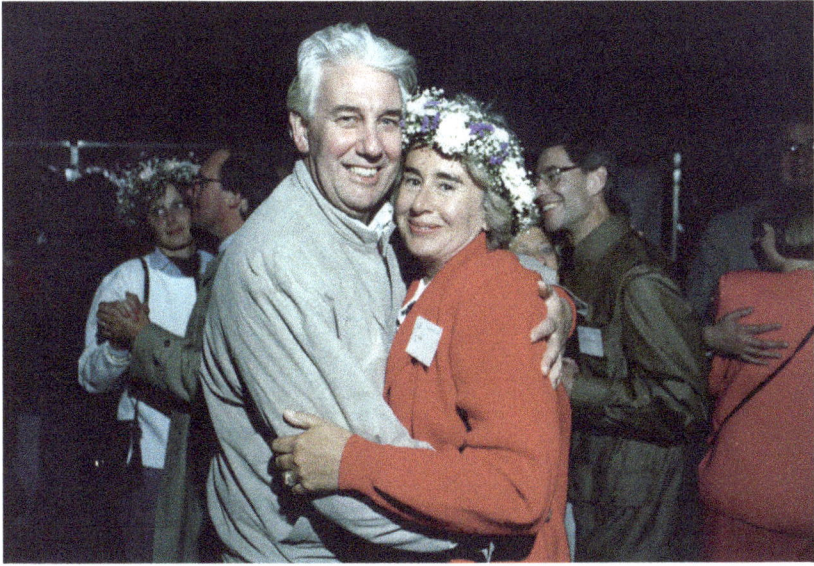

Peter and Pat Allen at an outdoor party during the C&L European
Partners Meeting in Stockholm in 1990.

With Kenneth Clarke, Chancellor of the Exchequer,
at Number 11 Downing Street in 1994.

Nicola's parents, Lesley and Sheila Scahill with their grandchildren in 1994.

Nicola at "Sweet Seventeen" – 26 years before we met in May 2004.

Dinner at Harewood House, at which we met John and Norma Major, in September 2004.

Nicola and her mother, Sheila, on holiday at Lake Como, Italy, in 2006.

Hugh and Beverley Grayson, Tony Wood, Jane Gibbs and Jo Wood
attending my "Cattles" retirement party in 2006.

Nicola and myself with former England rugby lock-forward, Martin Bayfield, who spoke at my Retirement Dinner held in the Chinese Suite of the Dorchester Hotel in 2006.

Sean and Pauline Mahon in 2008.

XIV

Home and Play

In the previous three chapters, I have concentrated mainly on my professional role within CB&Co/C&L over many years, referring only briefly to the private lives of my family and myself during this period. However, in Chapter XI, I mentioned our move in 1964 to a house at Totley in the south-west of Sheffield, where we lived happily and made several good friends as the children developed and attended their first nursery schools. Nevertheless, we had always recognised that this house, situated on a fairly busy road heading out of Sheffield into Derbyshire, would not be our long-term choice.

In 1969, we purchased a detached and rather larger property at Newfield Crescent, Dore. Although only a mile or so from our previous home, this house was in a more secluded residential area and quite close to the Derbyshire Peak Park boundary. There were numerous places for walking and other recreational activities nearby and ready access to the high-quality hostelries, restaurants and shops of Dore village.

As our new home was also within a reasonable distance of the private schools that Nigel and Michelle were then attending (and those they were scheduled to attend in the next few years), we believed that this would be our abode for the foreseeable future. Therefore, although the house was in generally good condition, there were a few areas where changes were required in order to suit our taste. One of these was in the entrance hall, which we felt was rather dark and forbidding. Therefore, we had the traditional staircase removed and replaced by one of open style in light coloured oak. While this work was in progress, Kath stood on a loose floorboard (which had not been secured by the joiner) and went through the floor with one leg down to beyond her knee. Her situation was not helped when two of the workmen, believing she had merely fallen to her knees, tried to hoist her to a standing position. It was some years later when she required a half-knee replacement operation! Maybe one could have claimed compensation, but fifty-plus years ago it was just a case of an apology – "Sorry, missus."

Two other recollections (of a somewhat selfish nature) of our days at Newfield Crescent were the acquisition in 1970 of my first Morgan car, a convertible, 1600, four-seater (provided the rear passengers were "legless or small children"!) and, secondly, my admission to membership of Sickleholme Golf Club at Bamford in the Hope Valley, of Derbyshire.

As regards the Morgan, I had fallen for the car on Press Viewing Day, which was held before the start of the Annual Motor Show at Earl's Court, London, an event to which I was invited each year as a guest of a client. I think that the waiting list for a new Morgan at this time was six to nine months and so I placed an order there and then to be ahead of the field. Hard of suspension and with a hood which had to be attached or removed by hand (great fun when it was raining!), the car could hardly be described as practicable. Nevertheless, I loved it and fortunately, the rest of the family were infected with my enthusiasm (or so I believed) and we were able to manage because of the small second-hand Hillman saloon car which Kath used.

Joining a decent golf club in Sheffield or the attractive areas of North Derbyshire at this time usually involved a wait of a year or more. Therefore, I was delighted when, after only a few months, I was contacted by Sickleholme GC, where several of my friends were members, and informed that a vacancy had arisen. I telephoned the secretary and accepted without delay. It was the following day when I discovered that my opportunity for membership had occurred because of the sudden death of my next-door neighbour! I felt very guilty to have benefitted from this tragedy. Nevertheless, I had already become a member and remained so for the next 42 years – although my golfing abilities were always mediocre.

As a family, we had settled very well at Dore, but unexpected events can change matters. I have mentioned in Chapter VIII that in 1972, which was only three years after our move, Ron Palfreyman and Sheila relocated from Longlands (their beautiful house on the outskirts of Chesterfield) to Abingdon in Berkshire. On making enquiries I found that Longlands, with its several acres of surrounding land, had been sold to Finnigans, a subsidiary company of FPA Construction Group, a listed company of which Ron was chairman and CB&Co were auditors and advisors. Planning consent had been obtained by Finnigans to erect several "Executive type" residences on the land surrounding Longlands but leaving the house with a substantial garden and well-screened by existing trees and shrubbery, to remain in its present form.

I had visited Longlands many times as a guest of Ron Palfreyman and greatly admired the house. However, because of its size and extensive grounds, I had believed that it was the type of property that would be outside my price range, at least for some years to come. However, my income had increased substantially in the eight years since admission to partnership with CB&Co, and the situation relating to Longlands, as outlined above, had also changed matters. Therefore, I contacted Bryan Ward, managing director of Finnegans, and a good friend, to make enquiries.

Bryan informed me that the intention had been to finalise the erection of the new houses and any other work required on access roadways and facilities, before the marketing of Longlands. However, as good progress had already been made on the development, he said that if I wished to acquire Longlands at the present stage, and be prepared to accept that there could still be a few inconveniences from remaining activities on the site, this could be arranged.

I replied that, although I should like to purchase Longlands, as the CB&Co partner in charge of the FPA group work, I needed to ensure that there could be no danger of this being seen as a conflict of interest. I suggested, therefore, that if Bryan agreed, the price should be at an independent valuation, carried out by an appropriately qualified professional firm, with which neither party had any relationship. Bryan was happy with this proposal and, in due course, I became the proud owner of Longlands.

I believe that all the family enjoyed our following years at Longlands, although in essence we were still Sheffielders, returning there to work (in my case), to shop and attend social functions, etc. Of course, there were some disadvantages, for example, my drive to the office took about 20 minutes longer than when we resided at Dore, with a similar extension of time for Kath when transporting the children to and from school. Both of our offspring had moved schools during this period, Nigel to Birkdale Preparatory School and Michelle to Brantwood School for Girls. However, we were fortunate to have very good friends in John and Ann Miln living nearby. John and I had been colleagues at CB&Co for several years, when he had assisted me on a number of special assignments. I believe that, had he remained with the firm, he would have achieved partner status, but he left to become financial director of Ann's family company. As the Milns also had two sons at school in Sheffield, Kath and Ann were able to share the daily chore of the school run, with John or myself stepping in when necessary.

Longlands was fitted with an intruder alarm system, which systems (in these days) were usually linked to a local police operations control centre. If activated (even if only by accident), the police would respond by an immediate visit to the property, having first telephoned the normal occupant or, if there was no reply, the nominated keyholder, to be present and available to provide access. On one occasion (for some unknown reason) our alarm activated when Kath and I (together with the children) were away visiting friends in Sheffield. Consequently, John Miln, our keyholder, was duly contacted and asked to be available.

As John and the police officer wandered through the property ensuring that all was well, the policeman (apparently impressed by Longlands and its contents) enquired, "What does this bloke do for a living?" At John's reply, "He's an accountant," the response came, "Oh, a bookie." One can only assume that the policeman's previous dealings with accountants had been with those of the "turf" variety. Whether this incorrect information (if reported back to control centre) increased or diminished my stature in their eyes, I can only guess.

Our family enjoyed life at Longlands for the next four and three-quarter years. Nigel, in particular, settled in well, making several local friends, and our large flat lawn proved to be excellent for cricket practice (but only with a tennis ball) or kicking around a football. However, in the winter of 1976, Nigel left his Sheffield prep school to become a pupil at Repton.

This was Nigel's choice after we had also visited two other "soccer-playing public schools" – Shrewsbury and Malvern. Because Nigel's birthdate was in December, he had been allowed to join following his 12th birthday at the start of the second term of the academic year. I had believed that this would be advantageous in saving a year at Repton before he could move on to university. However, this proved to be a bad decision on my part. Joining a new school in the second term when the other students have already established friendships, gained an understanding of the routines, and experienced the early stages of the syllabus, made it much more difficult for Nigel to settle in. Furthermore, several weeks after joining Repton, he was rushed into hospital in Derby for an appendix operation, thus losing even more school time.

On the day that Nigel was taken into hospital, I had been working in London and (in these days before mobile phones) arrived at the Midland Railway Station in Sheffield about 8.30pm without any knowledge of the above situation and to find the city under a heavy covering of snow and conditions worsening. My car was parked at the station and I was pleased to negotiate the icy slopes of Sheffield and arrive home, but only to be given the news concerning Nigel. I immediately left for Derby to visit the hospital, eventually getting back about midnight. It was not my most enjoyable day.

I suspect that Nigel was not very happy at Repton in his first year, but he never complained and, being proficient at most sports, he established himself with both pupils and staff over time, eventually becoming a regular in the first XI at football and a member of the tennis team which, I believe, won the National

Public Schools Cup. I am pleased that, after my error of judgement, Nigel appears to look back on his time at Repton with satisfaction and pride.

I have mentioned in Chapter IX that in 1975 (a few months before Nigel commenced his schooling at Repton), Michelle, for health reasons, had moved from the private school she had been attending to a special school for delicate children, which operated under the auspices of the Sheffield Education Committee. In order for Michelle to qualify for this placement, we needed to show residence in Sheffield.

After our happy years at Longlands, we recognised that this required move would be a wrench, and our initial search for a comparable home had been disappointing. However, to meet the deadline of having a Sheffield address, and while we continued the search, we purchased a small cottage in Dore village.

In fact, this cottage, which we held for about one year (and sold at a profit) proved quite useful in several respects. There was a difference in the finishing times of Michelle's new school and that of Birkdale, where Nigel was serving his final few months. Consequently, Kath had a convenient base for tea during the waiting period. We also made use of the cottage to spend the night on a few occasions after attending late-finishing functions in Sheffield, and in the winter months when the weather was particularly inclement and travelling in the Peak District difficult. However, this was only a temporary answer to the problem and our search for a suitable property continued.

After Kath and I had viewed several properties without finding anything of interest, I was contacted by Paul Procter, a friend but also a senior partner in Saxton & Co, a leading firm of estate agents. Paul said that he would send details of the Croft, a house in the very desirable district of Fulwood. The property was coming up for auction and Paul felt that it may be worthy of my consideration.

I had never attended a property auction, partly because I had always needed to borrow at least part of the purchase consideration for my previous houses. I was also reluctant to incur the time and cost of viewings and surveys without feeling a probability of success. Furthermore, on receipt of the auction brochure in this particular case, I considered that the house would be too large and, possibly, beyond my financial capabilities. I decided, therefore, not to spend time on attending the auction.

A week or so later, Paul telephoned to inform me that the Croft had not reached the auction reserve price and had been withdrawn without sale. He suggested that, despite my misgivings, I should at least visit the property and meet Jimmy and Betty Thompson (the owners), who had hived off part of the grounds, in which they had constructed their retirement bungalow. Paul said that a further plot had also been set aside for separate sale, with planning permission for the erection of a further bungalow. However, he said that the Croft still retained a substantial garden and was well-screened by high walls, trees and shrubbery which would ensure its privacy.

I accepted Paul's suggestions and Kath and I arranged to view the property. The Thompsons were likeable people and I felt that they would be good neighbours. I also sensed that they were tiring of the sale process and the constant viewings of their house, often they felt by people with no intention of acquiring the property. Jimmy, in particular, seemed keen to bring matters to a conclusion, so that they could settle into their retirement home, which awaited them beyond only a hedge of trees.

The Croft itself was much more impressive than I had imagined from the literature. Our viewing commenced in the formal entrance hall, from which a staircase with leaded stained-glass windows gave access to a galleried landing. The ground-floor accommodation included a large drawing room, study, dining room and snug. On the first floor was the master bedroom suite, four further bedrooms, a bathroom, etc. and a superb billiards room, complete with full-sized table, cues, balls and other equipment. A separate staircase provided access to the second floor, where there were three further bedrooms, a bathroom and storeroom. The property also included a large basement, wine cellar and a detached garage for 4/5 vehicles. Importantly, most of the principal rooms in the house faced south or south-east, looking over the landscaped gardens towards Mayfield Valley.

Built in 1909 for James Neill, chairman of James Neill & Co (still, at the time of our viewing, one of the world's largest manufacturers of tools for domestic and engineering use), the Croft had been designed by the Liverpool architects, Briggs, Wolstenholme & Thornley, a firm which had been involved in the construction of Stormont Parliament Building in Belfast (seat of the Northern Ireland Assembly). Arnold Thornley had subsequently received a knighthood in recognition of his architectural work.

Despite the size of the Croft, which had given me some initial concerns, Kath and I were greatly impressed with the property and unanimous in feeling that we would very much enjoy living there. There were a few areas which required updating, but nothing of major importance or which could not be dealt with over a shortish period of time. Consequently, the next step was for me to discuss the required purchase price with Jimmy. We quickly agreed upon a sum of £48,000, which was well within my financial capabilities and we shook hands on the deal, subject to contract, there and then. It was a decision I never regretted, and we lived at the property for the next 26 years, over which period it was the scene of many parties, celebrations, anniversaries and family occasions. The billiards room was also well used by Nigel and friends after nights out when home from school or college at weekends and in holidays.

The plot which had been hived off for sale and the construction of a bungalow was acquired by Bill Hallam (a veterinary surgeon with a practice in Sheffield) and his wife, Kath. The Hallams, with their family of two sons, proved to be excellent neighbours and the "two Kaths" became exceptionally good friends. This was an unexpected additional bonus from our move to the Croft.

In 2002, when we had decided to leave the Croft and it was being advertised for sale, I was contacted by Sir Hugh Neill, with whom I was acquainted mainly from my involvement in the Company of Cutlers'(of which Hugh had been Master in 1958) and certain local charities in which we both took an interest. A former Lord Lieutenant of South Yorkshire, and a High Sherriff of Hallamshire, Hugh had served as the third family generation, chairman of James Neill & Co for 26 years, before becoming honorary president. He was regarded as "a doyen of the Sheffield steel industry".

Hugh said that he had many happy memories of his boyhood days spent at the Croft and wondered if he could make a visit before it was sold with his young son Michael (who I think was about 9 or 10) so that he could see where his great-grandparents had lived. Of course, Kath and I were pleased to grant this request and the visit (also including Hugh's wife Ann) took place shortly afterwards when they were able to stay on for tea and refreshments.

About 10 years later, when I was enjoying the hospitality of Kevin and Donna McDonald at their impressive estate at Serlby following a shoot, their son (also named Michael) said that he would like to introduce me to one of the other guests – a very pleasant young man whom Michael described as "my best friend at school". This turned out to be "the small boy", Michael Neill, who told me that he well remembered his visit to the Croft all those years ago. As the saying goes – "it's a small world".

In Chapters XI to XIII I have referred in the main, to my role and duties with CB&Co / C&L in the years in which our family resided in the aforementioned properties. However, there are several aspects of my private and social life in this period which I consider may also be worth mentioning.

I have always had a great interest in sport, both as a participant and (in later years) a spectator. Nigel (and, to some extent, Kath) shared in this interest and Nigel, as he grew up and we competed against each other, would often (to my annoyance) demonstrate more natural ball skills and abilities than myself.

From my early school days, at the age of about nine years, until sometime in my late thirties, I regularly played soccer (overlapping for a couple of years with rugby when in Kenya). However, as the demands of work (and particularly the need to spend time away from Sheffield) increased, I found it difficult to give the necessary commitment to training and playing in regular team fixtures in the competitive South Yorkshire leagues. Therefore, I reluctantly decided to play only friendly games, usually for CB&Co against clients or other offices.

I was able to make the above change without concerns regarding physical fitness as I continued to make regular exercise runs and to play squash once or twice per week. My main problem was missing the camaraderie of being part of an established team and the competitiveness of league football, which I had always enjoyed. However, there were some compensations in the greater opportunity to attend major sporting events and to give support to Yorkshire County Cricket Club and Sheffield United FC.

A casual game of football which I well remember in this period (I think I was aged 43 years at the time) was a "fathers versus pupils" match involving Birkdale Preparatory School. I believe that this was in the winter of 1976 and Nigel, aged about 12, was a member of the Birkdale team and in his final months at the school before moving to Repton.

The game was played on a Sunday morning on the YMCA ground at Crimicar Lane, high on the south-western outskirts of Sheffield. The pitch was frozen and rutted and, in my ancient boots with long studs (more suited to muddy conditions), I found difficulty in staying on my feet let alone running. A bleak wind was blowing, and my hands were cold. The conditions could not have been much worse.

Captain of the fathers' team was Ian Porterfield (at the time, manager of Sheffield United). I had seen Ian playing at Wembley Stadium in 1973, when he scored the winning goal for Sunderland in the FA Cup Final against Leeds United. I enquired of him, "What kind of studs would professional footballers use on a pitch like this?" His rather unhelpful reply was, "Professional footballers wouldn't play on a pitch like this."

The game went ahead but, just before half-time, I pulled a hamstring muscle and (to Nigel's embarrassment) his father hobbled off, not to return. No substitutes were allowed in these days, but our 10 men battled on to win the game by the odd goal. We could then go for a dip in the large communal baths!

However, in my case, the trauma continued. I had to drive to Heathrow Airport (despite my gammy leg) for an evening flight to Oslo in order to attend the Norwegian partners meeting the next

luncheon guest, he proved to be an excellent raconteur, with a fund of cricket stories and (well-fortified by an extra bottle of wine) we overran the break by about 30 minutes.

Basil D'Oliveira had been batting for England at the start of the luncheon break and had clearly prospered when play had been resumed. However, as we eventually emerged from the marquee, there was a loud appeal and D'Oliveira was given out for a "fighting" 88 runs, but insufficient for England to avoid an innings defeat. Our small party had missed the best England performance of the day but, very surprisingly, we were able to read about the innings in some detail in Ted Dexter's newspaper column the next day!

In passing, it may be worth mentioning that Basil D'Oliveira will be remembered more for his role (although accidental, I think, to some extent) in bringing down South Africa's apartheid regime, than for his valuable exploits in playing cricket for England over his 44 Test match appearances.

Born in Cape Town of Indian-Portuguese heritage, D'Oliveira was labelled as "Cape Coloured", one of South Africa's racial groups defined under apartheid. However, he moved to England in 1960 to play cricket for Worcestershire, became a British citizen in 1964 and made his England Test debut in 1966. He was subsequently selected for the English squad to tour South Africa in 1968/69, despite warnings from South Africa that his inclusion would not be acceptable. As a consequence of his selection, the tour was cancelled, leading to the exclusion of South Africa from Test cricket for the next 22 years and having a massive impact in turning international opinion against apartheid.

While on the subject of cricket (and for the "education" of my Aussie born grandsons), I will also mention a game I attended in 1968, when a team selected from the Australian Touring Party of that year played against Yorkshire at Bramall Lane.

The Yorkshire XI, which included several stalwarts of the England Test side, batted first. Geoff Boycott opened the innings and made 86 and, the all-rounder Ray Illingworth scored 69 not out in a Yorkshire total of 355.

In response, the Australian team struggled and were dismissed in their first innings for only 148, of which Bill Lawry, captaining the side and opening the batting, contributed 58. Following on, the Australians were even less successful with Lawry out for a duck achieving a total of only 138, thus giving Yorkshire an emphatic victory by an innings and 69 runs.

In fairness, it must be admitted that over the five-match Test series against England, the result was a 1–1 draw, and Australia retained the Ashes. Maybe the full Yorkshire team should have been chosen to represent England!

In August 1998, my friend Matt Sheppard (the former chairman and, at the time, still a director of Sheffield Wednesday) invited me to join a small dinner party comprising the board and a few selected guests, to be held in the Directors Suite at Hillsborough Stadium.

The purpose of the dinner was to honour Sir Stanley Matthews, a footballing legend who had played 54 times for England. His league clubs had been Stoke City and Blackpool (both in the top division at the time) and he was widely regarded as having been the greatest player in the British game.

Stanley was the only player to have been knighted while still playing football, as well as being the first winner of both the European Footballer of the Year and The Football Writers' Association Footballer of the Year awards. However, more impressive than these awards, in my view, was that he had kept himself fit enough to be the oldest man ever to play in England's top football division (50 years and 5 days) and also the oldest player ever to represent England (42 years and 104 days).

I jumped at the opportunity to attend the dinner and meet "The Wizard of the Dribble" (as Matthews was known), who, previously, I had seen only in action on a football pitch and in black and white on a minute television screen, when Blackpool had won the FA Cup in 1953.

The occasion was well organised, with a pre-dinner drinks period, which allowed time for everyone to have a few words with Stanley and have a photograph taken with him as a memento. I had taken along a copy of Stanley's book *Feet First*, which I had chosen as my school prize in 1948 for obtaining the highest marks in the mid-summer examinations. Stanley, who I found likeable and very modest, kindly autographed the book and expressed surprise that it had survived for 50 years. He mentioned that a distributor had "gone bust" and that he had never been fully paid for these books.

Aged 83 years of age at the time of the dinner, Stanley appeared to be sprightly and in good health. However, sadly he passed away only 18 months later. I was grateful to have had the opportunity to meet one of my sporting heroes. The photograph, taken with Stanley before the dinner, is still on my study wall and *Feet First* survives in my bookcase.

On 15 of April 1989, a pleasant spring day, I attended Sheffield Wednesday's Hillsborough Stadium to see the FA Challenge Cup semi-final, between Nottingham Forest and Liverpool. This was a repeat of a game at which I had been present the previous year, on the same ground, between the same teams and at the same stage of the competition. My tickets were for two excellent seats, quite close to those occupied by the Sheffield Wednesday directors, and I had invited Tony Wood to join me. Both teams had some highly regarded players and we looked forward to an enjoyable afternoon. How wrong this proved to be!

Ten minutes or so before kick-off time, I drew the attention of Tony to the overcrowding, which seemed to be taking place in the central terrace in front of the Leppings Lane Stand. Access to this terrace was through a tunnel beneath the stand, and I recollected there being some problems in this area the previous year. However, on this current occasion, the situation appeared to be much more critical. Crowds of fans were still coming through the tunnel and attempting to exit, creating ripples as the fans standing on the steps of the already overcrowded terrace were being pushed forward and compressed. In contrast to the central terrace, the terrace pens on either side seemed to be quite sparsely occupied but barriers prevented the fans in the centre from spreading out into these.

An even greater problem was created by the high perimeter fences which, in common with most major football stadiums, had

SHEFFIELD FORGED AND TEMPERED

been erected at Hillsborough around the playing area to prevent access to spectators and to guard against the possibility of a ground invasion. These measures had been taken in recent years following hooliganism on several grounds, including, in particular, Heysel Stadium in Brussels. As the pressure increased, a few fans tried to climb over the perimeter fences to get out of the crush but, at this stage, they were being pushed back by the police.

In due course, the players and match officials came out on to the pitch, clearly unaware of the major disaster, which was building, and the game commenced on time. It lasted for only six minutes before the players left the field and the match was abandoned. By this time, the police appeared to have grasped the seriousness of the situation. The gates of the perimeter fences were unlocked, and injured people started to be brought onto the pitch, to be laid on the grass or on advertising boards, which had been ripped out of the ground to become makeshift stretchers. After a time, many of those lying on the grass were being covered by jackets and, to our horror, we realised that these people had passed away and were not simply injured.

A single ambulance arrived and was driven onto the pitch to be filled by injured people before driving away. I wondered why there were not more ambulances arriving. It was subsequently reported that they had been turned away by the police on the gate, who believed that a pitch invasion was in progress!

Sitting up in the stand, Tony and I were transfixed and shocked by the spectacle taking place before us. It was like watching a horror film, but with the knowledge that everything we were witnessing was real. In fact, the carnage we experienced was only part of the tragedy, many fatalities occurred in the tunnel and were discovered only later as work continued after we had left.

We sat for 20 or 30 minutes (I do not know how long) before leaving the stadium. I think we called at a public house on the way home to talk through events and recover our composure. When I eventually arrived home, Kath was in a state of agitation. There were no mobile phones to let her know the position, and it had not occurred to me that the disaster would have been appearing

234

live on TV. With no idea where we were in the stadium and an absence of contact from us, Kath was understandably worried that we might be involved.

In total, 95 Liverpool supporters died on the day with a further death, resulting from injuries sustained, over a year later. The disaster was caused when the police, under orders from David Duckenfield, the Chief Superintendent in charge, opened the large concertina exit gates at the Leppings Lane Stand in order to allow entry to fans who were still queuing outside and trying to gain access before the start of the game. This action allowed 2,000 people to enter, but the police failed to direct supporters away from the already packed central pens, to the less densely populated ones on either side.

There have been numerous words written with regard to the disaster and many views expressed as to those responsible. These included a thirty-one-day long inquiry (in the aftermath) by Lord Justice Taylor, who found that the main reason for the overcrowding was "a failure of police control". David Duckenfield was suspended after this report. A private prosecution of manslaughter was brought in July 2000, by the Hillsborough Family Support Group, against David Duckenfield and his deputy, Bernard Murray. However, after six weeks (and much to the understandable dismay of the group) the jury failed to reach a verdict and both men walked free. The judge ruled out a retrial on the grounds that publicity surrounding the proceedings meant a fair trial would be impossible.

As a result of the Taylor Report, it was decided that all football grounds in the top two divisions in England had to be "all-seaters" and that perimeter fences must be removed. Standing on terraces (the norm at football grounds for decades) was outlawed.

Presumably the above steps are regarded as "progress", but they are a far cry from the time of my boyhood and younger adult years when there was no segregation of fans and, despite a frequent "expression of views" between rival supporters, very little violence (so far as I can remember), even though the vast majority of spectators at the time were standing on the terraces.

SHEFFIELD FORGED AND TEMPERED

When grounds became crowded, children were passed hand to hand over the heads of spectators to sit on the grass surrounds of the football pitches and be collected by parents at the end of the game. One has to wonder if people have changed for the worse.

Having been a regular attender of football matches (when not playing) for most of my life from the age of about 10 years, up to and including the present day, I was surprised to find that I needed some time to recover from having witnessed the Hillsborough disaster. It was a horrific experience. I felt no appetite for the game of football for many months, and it was over a year before I could bring myself to attend another match. One can only hope that necessary lessons have been learned and the changes made are appropriate to resolve the problems.

XV

London

My schooldays were spent during the time of the Second World War and the period of austerity which followed. Five years of accountancy articled training in Sheffield, two years national service in the RAF and three and a half years preparation for and service with CB&Co in Kenya, took me to almost 28 years of age. By this time, I had spent no more than a handful of days in my own capital city of London.

However, I had always been a traditionalist and brought up to be patriotically British. Therefore, I grasped the opportunity in the early sixties to spend several months working for Wilfred Molyneux in London (see Chapter VIII), with the hope of seeing something of our capital city. In fact, I found that my working days were to be spent mainly in the Docklands of the East End but, at least, I returned to a hotel in central London each evening.

Still only of manager grade at this time, the hotels I used were usually in the category of "good modern" and situated mainly in the Bloomsbury area – for example, the Russell, Marlborough and Holiday Inn. They were adequate but by no means luxurious. However, all were well located for the theatres, cinemas and eating places of the city and I found that I could afford to visit a trendy (but not too expensive) restaurant once or twice each week.

Although rather touristy, one of my favourites at the time was Rules, near to Covent Garden. Established in 1798 and one of London's oldest restaurants, the walls of Rules were adorned with old prints, sketches and photographs of famous theatrical characters and there was always a great atmosphere. I also liked Simpsons-in-the-Strand. Carving roast beef at your table from a trolley containing three joints – rare, medium and well done, would be a waiter in long white apron (looking like a character from *Hello Dolly*). I was told by a colleague that the important thing was to place a half-crown on the trolley in order to ensure a large portion. However, from my observation this was a waste of money – everyone seemed to receive a large portion.

Moving some years ahead (and after I had become a partner) my need to spend time in London was increased, partly from a growing role within the firm but also from the early sixties, because of involvement in several client assignments relating to stock exchange documents for listings, acquisitions and disposals. These required close involvement with the merchant banks (these days called investment banks) and the City firms of brokers and lawyers. I greatly enjoyed the work, but it often required the production of information in a demanding timeframe, involving much late-night working. The role of the merchant banks was, no doubt, essential but, in my view, their remuneration was excessive when compared to the fees of the professional firms. However, this was not an observation I made at the time, otherwise the next assignment might have gone to Peat, Marwick and Mitchell!

As I progressed with the firm, I was also able to justify moving up the scale of hotels which I could use. My first change was to stay at the Waldorf and, a few years later, the Berkley on Wilton Place. My final choice was the Howard at Temple Place. This provided exercise in walking to the main C&L office which, by this time, had moved to Plumtree Court, off Farringdon Street. If entertaining clients, for lunch my choice would usually be the Savoy Grill, and for dinner, Wiltons on Jermyn Street – both very much up-market from the days in Bloomsbury. However, entertaining of this nature was not a regular occurrence.

In 1978, with my need to visit London increasing, I had become a member of the Naval & Military Club (better known as The Inn and Out, because of the separate entrance and exit for vehicles onto Piccadilly). A former home of Lord Palmerston, the building was impressive but (for no reason that I can now recollect) I rarely stayed there, although I sometimes made use of the squash court. I still have my 25-year membership tie, but I resigned in 2007 when my visits to London had declined, donating the value of my share to the club.

C&L's merger with Deloitte took place about four years before my expected retirement date (see Chapter XIII), and this resulted in spending even more time in London. Therefore, I purchased a smallish apartment in Rosebury Avenue. This was roughly equidistant from St Pancras Railway Station (where the trains from Sheffield arrived) and the C&L office in Plumtree Court (about a 20-minute walk to or from each of these destinations). There was a basement parking place allocated for the apartment and a pleasant private garden to which owners of the 12 flats in the block had access. However, I rarely made use of either of these facilities.

An obvious advantage of the apartment was to be able to travel light on business visits to London, but it also proved useful on two or three weekends for Kath and myself to accommodate friends before going to the opera at Glyndebourne. However, looking back, I consider that I failed to make adequate use of either my club membership or the ownership of the apartment. Nevertheless, I enjoyed having these "assets" and the greater sense of belonging which they gave me when in London.

In Sheffield, I had become involved in several charitable appeals and unremunerated good causes. These were not necessarily activities which I had sought but arose from my position with C&L or membership of clubs or organisations such as the Chamber of Commerce. However, to my surprise, these involvements in South Yorkshire sometimes gave rise to invitations to events in London, where the sponsors or patrons of the charities were based.

One such invitation came from Kenneth Clarke, chancellor of the exchequer, for my wife and myself to attend a cocktail party at Number 11 Downing Street. We were pleased to accept and enjoyed the occasion, at which Kenneth proved to be a very relaxed and friendly host. Some years later, I found that I was to be seated next to him at a dinner to be held at the Queen's Hotel in Leeds. Arriving at the table, I started to introduce myself with the words, "You will not remember me, Mr Clarke but—" Before I could finish the sentence, Kenneth said, "I do remember you. You are Barrie Cottingham." I concluded that Kenneth either had an exceptionally good memory or a very efficient referencing system – whichever of these, I was very impressed.

Another invitation which I received was from Betty Boothroyd, the Speaker of the House of Commons, to join a small group of people for a tour of the House. Ms Boothroyd, a charming and down to earth lady from Dewsbury in West Yorkshire, was the first woman to hold the position of Speaker. At the end of the tour, she kindly invited us to see her private apartment, which included a sitting room and splendid bedchamber. Apparently, the Speaker is the only person in the Commons to be provided with facilities of this type.

Although my knowledge of London increased over the years, there were places, such as the great halls of the City, which were not readily accessible to the public. However, over a period, I had chance to visit many of these. Probably my first opportunity (in my early years of CB&Co partnership) came from an invitation to attend a formal dinner at the Mansion House, the official residence of the Lord Mayor of London. The invitation was from Barry Reed, chairman of Austin Reed (a client company) and I believe it was Barry's year as president of the trade association of which his company was a member.

Tall and distinguished in appearance with a modest and gentlemanly manner, I found Barry to be likeable and an excellent host. It was an enjoyable occasion. Some months later I discovered that Barry also possessed a strong and determined character, in that during his two years national service in the Middlesex Regiment, he had served in the Korean War, where he had been commissioned and awarded the Military Cross for bravery! Barry's experience was quite a contrast to my "cushy number" (RAF slang) in the comfort of the officer's mess at Leconfield.

Moving several years on, in 1988, Kath and I received an invitation from Alderman Sir Greville Spratt, Lord Mayor of the City of London, to attend a reception and banquet at the Guildhall in honour of His Majesty, the King of Norway (Olav V).

I had assumed that the invitation was in connection with my role as liaison partner to the C&L firm in Norway and considered that one of my London partners, Alderman and Sheriff Brian day. I think that this was the point when I decided it was time to hang up my football boots.

Moving to a different sport, in the mid-1960s I became a member of the "100 Club" at Headingley Cricket Ground in Leeds, Headquarters of Yorkshire CC. No doubt the 100 Club is long gone (at least in its original form) and its premises (above the players' changing rooms), situated at that time between the cricket ground and the rugby league pitch, will have disappeared with the many new buildings and developments which have taken place at the ground over the years.

Ray Emmitt and Brian Buckley (mentioned in Chapter XII) were also members of the 100 Club and, as we were each allowed to invite a guest, we would often bring together a small group of friends to attend matches. Furthermore, one could sometimes meet interesting people, who were present as the guests of other members. The club was an excellent facility, if somewhat costly.

I remember one particular occasion meeting and enjoying a long conversation with Godfrey Evans, one of my boyhood heroes, who played in 91 Test matches for England between 1946 and 1959 and was described in Wisden as "arguably the best wicketkeeper the game has ever seen".

However, possibly my most vivid recollection of these years was the 1966 Test Match against the West Indies, when Brian Buckley invited his friend of Cambridge University days, Ted Dexter, the Sussex and England all-rounder to join us for lunch in the members' marquee.

Dexter was one of the games great characters. In 62 appearances between 1958 and 1968, he captained England on many occasions and could be a batsman of ferocious power, scoring over 4,500 runs at an average of 48 and taking 66 wickets at 34.93. However, as a captain, his dictatorial manner on the field was not always appreciated by other players and he gained the nickname of "Lord Ted" because of his aloof self-confidence.

Outside cricket, Ted Dexter was a man of many interests. A talented golfer (an amateur champion) and owner of Jaguar cars, Norton motorbikes, greyhounds and racehorses. He also worked as a journalist for the *Observer* and the *Sunday Mirror*. As a

Jenkins (who was in line to become Lord Mayor in 1991) may have had something to do with it. However, Kath and I were very pleased to accept.

As one might expect, there was a good deal of pomp and ceremony and the proceedings were very formal. My recollection is that dress for the occasion was white tie and decorations (not that I had any). Present were Her Royal Highness, The Princess Royal, and Captain Mark Phillips, and the total attendance was about 730 people.

Music was provided by the Orchestra of the Coldstream Guards, with the trumpeters of the Blues and Royals. The Guard of Honour for His Majesty was provided by the Honourable Artillery Company, and the State Trumpeters of the Household Cavalry were also present – all very impressive.

Unsurprisingly, the wines and food at the dinner were excellent and Kath and I were well positioned to see the proceedings. After dinner, there were toasts to the Queen and to His Majesty the King of Norway, which were followed by several speeches and responses.

I think that it was in course of these speeches that mention was made of an occasion in World War II, when Norway had been occupied by the Nazi forces, and King Haakon VII (father of Olav V) had fled to Britain. Having arranged to make a broadcast of encouragement to the Norwegian people on the BBC overseas channel, King Haakon duly reported to the reception desk at Broadcasting House. He informed the commissionaire who he was and the purpose of his visit and also enquired to which studio he should make his way.

At this point, the telephone on the reception desk rang, and the commissionaire said to King Haakon, "Just one minute, sir." He picked up the phone and dealt with the call. On completion, he turned back to the King with the words, "Now then, sir, which country did you say you were King of?"

One regret in relation to my time spent in London was in not taking up an invitation to compete in the marathon. This opportunity followed the General Partners' Meeting of the firm at Eastbourne. With conclusion of the formal business in the morning session of the last day, a fun run had been arranged for the afternoon (to take place along the promenade) for any partners wishing to participate. Announcement of leading placings and any award of prizes were to take place in the evening at the concluding dinner.

I believe that the firm had about 250 partners at the time and 134 of these had put their names forward to take part in the run. These were mainly in the 30 to 45 year age group but, in order to encourage some of the "more mature" people to become involved, the organisers decided that there should be a deduction from the finishing times of partners over a certain age (45 years, I think). Although aged 55, I had always kept reasonably fit and decided to enter.

First person past the winning post was a thirty-one-year-old partner (and champion squash player) from Sheffield in a time of 8.2 minutes. I was pleased to come in sixteenth in 9.27 minutes which, after the time deduction, made me a very clear winner! At the evening dinner, I received my medal and the greater reward of a bottle of vintage champagne.

As a result of my performance, I was also offered the opportunity to take up one of the firm's three allocated places in the London Marathon, to run for the "I Can" charity for disadvantaged children. It was a decision which had to be made quickly and I was conscious that I had a heavy workload coming up, which would leave little time for training. I was also aware that there were many better athletes in the firm than myself. Therefore, I decided to leave the place for someone else. It was a decision which I subsequently regretted as I never had another opportunity to enter the London Marathon.

In foregoing paragraphs, I have tried to give an impression of my feelings and experiences during the time I spent in London in course of dealing with the firm's affairs. There are numerous other incidents and events which I could have mentioned, but my intention has been merely to give a flavour of life in these years. In summary, I gained a genuine affection for the city and developed some sense of belonging over the years. Nevertheless, I have to admit that life in London was not an existence which I would have chosen in exchange for my days in Sheffield.

XVI

A Second Career

In 1993, as I moved towards my expected date of retirement from C&L, I was contacted by Patrick O'Reilly (Pat), a partner in the City stockbrokers, Panmure Gordon. Pat was a well-known character in the north of England, where he had involvement with several listed companies. Although quite small in physical stature, he had an impressive personality and was always popular, both at business meetings and private parties where, if encouraged, he could sing in an excellent tenor voice.

Pat said that he understood I would shortly be retiring from C&L and he wondered if I would be interested in considering non-executive directorships. This was, of course, a time when listed companies were being encouraged to give greater attention to corporate governance, and the appointment of appropriate non-executives to their boards was a move in that direction.

Although partners in C&L were not normally permitted to take remunerated appointments outside the firm, this rule was relaxed in their last two years before retirement. Consequently, I informed Pat that I would be interested, provided the opportunities were with companies of good quality. A few days later, Pat phoned again and said that I should get in touch with Norman Adsetts, chairman of Sheffield Insulations Group plc (later to become SIG plc. SIG), who would be pleased to see me.

I had met Norman Adsetts (Norman) some years earlier when I had been involved with the Sheffield Chamber of Commerce, of which Norman was a former president. However, my recent duties with C&L had taken me away from the Sheffield business scene and I had not had any recent contact with Norman. Nevertheless, when I telephoned, he was very friendly, and I arranged an appointment at his office.

The meeting was both pleasant and informative. Norman gave me a brief résumé of the history of SIG, since the establishment of the business in 1956 by his father, Ernest. After an initial period of expansion, the group had experienced difficult times in the early 1980s but had recovered and obtained a listing on the London Stock Exchange in April 1989.

Norman had joined his father at SIG in 1966, having proved his abilities working for Fibreglass Ltd, part of the Pilkington group. He was appointed managing director in 1970 and held this position for 24 years (ending only a short time before our meeting), when he became chairman.

In course of the visit, I also had the opportunity to meet Bill Forrester, who had succeeded Norman as group managing director, and Frank Prust, the finance director. Contact with the remaining executive member of the board, David Williams, was left for a later stage. I was impressed by everyone I had met and when offered the opportunity to join the board, as SIG's first non-executive director (NED), I was pleased to accept.

I quickly settled to my new role, but as explained in Chapter XIII, I had extended my service with C&L beyond their normal retirement age of 60 years until mid-1995. However, as this additional period was spent at the Sheffield office, it did not give rise to any difficulties with regard to duties with SIG.

During this same period, Norman was finding that his several commitments connected with the regeneration and development of Sheffield (particularly his role on the partnership board of the Development Corporation) were requiring a great deal of time and taking him away from his involvement with SIG. Consequently, in 1995, I was appointed deputy chairman of SIG in order to provide Norman with extra support. However, in 1996, Norman took the decision to fully retire from the board and he was elected as honorary life president of SIG. Moving a few years ahead in order to complete the story regarding Norman, in 1999 he received a well-deserved knighthood for "services to the community in Sheffield".

Norman's retirement fitted well with my final involvement with C&L and greater availability of time, and I was proud to succeed him as non-executive chairman.

I greatly enjoyed my 11 years' service with SIG and felt that I made a useful contribution. I fully recognised that Bill Forrester was a decisive manager with a sound knowledge of the industry, but I found that I could help in certain respects and particularly by providing support to Frank Prust (with whom I developed a very good relationship) in such areas as accounting standards and best practice, stock exchange requirements and areas for consideration on acquisitions and disposals.

Bill and I would always touch base before board meetings to ensure that we shared similar views or, at least, that there were no surprises. However, we were always prepared to poke a little fun at each other. I remember Bill suggesting (tongue in cheek, I think) that non-executive directors were like bidets, nice to have but no one was quite sure what use they were. However, I think I squared things by stating that I had met a member of his golf club who, on being asked if he knew Bill, said that he had played a round of golf with him and "remembered him as a wit and a shanker". I added, "At least, I think that is what he said."

During the years with SIG there were major developments in the area of corporate governance. These had commenced with the publication of a report produced by a committee chaired by Sir Adrian Cadbury in 1992 in response to several major corporate scandals. In 1994 the principles of this report were appended to the Listing Rules of the London Stock Exchange which were overseen by the Financial Reporting Council.

Other reports on aspects of corporate governance followed, including one (dealing with executive pay) under the chairmanship of Sir Richard Greenbury, and, another from a committee chaired by Sir Ronald Hampel, which resulted in a consolidation of all the various recommendations into a "Combined Code". I will not bore readers with the issues dealt with in the above documents or the subsequent developments in corporate governance, which continued well after my service with SIG and resulted in 2010 with the UK Corporate Governance Code and subsequently with the 2018 Corporate Governance Code!

However, one aspect of particular relevance to SIG was a recommendation for listed companies to move towards a balancing of boards between executive and non-executive directors and to include at least three NEDs. Consequently, in 1999 the SIG Board (all executives except myself) requested me to make suggestions for additional NEDs. I put forward two names – David Haxby, the former managing partner of the London office of accountants Arthur Anderson, and Sir Timothy Kitson (see below). These suggestions were approved and both individuals accepted the offers of appointment.

My previous contact with Tim Kitson had been as the senior C&L partner dealing with Provident Financial Group, of which he had been chairman for 12 years up to 1995. In this period, I had assisted Tim in finding a suitable replacement, following the sudden and tragic death of the managing director of the group and I felt that a good rapport had been established between us.

A Yorkshire farmer, who loved hunting and racing but had also served for 24 years as a Conservative MP (including 4 years as parliamentary private secretary to Edward Heath during his term as prime minister), I believed that Tim would prove a valuable addition to the SIG Board and provide a different perspective on many issues.

However, to digress from the main subject for a little light relief, Tim, who was quite a character, had enjoyed some unexpected publicity in 1967 when, together with his colleague William Elliott, he entertained Jayne Mansfield (who had been staying in his constituency while appearing at clubs in the North East) for lunch at the House of Commons. Following lunch, he had taken her into the Speaker's Gallery to watch the Commons in session. Miss Mansfield, in a mini skirt and "striking white blouse" sat in the seat usually reserved for the prime minister's wife! The resultant buzz of conversation from the members had drowned out questions in the House, compelling the Speaker to call for order. Apparently, Tim subsequently commented, "I was just a bit of a chaperone."

People not of my vintage (most people) may not have heard of Jayne Mansfield, who was an American film, theatre and television actress. She was also a nightclub entertainer and singer and one of the early Playboy Playmates. A major Hollywood sex symbol during the 1950s and early 60s (while under contract to 20th Century Fox), Jayne's career was infamously fuelled by a rivalry with fellow "bombshell" Marilyn Monroe and both were often typecast in film roles as dizzy blondes. However, it appears that Jayne's IQ was notably high. She was fluent in no fewer than five different languages and in 1957 had shown her acting ability by winning a Golden Globe Award. Nevertheless, Jayne had apparently complained that the public didn't care about her intellect but were only interested in her measurements – 40-21-35 for chest, waist and hip!

Very sadly, only weeks after her appearance in the House of Commons, Jayne died in a car crash at the age of only 34. Maybe this shortening of her life explains, in part, why she appears to be less well remembered than some of her contemporaries.

I enjoyed my years with SIG and many events of these days come readily to mind (although maybe not always in the correct sequence). One memorable occasion was a trip undertaken by Bill Forrester and myself over the course of about seven days (I think we "lost" one day travelling west to east), when we flew first class, carrying only hand baggage, so that we could board and exit planes with a minimum of delay.

Flying from Heathrow, first stop was Houston (my first ever visit to Texas), where we were visiting a company for possible acquisition. Everything in Texas seemed big and impressive. (I wondered if the target company should be acquiring us!) We were taken for lunch at the Petroleum Club, situated in a skyscraper with magnificent views. Several of the other diners were "big hitters" in the Oil Industry. We were well entertained again in the evening, at a restaurant which appeared to specialise in providing a wide range of expensive cigars! This was lost on myself as a non-smoker. Nevertheless, I survived the smog, and we met the company management again the next day when, in principle, we agreed to make the acquisition.

I will not bore readers with details of the rest of our trip, which was devoted to visiting suppliers where, in some cases, we owned minority shareholdings. This was the case for two companies in China, where we purchased about 80% of their production but held only 10% of the equity. We were being pressurised by the Chinese government to increase this stake but were not prepared to do so. In total, in course of our trip, we made 10 separate flights (including the initial one to the USA). These comprised flights to two different locations in China, two in Manila, one in Taiwan, plus calling-back twice to Hong Kong (still independent at the time). I found it an incredibly interesting experience.

Two other events worth mentioning in these years were an attempted takeover of SIG by a large Irish group, (I think this was in 2000), which we successfully repelled, and, in contrast, a proposed management buyout by our three executive directors (at a time when the stock market was in decline and our share price low). I was not satisfied with the price offered and, with the support of our merchant bank, successfully fought off the bid.

We had met (together with our respective advisors) in London and once the decision had been made, Frank Prust and David Williams caught a train back to Sheffield, while Bill Forrester and I remained in London for a time and agreed what should be said to the press, institutional shareholders and other interested parties. We then sat opposite each other, with two telephones, in the offices of our brokers and fielded the calls as they came in. That done, we caught the "Master Cutler" Pullman train to Sheffield, dining together (with a decent bottle of wine). Next day we were all at our desks in the SIG offices, attending to duties as normal. Although the executive directors must have been disappointed, to the best of my knowledge, there were no bad feelings between us, and we remained friends. I also felt satisfied, as the months passed, that I had achieved the best decision for the shareholders.

I cannot remember the exact date, but Frank Prust experienced serious medical problems in the second half of my service with SIG. These necessitated his absence for several months. Typical of Frank, he returned to work at the earliest possible opportunity and probably before it was wise. Frank struggled along for a time but never seemed to be his previous energetic self and he eventually took early retirement. This was sad for SIG and a blow for me, as we had always enjoyed a good relationship.

In 2000 at the Annual Business Awards Dinner held at the Queens Hotel in Leeds, SIG won the Board of the Year award. I was delighted to accept the large silver platter, and to have the opportunity to say a few words paying tribute to my fellow directors and the employees of the group.

This public recognition of SIG's success came at an appropriate time as, in November the following year, Bill Forrester reached his retirement date and was able to depart on a high note, particularly as the group turnover had exceeded £1 million and employees more than 5,000. Bill had been an excellent chief executive but fortunately, in David Williams, there was a ready-made successor with a sound knowledge of the group's activities.

Nevertheless, with the loss of Frank and now Bill, the team, of which I had been part, had changed and, inevitably, the new management would need time to settle in and establish its own identity and style of operation. I was also conscious that I was approaching the number of years, which corporate governance deemed should not be exceeded by a non-executive director and that a new chairman would be required in the not too distant future.

I eventually retired as chairman and board member in April 2004, following an excellent send-off at a leaving dinner (attended by the board, bankers and a few senior professional advisors) at Baldwin's Omega Restaurant in Sheffield. I had greatly enjoyed my years with SIG and felt proud to be part of a team (albeit as a non-executive) that, in my eight years as chairman of the group, had enjoyed a profit growth of 570%.

Going back in time to 1993, shortly after Pat O'Reilly had contacted me with regard to SIG, he telephoned again to say that he had been in touch with Eddie Cran, chief executive of Cattles plc, a financial services company operating in the same areas as Provident Financial Group (Provident). Although still much smaller than Provident, Cattles was growing rapidly under Eddie's leadership.

Pat informed me that Cattles' chairman was due to retire and Eddie (a former employee of Provident, who had met me in the past) considered that I would be the ideal replacement.

Consequently, a week or so later I met with Eddie and his financial director, Grant Clappison. It was an excellent and good-humoured meeting. Eddie, in particular, impressed me with his energy and ideas, and I felt that I would enjoy working with both of these people. However, I said that, as I had agreed to remain with C&L for at least another year, Provident would need to be informed as a matter of courtesy before I could accept.

Unfortunately, when informed of the proposal, Provident strongly objected, stating that in their view, for the C&L partner, who had been in charge of their work for many years, to be allowed to join a competitor was not acceptable and would damage the relationship between Provident and C&L. To be honest, this response did not surprise me. Therefore, I contacted Eddie and explained that I would not be able to accept the offer to become chairman.

In 1995, when I finally left C&L, Eddie telephoned again. He said that, as I would be aware, the position of chairman had been filled but he wondered if I would be free to join the board as a non-executive director. By this time, it was three years since I had been involved in any work with Provident and, of course, I was no longer a partner of C&L. I could see no reason why I should not accept Eddie's offer. Therefore, I told him that I would be delighted to join the Cattles board.

Four years later on, 1 July 1999, I was appointed chairman of the board and remained in that position for the next seven years until my retirement from Cattles in 2006.

Cattles is quite an unusual name and several people have enquired as to its origins. In fact, it dates from 1927, when the business was founded in Hull by Joseph Cattle. I remember an occasion when I had played golf with someone I did not know very well. As we walked towards our cars after the game, he said, "Someone told me that you farmed cattle, do you have sheep as well?" He had obviously been misinformed on the first count but his question, I found, was based upon my car number plate – 551 BAA.

At some time in 2000, Eddie informed me that he wished to give some months warning that he had decided to resign from his position at Cattles. He was an excellent chief executive and there had been a great rapport between us, but he had clearly made up his mind. Eddie's elder brother was establishing a strong reputation as an entrepreneur in the Huddersfield and surrounding areas, and I wondered if Eddie intended to join him in certain ventures. However, I was also aware that Eddie's daughter was a very proficient tennis player and starting to qualify for tournaments around the country, which he was keen to attend. Whatever his reasons, I accepted that I would need to find a new chief executive.

I agreed with Eddie that for the present I would not report his decision to the board but would give the matter my immediate consideration. I could not think of any obvious contenders for his role and believed that we may need the services of recruitment consultants. However, I first wished to establish, in my mind, the main requirements for the job.

We were a financial organisation, and I felt that the candidates would need to be qualified accountants or hold other appropriate qualifications. However, probably more important, it had to be recognised that we were a "people company" and the successful applicant would require the communicative skills to deal with the board, the consortium of banks from which we received our funding, City institutions, the financial media and major shareholders. It was a tall order.

At this point, I think it relevant to depart from the subject of Cattles, to make a few observations on C&L and the changing nature of the accountancy profession. In Chapter XIII, I referred to the C&L and Deloitte merger, the differences in culture and management styles of these two firms and that (despite the benefit to my personal position) this was not my happiest time with the firm.

In 1995 the enlarged entity entered into a further merger with another "Big Five" firm, Price Waterhouse. The name of this combined organisation, PricewaterhouseCoopers, was, thankfully, subsequently shortened to PWC. I was grateful to be retiring before the post-merger rationalisation was implemented when it appeared to me that the C&L culture and the operational structure in the regions were gradually being replaced by those of Price Waterhouse.

Furthermore, the concept of "partnership for working life" and the esprit de corps which this engendered, seemed to be disappearing. Many partners were seeking opportunities to leave the firm well before the retirement age of 60 years in order to move into industry or commerce, where there was a possibility of management buy-outs or takeovers and capital profits, with the much lower tax burden than applied to earned income.

Having aired my above views, I found at the time that I could benefit from at least one of the changes taking place. Sean Mahon, my friend and colleague of many years, had decided to take early retirement from C&L. I telephoned to enquire what he intended to do and was informed, "Take a sabbatical." I said, "Forget the holiday, I need you at Cattles." Sean was duly interviewed by a committee of directors and joined the company as a director in 2000, for a short period of overlap with Eddie before becoming chief executive in May 2001.

Grant Clappison had retired some years earlier and had been replaced as director of finance by Mark Collins (who had spent some time at SIG and been recommended to me by Frank Prust). However, Sean decided that, in view of the importance of close liaison with the consortium of banks and other providers of funds, which were essential for Cattles to carry out its lending activities, this responsibility should be separated from the duties of director of finance, and undertaken by Mark as treasurer and risk director. James Corr, a former director of finance with C&L client Polypipe, was recruited for a similar role with Cattles. Together with Ian Cummine, the existing chief operating officer, and Sean as group chief executive, these four comprised the executive membership of the Cattles Board.

At this stage, as I was approaching my final years with SIG, I moved my office to Cattles, and could normally be found there two or three days each week. Therefore, I was readily accessible to Sean, James or any of the other executive directors or senior managers if required. As a "people person", Sean created an excellent working atmosphere at Cattles and his involvement with charities and various local community activities enhanced the group's reputation in the Leeds area. My recollection is that on one occasion, in aid of a charity, Sean was being driven around the city (sweating profusely) in some sort of animal suit with a tail and removable head! Probably he will provide the details if asked!

As regards the business, the group continued to flourish under Sean's leadership and in 2003, Cattles became the second company, of which I was chairman, to be awarded the Board of the Year trophy at the Annual Business Awards Dinner at the Queens Hotel in Leeds.

Presenting the trophy was Christa Ackroyd, who currently provides an amusing weekly column for the *Yorkshire Post* but, I believe, was with Yorkshire Television at the time. She enquired, "Aren't you the company which makes loans at exorbitant interest rates to poor people?" I felt that these were offensive and misleading remarks for the occasion. Therefore, I replied, "Oh, do you need a loan? I can probably arrange one at a slightly better rate than usual." The audience laughed, but I think Christa was not amused.

In the latter part of 2005, as I moved towards my proposed date of retirement from the chairmanship and board of Cattles, I started to handover some responsibilities to Norman Broadhurst, my designated successor as chairman. There were several changes to be made in non-executive directors and, as the board would be Norman's responsibility in the future, I considered it appropriate for him to take the lead in this connection. By the time of my retirement in May 2006, I had served for 11 years as a director, with the last seven as chairman. The annual pre-tax profit of the group had increased from £16.7 million in 1994 to £138 million in 2004, not much to do with me, of course, but a performance of which I felt everyone in the group could be proud.

To mark my retirement, Cattles gave me a splendid party in the banqueting suite on the top floor of the Dorchester Hotel, with its wonderful views over London. This was attended by my former board colleagues, our bankers, professional advisers and a few other selected people.

Well aware of my sporting interests, a special guest and after-dinner speaker, invited by Sean Mahon, was Martin Bayfield, the former England lock-forward. In course of Martin's amusing speech, I remember, in particular, a story concerning Wade Dooley, "the Blackpool Policeman" (rugby union was still an amateur sport at the time), whom Martin had partnered in the England second-row on several occasions.

Six foot nine inches tall and built like a "brick closet", Dooley was the team's "enforcer" in times of rough play. He was a great favourite with the fans – and particularly the girls, who could often be found waiting outside the hotels where the team was staying or meeting the motor coaches as they arrived at the grounds. On one occasion, as Dooley was leaving the coach, one of the groupies said, "Oooh, Wade, you are a big boy and six-foot-nine tall. Is everything in proportion?" With no hesitation, Wade replied, "No, luv, otherwise I would be seven foot-nine."

In April 2006, I was invited, together with the four executive directors of Cattles, to a luncheon honouring my retirement, held in the Executive Suite of the Royal Bank of Scotland in their offices at 280 Bishopsgate. It was the first time I had visited one of these new skyscraper buildings, stretching down to the Canary Wharf area in East London, where many of the banks, financial institutions and professional firms had relocated.

The hosts were Johnny Cameron, chief executive corporate markets, and four of his colleagues, who had dealt with Cattles over the years. It was a very pleasant occasion, and I was presented with a suitably engraved silver plate (the largest in my growing collection – as one might expect from a bank!).

The redevelopment of this area of London had taken place mainly after my years with C&L. It was very impressive, but I felt grateful to have been able to spend most of my time when in London in the historic City area, surrounded by such buildings as St Paul's Cathedral, the Bank of England and the London Stock Exchange.

In September 2006, about four months after my retirement from Cattles, I was contacted by the West Yorkshire Society of Chartered Accountants and informed that I was one of three members to be shortlisted for their Lifetime Achiever Award. The winner was to be announced at the Annual Gala Dinner a few weeks later. Sean was away, but James Corr arranged a table at the event to include myself and some of the other chartered accountants employed at Cattles. I was pleased not to let down these former colleagues and be chosen winner of the award, which was presented by the national deputy president of the Institute of Chartered Accountants. It was a happy conclusion to my service with the Cattles Group.

From 1993 (when I had accepted my first appointment) and for the next 20 years until I retired at the age of 80, I enjoyed a second career as a non-executive director with a variety of companies. Although the main demands upon my time in this period had been in connection with SIG and Cattles, particularly in the years when I served as chairman of both of these companies, I had the opportunity to enjoy several other interesting roles.

In early 1996 I was approached by an executive recruitment organisation in connection with a possible NED appointment with Vibroplant plc (later to be named VP plc). The company, which had headquarters in Harrogate, was engaged in plant hire and tool and equipment rental through a network of depots in the UK. In due course, I met with Jeremy Pilkington, chairman and chief executive, and his financial director. Jeremy was son of the founder of the company, and the Pilkington family still held a controlling interest. It was a good meeting, and I was impressed by Jeremy's style and enthusiasm. Consequently, when offered the position of non-executive director (to replace their single NED who was retiring), I was pleased to accept.

Some months later, there was a change in financial director when the role was taken by the recruitment of Neil Stothard. Neil subsequently became managing director, and the financial director position was filled by Mike Holt.

With Jeremy as leader, this executive team operated for much of my 13 years' service as a NED, steadily expanding the activities of the business, by acquisitions of companies and investment (both in the UK and overseas) into such areas as:

excavation support and shoring,

rough terrain material handling equipment,

oil field service equipment,

equipment in railway renewals and maintenance; and,

tracks, barriers and bridges for events.

Although my contribution as a NED was small in relation to these activities, I felt able to give some support to the board in matters such as stock exchange requirements, accounting standards and policies, areas for review on investigations and group pension scheme issues. Consequently, I always felt a useful part of the team.

I retired from the board in 2009, enjoying an excellent farewell dinner attended by my board colleagues and senior management at the trendy boutique Hotel du Vin in Harrogate. I had thoroughly enjoyed my years with the group.

A year or so after my retirement from C&L, I had been contacted by the chairman of Smith Self Drive, a substantial private company based in Rotherham and engaged in car and vehicle hire. He explained that, although the company was still owned by the Smith family, with himself as the main shareholder and executive chairman, he wished to retire in about a year's time. As there was no one in the family who would wish and be suitable to take over the running of the business, he believed that the way forward should be either flotation or a trade sale. In either case, he considered that some preparation would be needed for the event. Mr Smith said that he was contacting me, at the suggestion of Kevin McDonald, as someone who would be suitable to join his board and assist in ensuring that the necessary actions were taken.

I accepted the offer to join the board and help in reaching the decisions needed to achieve the objectives mentioned. In fact, I found that the company already had an able financial director in Steve Jago (not a shareholder), who with some support was well capable of implementing the actions required. We carried out the necessary work over the next 12 months or so and appeared to be on track for flotation but, at a late stage, a large American group made an offer, which the family owners considered could not be refused. Consequently, the trade sale took place and I resigned from the board, feeling satisfied that I had served my purpose.

In July 1997, Hugh Grayson, a good friend (who I had known since he spent time working for C&L in the 1970s) asked if I would join the board of Dew Pitchmastic plc, a public but unlisted company of which he was chairman and of which the family owned control. The company had two quite different activities: firstly, building and construction and other services for the construction industry; and secondly, the construction of timber leisure buildings and the operation of holiday parks.

I accepted Hugh's offer and became non-executive deputy chairman of the company. Subsequently, the timber leisure buildings and holiday park activities were hived off into a new company named Pinelog Group Ltd (Pinelog) of which I also became deputy chairman. In July 2005, I resigned from Dew Pitchmastic but continued my role with Pinelog.

The Pinelog operations comprised a manufacturing unit, based in the attractive Peak Park village of Bakewell, where the timber buildings (including lodges for the holiday parks) were produced. The main park (Darwin Forest Country Park) was located just outside the Peak Park boundary, which, I believe, was helpful as regards planning applications. Hugh was a perfectionist, and the lodges, which varied in type and size, were of the highest standard – older lodges often being sold off and replaced by new models. The park had a large spa, with an impressive pool and various treatment facilities, there was a pub/restaurant and a superb (newly erected) children's play centre (named the Little Monkeys), with a café for use by supervising parents.

It was at this park that Hugh and the Pinelog financial director, Paul Daley, shared an office, and where Hugh's daughter, Lindsey, was also based and involved in the park management. Hugh's son Nick was located at the manufacturing unit in Bakewell, becoming director in charge in March 2010 on the retirement, after 36 years' service, of Alistair Grey.

Mention of Alistair reminds me of his retirement party, held at the Little Monkeys play centre and well attended by the directors, old friends, suppliers, trade distributors, etc.

Hugh, probably with the assistance of Beverley, his able and attractive wife, had meticulously planned the evening and taken on the responsibilities of master of ceremonies to ensure that Alistair had the send-off he deserved. However, I suspect that Hugh had the secondary objective of introducing the guests to this splendid new play centre and, as the meal was reaching the concluding stages, Hugh suddenly appeared high above the proceedings, microphone in hand, at the top of the stairs which ran down the side of a magnificent slide. Hugh appeared to be speaking into the microphone, but nothing happened – it was not working! Hugh continued speaking – but it proved to be only to himself. The guests, with no idea why Hugh was "up in gods" in the first place, carried on with their gossip with the usual buzz of conversation. It was a case of the best-laid plans etc. However, probably few people noticed, and the evening was a great success.

Pinelog was the last of the companies for which I served as non-executive director, retiring in 2013. Board meetings had always been well conducted and Hugh would be clear in his objectives, but there were usually subjects where I felt able to make some useful contribution. Of course, Hugh and I were old friends and there was usually time for a little banter and humour in addition to the serious business. The board meetings were often followed by a relaxed lunch at the Peacock Hotel in the nearby village of Rowsley – members with pressing matters for attention being excused.

Very sadly, Hugh passed away in 2019 after a long and brave fight against cancer. He had explored numerous possible treatments to combat the illness but was beaten in the end. He was a good friend and is badly missed.

I have referred to the non-executive director roles which are mentioned in this chapter as my "second career". Spanning around 20 years, of which the 10 overlapping years as chairman of either or both SIG and Cattles were the busiest and most rewarding (both financially and in terms of personal satisfaction), it was an enjoyable and, I feel, necessary period of adjustment following life at CB&Co/C&L, although I would not pretend that it provided the camaraderie and pride that emanated from partnership with the firm. Nevertheless, it gave me a different perception on the world of business and also the opportunity to meet several interesting people and make some new friends.

This chapter has been confined to my business activities in these years. There were many other experiences and events of a non-business nature, which I think are worthy of mention, but I will deal with these in a later chapter.

XVII

Family, Colleagues
and Friends

In Chapter IX I have discussed at some length the Prader-Willi condition of my daughter, Michelle, and her death on 6 February 1998 at the age of 36 years and only 13 days after Mum had passed away. These deaths were devastating for all the family. Kath, who had devoted so much of her time to the care of Michelle, was probably the most badly affected. However, Nigel, with the need to return to Australia only days after the tragedies in order to retain his residency, was also clearly depressed.

Kath and I continued to live at the Croft for the next four and a half years, but things had changed. It seemed too large a house for two people and there were many sad reminders of Michelle. We were not in party mood and the Christmas get-togethers (which had become traditional at the Croft) were different and smaller. Many of Mum's and Dad's contemporaries had passed away and, of my maternal cousins, only John and Jenny, with their children Duncan and Adele, still lived in Sheffield. Linda had moved to Bournemouth, and Ian and Rená, with children Jenni and Chris, had settled in Hampshire. We also missed Nigel (when in Australia) and his younger set of friends.

In 2002, having decided to sell the Croft, we commenced viewings for a suitable replacement property. By this time, Nigel had returned from Australia (ostensibly for good) and taken a position with a company in Lancaster. Nevertheless, he assisted with our search and we eventually decided upon a house in Belgrave Drive, Fulwood, only 400 yards or so from the Croft. Although much smaller, the property had a good deal of character. There were four bedrooms and, therefore, plenty of room for visitors and although the garden was small, it was well landscaped and secluded.

However, in 2003 there was a very major occurrence in the lives of Kath and myself in that, after more than 47 years of marriage, we separated. This was at my instigation, and I have decided that as it is a very personal matter, which concerns only Kath and myself, I will not discuss the subject or try to give explanations in these memoirs, except to say that I attach no blame to Kath.

I think that most marital separations, unless desired by both parties, give rise to feelings of hurt and resentment. These emotions can often escalate into hate because of disputes on matters such as the division of assets. I was determined to do everything I could to avoid this situation. I recognised that Kath had made a full contribution to our marriage, particularly in the way she had cared for and supported Michelle, and, therefore, that she was entitled to an equal share of the assets and pension rights, which we had built up over the years. Of course, one could not divide everything down the middle. Therefore, we agreed that Sean Mahon, a friend of both of us and someone we trusted, should be asked to act as arbiter in deciding how we arrived at the final allocations.

Having separated from Kath, I had no clear long-term plan for the future. As a temporary measure, I rented an apartment next to Abbeydale Sports Club, where I played squash. This was relatively near to Belgrave Drive where Kath still resided, and in the district where we had many friends in common and used the same shops and professional practitioners such as opticians and dentists. Consequently, it was inevitable that our paths would cross, and I wondered if, in these circumstances, it was desirable for me to move away from Sheffield. Another consideration was that my two main business activities at this time – Cattles and VP, were both located north of the city, necessitating longish journeys, which could be slow at peak times.

Therefore, in October 2003, after a brief exploration of the area, I purchased a cottage at Number One, Old Mount Farm, in the pleasant village of Woolley, which is located between Wakefield and Barnsley but, importantly, accessible to the M1 motorway in only a few minutes. This substantially reduced the travelling time to the two companies mentioned above.

The stone-built cottage, which had been created from the original Old Mount Farm and Outbuildings, was part of a development of seven individual dwellings built around a square, which was accessed under an archway. There were two cottages for sale, and I chose the one which I considered had the most character, with a minstrel gallery overlooking the sitting room.

A few weeks later the second cottage (Number 3) was acquired by a very attractive and elegant young woman named Nicola, who I felt I would like to get to know. From my brief initial contact, I discovered that she had two children, a son (Charles) aged 14 and a daughter (Sophie) of 10 years. The family had moved from North Yorkshire so that Charles and Sophie could attend school (as day pupils) at Ackworth – about a 20-minute drive away, in order to take "O" levels prior to moving onto Oundle and Repton, respectively. So far as I could ascertain, Nicola had no husband!

A disadvantage of my new home was that it had only one garage, whereas I had two cars – a Mercedes soft-top convertible, which I decided to keep in the garage, and an Audi 8, which, therefore, had to be parked outside. In the winter of 2003, I went on a golfing holiday to the Algarve with my son Nigel. On return, I found that because of an electrical fault (I never discovered the cause), all the windows of the Audi had opened shortly after we had departed, leaving the car vulnerable to the rain and sleet. Very kindly, two neighbours (Nicola being one of them) had cling-filmed the windows to keep the car dry, leaving a note on the windscreen explaining the circumstances.

Next day, I called at the houses of these two "Good Samaritans" with thank-you bottles of wine. This also provided an opportunity for me to start getting to know Nicola.

A few weeks later, I asked Nicola if she would like to join me in seeing the Northern Ballet company perform *Midsummer Night's Dream* at the Lyceum Theatre in Sheffield (I explained that I had a spare ticket, having been let down by a friend). My suggestion was that we should join my good friends, Sean and Pauline Mahon (who Nicola had not met) and have dinner with them after the performance at Milano, my favourite restaurant in Sheffield. Nicola accepted and I arranged a car to take us to the theatre and, subsequently, pick us up from the restaurant for the return journey to Woolley.

Sean telephoned me on the day of the event. He said that he felt I ought to be aware that Kath, my estranged wife, would be attending the same performance at the Lyceum as ourselves. I decided not to mention this to Nicola until we were well on the way to Sheffield, when I hoped it would be too late for any second thoughts! Fortunately, this proved to be the correct decision and the evening was a great success.

Between our cottages at Woolley lived Denise and Steve Knighton. They were very good neighbours and Denise, in particular, was always helpful. I was also aware that Denise and Nicola, in the short period she had been at Woolley, had become very good friends. Therefore, indebted to both these people for their kindness (at least, this was my excuse), I invited them for lunch at Pool Court, a highly regarded restaurant at 44 The Calls in Leeds. It was an enjoyable occasion – the only blip being that, to the horror of Denise, a waiter removed her champagne glass before it had become empty! If I had noticed, she could have had a refill.

Following our "chaperoned" evening at the theatre and the lunch, where we were accompanied by Denise, I felt it was in order for me to invite Nicola for lunch again, but this time for it to be just for the two of us. Nicola accepted and, in course of the meal, she told me that it was her birthday (3 May). I also discovered that she was 28 years my junior! However, I decided that "she was not too old for me" and this luncheon was effectively the start of our relationship. This developed steadily over following months and years, when we first became best friends and confidants and eventually, although not living together, life partners, and recognised as such by all our friends. Consequently, Nicola accompanied me to many of the retirement functions to which I have referred in Chapter XVI, including the splendid dinner at the Dorchester Hotel, when she was seated next to Martin Bayfield, and the happy VP occasion at the contemporary style Hotel du Vin, where the ornate bath was at one end of the large bed/sitting room!

Also, during these years, we enjoyed a number of overseas holidays, to include Nicola's children when school commitments permitted and attended many interesting functions and events.

One of these was a meeting at York Races which I remember particularly well, when we were guests of Stuart Doughty and his attractive wife, Penny. I had got to know Stuart when, for shortish periods, we served together as non-executive directors at VP and Dew Pitchmastic. With our different professional backgrounds and experience, I felt that we made a good combination. However, Stuart was quite a few years younger than me and still in demand for executive roles.

In 2001 Stuart was appointed chief executive of Costain and in the next six years or so he restored the group's reputation as one of the UK's leading contractors and achieved a massive rise in the share price.

However, to return to the visit to York Races, Stuart had two other guests and, in order to avoid the congested road traffic, we all met at Sherburn in Elmet airfield to be transported for the relatively short distance to the racecourse by air.

Awaiting us were two four-seater helicopters, each to accommodate a pilot and three of our party of six. I found the journey interesting and a reminder of RAF days but, unfortunately, because of the volume of traffic, we were delayed for quite a time before landing, having to go round and round in circles waiting for a slot. I chattered away, pointing out various landmarks before I noticed Nicola's face. She was suffering from nausea and was desperate to return to firm ground. Fortunately, she managed to hang on and quickly recovered after landing. Stuart was an excellent host, and it was a very enjoyable day, except possibly for my selection of horses upon which to "invest"!

In course of 2004, I had the opportunity to get to know (and like) Nicola's parents, Sheila and Leslie. In particular, I remember one happy occasion when we all travelled to London for a day's sightseeing and a visit to Oxford Street. However, Leslie was not in good health and, very sadly, he passed away in June 2005, after a long fight against prostate cancer. Sheila was devastated and Nicola was greatly concerned about her. By chance, the small cottage (Number 4) next to Nicola's had come up for sale a few months earlier and been purchased by myself as an investment. Sheila was persuaded to move in so that Nicola could be close to hand during this difficult period of mourning. My recollection is that Sheila remained in the cottage for about a year after Leslie's death, before returning to her home at Lepton near Huddersfield.

As Nicola and I became closer, I found that she had experienced a sad marriage, from which she had managed to extricate herself, but in 2006 I became aware that a further dispute with John, her former husband, had arisen in relation to maintenance. She was clearly upset and in need of guidance and protection. I offered to help in any way I could. I found that the point had been reached where John wished to terminate maintenance payments for a capital sum in settlement, which amount, in my view, appeared ridiculously low.

At Nicola's request, I accompanied her to see her solicitor in order to discuss the matter. However, before this visit, I had the opportunity to read through the information relating to the previous proceedings. It seemed to me that a matter of prime importance, for future hearings, was that Nicola should be represented by a barrister of equal calibre and eminence as the one used by John, even though this could result in increased costs.

Over several months, I spent a good deal of time in helping Nicola to provide the information required by her barrister for the court hearings at which Nicola appeared in person for cross-examination and (I understand) performed exceptionally well. The outcome was that Nicola obtained a financial settlement, which she regarded as acceptable and was much in excess of the sum which had been put forward by her former husband. She was also awarded all her legal costs.

Having returned to Four Firs, the family home at Lepton, Sheila was the sole occupant of a residence of six bedrooms, surrounded by four acres of gardens, woodland and fields. With

Charles away at Oundle and Sophie able to travel daily to Ackworth by a school bus, which picked up students living in the Lepton area, Nicola wondered if she should move closer to her mother at this difficult time. After discussing this with Sheila, it was decided that Nicola would sell her house at Woolley and purchase a 50% interest in Four Firs, which was already divided into two separate areas of living accommodation.

This decision of Nicola's coincided with my feelings that, while I had been happy at Woolley, it had been only a temporary expedient, made in the light of matters referred to in an earlier paragraph. I now felt ready to seek a more permanent residence in an attractive location, which provided more living space and would be convenient for travel to both Sheffield and Lepton. After some consideration and exploration, the choice of location was not difficult – the historic village of Cawthorne, on the western side of the M1 motorway, which had previously been holder of the "South Yorkshire's Best Village" title.

I had been aware of the facilities of Cawthorne for some time, with its historic All Saints' Church, Spencer Arms tavern/ restaurant, antique centre, local museum, etc. However, in my view, the major benefits came from the adjacent properties of Cannon Hall Farm (an award-winning visitor attraction) and, in particular, Cannon Hall itself, with its surrounding 70 acres of parkland, lakes and gardens.

For 300 years, the estate had been the home of the Spencer– Stanhope family, but in 1951 it was acquired by Barnsley Metropolitan Borough Council and, after much restoration, the Hall and grounds were opened to the public in 1957, providing an excellent facility for people living in the surrounding area.

For anyone interested in history, it was from Cannon Hall that the 13/18th Royal Hussars and Light Dragoons were raised to form the Light Brigade, which during the Battle of Balaclava in 1854 "Charged into the Valley of Death", as immortalised in the famous poem by Alfred, Lord Tennyson.

Accompanied by Nicola, I visited two houses which were for sale in Cawthorne and quickly made my choice – Waterstones, an architect-designed property (built only four years earlier) in a good-sized landscaped garden and located about 400 yards from the village centre, and an even shorter distance from an entrance to the Cannon Hall Estate.

I completed the purchase of Waterstones on 30 October 2006 but continued to live in Woolley for a few months before moving and while my two properties (numbers 1 and 4 Old Mount Farm) were put up for sale. Both were eventually disposed of at satisfactory prices. These 14 years later, Nicola and I live at Waterstones, still enjoying the facilities of the village and walking most days in the beautiful and well-maintained grounds of Cannon Hall.

On 17 December 2008, the decree absolute ending my marriage to Kath came through. The decisions Kath and I had agreed regarding equitable division of assets at the time of separation 17 years earlier had worked well. With the initial emotions behind us, we are good friends with several things in common – not least, three grandsons in Australasia, in respect of whom we regularly exchange information. We keep in touch, liaise on the maintenance of the family grave (which includes the ashes of Michelle and my mother) and occasionally have lunch together.

On a holiday at Reids Hotel in Madeira, about 10 years after we had first met, I proposed to my darling Nicola, and she agreed to be my wife. The wedding took place on 27 June 2012 in a civil ceremony at Fischers Hotel/Restaurant in Baslow, an attractive village in the Peak District of Derbyshire. The witnesses were my son Nigel (having returned from Australia for the occasion) and Nicola's son Charles. Including ourselves, there were 31 people at the luncheon that followed the service, including Nicola's close family – her elegant mother, Sheila, Charles and, acting as a lovely bridesmaid, Sophie. Most of our close friends were able to attend. Faith Douglas made readings, Sean Mahon an amusing speech, and Nigel almost stole the show in an unscheduled wind-up speech, in course of which some of the male guests were beginning to look puzzled and slightly annoyed in the mistaken belief that they had been left out of an eventful stag party! It was typical Nigel and, in all respects, and excellent occasion.

On a change of subject, over the years I have been fortunate to have had contact with many likeable and talented people, either socially, in course of business situations, or both. I have been grateful for these relationships, particularly where they have developed into friendships. However, with the passing of time, retirements and distances to travel, I currently have little contact with many of these old friends and colleagues, although several will already have been mentioned in these memoirs. Therefore, in this current chapter, when naming my "close friends", I have considered it realistic to include only those with whom I have regular contact at this time. If I fail to mention anyone who should have been included, I hope I will be forgiven.

My oldest friendships, which have existed for 70 years or so and still continue, have been with Ted Machon and Bryan Hancock. Although none of us now reside in Sheffield, we keep in touch, and periodically, Nicola and I meet up with Ted and Margaret and Bryan and Liz for lunch, dinner or theatre visits. All the three men are supporters of Sheffield United (the Blades) and, until about a year ago, we would have seen each other regularly at Bramall Lane during the football season. However, because of health issues, I am left as the only current attender. Maybe this is a good thing in the case of Ted, as we usually disagree on some subject or other!

Several other close friends (who have now also become friends of Nicola) were with the firm in the sixties and early seventies when we were building up the practice from a Sheffield base. These include Tony Wood, Sean Mahon and Paul Southern. Tony and I first met in 1961 and, in addition to being friends and work colleagues, for many years, we were antagonists on Sickleholme golf course every Saturday morning, when civilities between us were sometimes less well observed than in the office.

Nicola and I meet with Tony and Jo and Sean and Pauline quite regularly for dinner, theatre visits or other social occasions and I know that Nicola, Jo and Pauline communicate quite regularly. However, we see less of Paul and Sally, who reside in Sutton Coldfield. However, as a staunch "Blade", Paul is a regular attender at Bramall Lane in the football season, usually accompanied by son, Jack, and often Sally. With seats only a few rows in front of mine, at least I can see the back of their heads!

Other good friends, who served in Sheffield or Leeds offices in the above-mentioned period were Alan Young, Patrick Andrews and Robin Wight. Alan and Patrick were taxation partners in Sheffield office, and Patrick has recently joined Sean and Paul as "the young man" of my named executors, just in case either of the other two decide to expire before me.

Robin, who was a partner of Leeds office in its early stages, moved to Scotland, on my recommendation, to become regional partner in charge. Robin and his wife, Sheila, were good friends of my former wife, Kathleen, and myself, and we usually joined up each year to share rented accommodation for the duration of the Open Golf Championship. In the rugby season, we usually stayed with the Wights when attending Calcutta Cup games at Murrayfield. We supported different sides, but this never spoiled after-match celebrations. However, Robin's insistence on playing "Flower of Scotland" on the car radio if his team had won could be irksome.

Another colleague of these years, who was not a C&L partner but chose to develop a career in industry, was John Swynnerton. Apart from being my regular squash opponent for about 30 years (I rarely won), I had dealings with John in his roles with various client companies. Nicola and I also met with John and his wife Liz from time to time and on several significant family occasions. When John became redundant, following a rationalisation in the steel sector, he was the ideal person to join SIG as company secretary during my years as chairman. One way or another, we were colleagues for most of our working lives.

An amusing event in April 1979 (although possibly not for those involved) concerned Tony Wood and Paul Southern. Paul had been attending the Partner Induction Course near London (to which event he had travelled in his car) following his recent admission to partnership. By chance, the timing of Paul's return journey coincided with Tony wishing to travel north, having been attending the Annual General Meeting of Spear & Jackson plc, a C&L client. Derek Stoddart (ex CB&Co), the financial director of the above company, also wished to return to his home in the Derbyshire Peak District.

Paul, no doubt proud of his new status, was pleased to offer lifts to both Tony and Derek and the party set off travelling up the M1, Paul driving, Derek in the front passenger seat and Tony in the rear – with nothing for company except Paul's new dinner jacket, acquired specially for the formal concluding dinner of the induction course.

Unfortunately, this was the occasion of a freak and entirely unseasonal snowstorm, with conditions rapidly deteriorating as the car moved north. Paul eventually turned off the motorway to head towards Derek's home, but this proved to be a mistake. Travel became impossible and the car (amongst several other vehicles) came to a halt, with snow still falling heavily. There was nothing for it but to accept that they were marooned for the night.

Tony solemnly shared his bar of chocolate – the only food between the three of them, and the car engine was run from time to time to generate a little heat, but it was a cold and miserable night. As dawn broke, Paul looked behind to see how Tony had fared. He found him to be asleep, having used Paul's new DJ as a blanket with his feet stuffed firmly down the sleeve holes.

A few words about Sean Mahon. I had recruited Sean in 1969, shortly after he qualified. He came into partnership with C&L in 1977 and for the following years up to my retirement in 1995, we worked together on numerous and varied client assignments. As our homes were only 400 or so yards apart, we also met socially and became well acquainted with each other's families.

If on my retirement, Sean thought that he was getting rid of me after 26 years of working together, he was mistaken. As explained in Chapter XVI, I called for his support at Cattles and we became colleagues for another four years. However, even between these periods of working together, we were (and continue to be) involved as president and vice president/treasurer respectively of Boys and Girls Clubs of South Yorkshire, a charity supporting young people through clubs which are often located in the most deprived areas of the county.

Since retirement from C&L, Sean has also taken part in a number of local business initiatives and charitable activities, which efforts have been recognised by several awards, including:

2004 An honorary doctorate from Hallam University,

2007 The *Yorkshire Post* Award for Individual Excellence; and, in

2008 The Institute of Chartered Accountant's Outstanding Achievement Award.

I suspect that Sean is still looking for other good causes to champion, but recent knee and back problems (not just his usual fraudulent efforts to gain an extra stroke when we play golf) could make this difficult.

However, I enjoyed his wife Pauline's account of a recent incident when they were returning home after an evening out –

Sean, with his gammy knee, was experiencing difficulty in lifting his foot over a high kerb. A passing young man put his arm around Sean's shoulder and helped him along with the comment, "You have obviously had a good night, pops."

Pauline, following in the rear, replied, "He has, luv. I'm just taking him back to the care home."

Another former colleague, who I regard as a good friend, is Peter Allen (already mentioned several times and particularly in Chapter XIII). Peter was an excellent C&L managing partner, very likeable and with good people skills, but also the ability to make tough decisions when required. I greatly enjoyed working with him in my role as EPIC of the Regions and felt that I always had his strong support when required. Peter's wife Pat is a "Sheffield girl" but, for health reasons, I think that they rarely make the journey north these days. However, Peter and I keep in touch by telephone, and it is always a pleasure to speak to him.

In addition to former C&L colleagues, Nicola and I have several good friends who I wish to mention. Kevin McDonald comes immediately to mind. An important client from my early years as a C&L partner, he is referred to at some length in Chapter XI. However, in more recent years, I have greatly appreciated the hospitality of Kevin and his attractive and charming wife, Donna, when invited to shoots at Serlby Estate. Nicola and I were also privileged to attend Kevin's "surprise" (to him) 80ᵗʰ birthday lunch at the Roux Brothers Waterside Inn at Bray. For Nicola, having attended a cordon bleu course under Prue Leith, this was a particularly interesting and enjoyable experience.

Although being somewhat geographically dispersed, Nicola and I, Sean and Pauline Mahon, James and Brenda Corr and Kevin and Donna, try to meet up for dinner at least once each year to remember old times and have a general catch-up of news.

Some time after retirement from C&L, I became very friendly with Gordon Bridge, who served as "Master" of The Company of Cutlers in Hallamshire (a trade guild established in 1624). Gordon and his wife Janet were already friends of the Mahons and Woods and, therefore, part of a group which Nicola and I regard as close friends.

During his year in office, Gordon launched "The Master Cutler's Challenge", in which member companies would compete each year to be chosen as the most innovative and successful in raising monies for distribution to selected charities and good causes. Amazingly, I believe that since Gordon's year as Master Cutler, a sum of around £2 million has been raised and distributed.

Having established the Challenge, Gordon continued to play an active part every year until his retirement in 2018, by sponsoring a dinner/auction evening at the Pizza café in Sheffield. With around 50 attenders, Gordon paid for everyone's meal and wine, but invited guests to make a donation. My recollection is that the event raised over £20,000 for the Challenge each year until Gordon's final occasion, when the proceeds of £23,000 were increased by a donation of £100,000 from a regular attender (who I feel it is not appropriate for me to name) in honour of Gordon's efforts over the years.

Mention of Gordon leads me to name another good friend of Nicola and myself, Faith Douglas, who (in addition to her own separate charity fundraising activities) has assisted Gordon on several occasions. Never short of ideas, in April 2018, Faith organised a very enjoyable "Gordon's Desert Island Discs" evening, to raise funds for St. Luke's Hospice in Sheffield. Faith interviewed Gordon, between playing discs of his favourite music in order to bring out past memories. Faith was awarded a well-deserved MBE in 2019 for her charity involvements.

Other members of the group of friends, with whom Nicola and I meet up at parties or other functions several times in course of a year, are Janet and Peter Flint, and Beverley Grayson and Jane Gibbs. I have previously mentioned the death of my friend and former colleague, Hugh Grayson, and Clive Gibbs also passed away in 2019. Both are sadly missed but we are fortunate to still see Bev and Jane.

Moving on from colleagues and friends to family, the only remaining male members from my original family who bear the Cottingham name are myself, Nigel and his sons – Jack, Sam and Ned. Several of Nigel's actions and deeds have been mentioned in previous chapters, but some further information is given in following paragraphs.

Nigel was born on 13 December 1964, less than nine months after I had been admitted to salaried partnership with C&L. However, I felt confident that I could make rapid progress in the firm and generate the increased income that this should bring. Consequently, I was determined to ensure that Nigel (and, if appropriate, Michelle) should obtain the best education and life experiences that I could provide, and which had not been available to myself. Therefore, after his original kindergarten classes, Nigel became a pupil at Birkdale Preparatory School in Sheffield, with a view to attending a public school in due course. As mentioned earlier, the eventual choice of school was Repton.

Nigel's years at Birkdale require little comment. His classwork was satisfactory, his sporting abilities above average and he made several good friends. I greatly enjoyed having a son and, in the last two or three years before Nigel moved on to Repton, we regularly kicked a football around in the local park, practised batting on our lawn and, occasionally, attended football games at Bramall Lane to see the Blades. I also introduced Nigel to the game of squash, giving him an appropriate number of points start, which I reduced as he steadily improved.

In the winter of 1976, Nigel became a pupil at Repton. His unfortunate start to this phase in his life is referred to in Chapter XIV. None of us had mobile phones in these days, but I remember Nigel calling early one morning from the public box in Repton's main street, only a few weeks after he had started at the school. Obviously unhappy, he announced that he had "run away". Kath and I were probably more upset than Nigel, but this was not the time to show this, so I enquired, "How much money have you got?" I believe that the reply was two shillings and sixpence or some such trivial sum. I responded, "That will not get you very far. I think it would be best for you to go back."

I immediately phoned Nigel's housemaster, the Reverend Grew and suggested that he should send someone to find Nigel and escort him back before he acted in a stupid way.

As time passed, Nigel settled to life at Repton and seemed to develop some pride in belonging to the school (although I have never discussed this with him). I think that his sporting prowess (particularly in football and tennis) may have helped in this connection. He also became involved in the school theatrical society, which he clearly enjoyed. I remember attending the society's production of *West Side Story*, in which Nigel appeared as Officer Krupke. However, on the evidence of this particular performance, I considered that Sir Lawrence Olivier need have no worries.

After the first year, when pupils were encouraged to remain at school during weekends, students were allowed to leave after lessons on Friday and return to Repton on Sunday evening. This enabled us to see more of Nigel and he could also keep in touch with his friends in Sheffield. In addition, Nigel and I usually managed to fit in a game of squash, although by this stage he was not receiving any points allowance! I remember that following the first time Nigel won a game on this basis, he enquired, "Would you like me to give you a start next time, Dad?" This nearly earned him a thick ear, but subsequent experiences proved that I should have accepted!

After completing schooling at Repton, Nigel moved to Oxford Brookes to take his degree. He continued to play football in these years, but suffered a bad knee injury and snapped tendon, requiring surgery. Although this injury never fully mended, Nigel returned to playing football wearing a knee support and continued until his mid-forties! Thereafter, with steadily deteriorating mobility, he struggled along for another 10 years before having surgery in 2014, which necessitated a complete knee replacement.

Kath (my former wife) and I visited Nigel in Oxford on several occasions but, as this was before the major road improvements to the A43, the journey was much slower and more tedious than in the present day. My recollection is that Nigel was originally accommodated in one of the college halls of residence, but he moved out to share a house with two other students. The house was in a reasonable area, but the furnishings were not the most luxurious. I remember that Nigel's bed had a broken leg and was supported at one corner by house bricks! Nevertheless, he seemed happy and, in addition to his studies, had continued with an involvement in amateur theatricals.

Our final visit to Oxford was in June 1986 to attend the ceremony at which Nigel received his degree.

For a year or so after obtaining his degree, Nigel remained in Oxford. He then moved to the London area, where he resided for a further five years. He was employed throughout both these periods, in quite good jobs by several different organisations, but I felt that none were likely to develop into the type of career which Nigel desired. I felt that Nigel's ideal occupation would have been in dramatic arts or some other branch of entertainment, but this was a difficult area to break into. Fortunately, he had excellent presentational skills and an ability to express himself clearly and in an interesting way, both orally and in writing.

A brief employment in the above period, which required none of the qualities mentioned, was "chalet maid" at a Ski Resort. Nigel had taken the job so that he could improve his own skills on the slopes in off-duty hours. It has proved to be a good decision, particularly as my grandsons are now enthusiastic skiers.

At some stage in these years (I cannot remember the timing) Nigel took a sabbatical of several weeks (possibly months) for a trip around South America. In the absence of mobile phones, there were often quite long periods without any contact. We subsequently discovered that, at one stage, he had been very ill having picked up an infection when swimming in a lake. He lost a lot of weight, and a message placed on the door of his room in the hostel where he was staying asked new travellers to make sure that the "sick gringo" was given water.

The next time Nigel got in touch was from a public phone box in Buenos Aires to say that he was running out of money. I arranged for funds to be available at the local C&L office and Nigel duly attended. He was shown into the office of a friendly young partner, who called for coffee and chatted away pleasantly about various topics, including, apparently, the prospects of the Puma's rugby team in the forthcoming season! Eventually, concerned that he might miss his flight to the next stage of his travels, Nigel enquired, "Would it be possible to collect my money?" The reply was, "What money?" No one had mentioned the arrangement to the young partner – he was just being friendly to the son of a UK colleague. Fortunately, all ended well.

Nigel subsequently wrote articles on places he had visited in course of his travels in South America, and I still have a copy of a publication by AFTA (The Australian Federation of Travel Agents) containing an article by Nigel on Brazil – "An Affair of the Heart", nine glossy pages of writing and photographs.

Towards the end of the above period (around 1992), Nigel had taken employment with a small public relations/advertising consultancy. This firm had a relationship with a similar organisation in Australia, and the two companies were often able to co-operate for their mutual benefit. Although I am not clear on the details (which, no doubt, Nigel could provide), the companies agreed to the formation of a joint venture in Australia. Nigel was pleased to volunteer to move to Australia and become the UK representative in this new undertaking.

My first visit to Australia (accompanied by Kath) was in 1992 in order to attend the C&L International Partners Meeting in Sydney. However, this must have been before the arrival of Nigel in his role referred to above as I have no recollection of meeting up with him. After the two and a half-day C&L meeting, Kath and

I took a plane to Cairns and a boat to Hayman Island on the Great Barrier Reef where we stayed for about five days. It was a superb holiday. Except for the hotel complex, with its private harbour and beach, the island was completely undeveloped at the time, and both land and sea were ideal for exploration.

Having related (in the above paragraphs) my best recollections of events concerning Nigel, in the half-dozen or so years from him leaving college at Oxford to moving to Australia, I recognise that there could be some factual inaccuracies, particularly in the dates stated. If so, I apologise to him. Nigel can always put the record straight by writing his own memoirs!

According to my records, from 1992 onwards, Nigel spent only 12 ½ out of the next 15 ½ years in Australia. He returned to the UK for a one-year sabbatical in 1997/8 and again for about two and a half years between 2001 to 2004. In this latter period, Nigel took up an appointment with a company in Lancaster in the belief (at that time) that he would be returning to the UK for good. In most of the years when Nigel was resident in Australia, Kath and I had opportunities to see him, either on his brief visits back to the UK or in course of several excellent holidays (when we were accompanied by Nigel) visiting different parts of Australia.

I think it was early in the 15 ½ year period mentioned above that Nigel had some success with regard to his acting ambitions when he had a major role in an award-winning documentary film. I believe that he also had a few minor appearances in other films, including one as stand-in for the star of an Australian TV soap, when he had to jump into a moving boat (keeping only his back visible to the cameras). I assume that he was considered to be expendable if he missed his footing!

Nigel also had some bad experiences in this period, but I feel that these are best left for his own thoughts. However, I will record one of the most important and happy events in his life, the marriage on 24 January 2009 to Lisa, a very attractive and sporty young Australian-born woman.

The wedding of Nigel and Lisa took place in the beautiful wine-growing area of Hunter Valley, about 70 miles from Sydney. For bridesmaids, Lisa had chosen her sister Pippa and a close friend. Nigel's best man was Dave Griffiths (Griff) his best friend from schooldays at Repton. In addition to myself, Nigel's mum, Kath, and her friend of many years, Pam, were attending from the UK.

Most of the guests were staying at the same hotel, which was situated on a golf course a few miles from where the wedding ceremony and following celebrations were to take place. My recollection is that a golf competition, for any guests wishing to participate (of which I was one), had been arranged for the day before the wedding. I believe that I also played a few holes on the morning of the "big day". Transport was provided to the venue, and the wedding service, reception, weather, dinner and speeches were all excellent.

I believe that I was slightly led astray in the bar on return to the hotel, by two of Nigel's friends, who I knew quite well from previous visits to Australia. However, I felt entitled to celebrate at the wedding of my only son. Griff had been instructed by Nigel to "keep an eye on me" and make sure that I found the way back to my room!

Next day, a cricket ground with a clubhouse had been reserved, with additional guests arriving who had not been at the wedding. In addition to the drinking, eating and socialising, a cricket match took place between Australian and English teams – Lisa (quite a useful cricketer) and Nigel playing on opposite sides. I think that I was suffering from the previous day's festivities and scored only 5 runs. However, Nigel, batting well down the order, played the innings of the day and steered England to victory. The whole of the day had been enjoyable and an excellent conclusion to the wedding festivities.

At 6.50am on 9 August 2009, in Sydney, my first grandson, Jack Harvey Cottingham, was born. However, it was six months later before I had the opportunity to fly out to Australia for our first meeting.

In late August/early September 2010, Nigel, Lisa and baby Jack (just over one year old) travelled to New York for the marriage of Lisa's brother Jamie. He had met his bride during her secondment to Sydney by a US investment bank. The relatively short flight to the USA (compared to Australia) was too good an opportunity to miss, and I flew out to join Lisa and Nigel for a few days. I found them looking the worse for wear. Jack was still on the Australian time clock, and at his most active when the others were hoping to sleep! At least it gave me the opportunity to spend some time with him in the daytime when his parents tried to catch up on their rest.

On 1 December 2010 at 12 noon, my second grandson, Sam Gordon Cottingham, came into the world. Nicola and I flew to Sydney to see him, and stay for a two-week holiday, during June 2011. Lisa's stepfather owned (jointly with his sister) a beautiful holiday home at Palm Beach, a very impressive resort about 25 miles north of Sydney and for part of our visit, we spent a few days there, together with Nigel and family. It was a wonderful opportunity to get to know Jack and Sam, even though they were still very young.

In September 2011, Nicola and I returned to Sydney (staying at the Quay Grand, our usual hotel) but, together with Nigel, Lisa and the two boys, we flew north into Queensland for a few days to visit Noosa, a superb resort with excellent beaches. By this time, both boys, although different in looks and nature, were showing a great deal of character.

On 4 July 2013 at 15:18 hours, my third (and final?) grandson, Ned Cooper Cottingham, was born. In this case, our first meeting with him was in Bali, where we had arrived, via Bangkok, on 13 September for a two-week visit. Nigel and family joined us a short time later, having been in the country a few days before us to attend the wedding of Lisa's sister (Pippa).

We stayed at the Westin Hotel, Nusa Dua, located in a very plush seaside development with strong security arrangements. This was one of several high-quality hotels in the resort, although the surrounding areas were still very undeveloped, with little obvious change since a holiday I had taken in Bali some years earlier. I was surprised by the number of attractive young women staying at our hotel until I discovered that it was the venue for the Miss World competition a few days later.

At this stage, Ned was only two and a half months old, but he accompanied us everywhere in a carrycot and was amazingly content. Nicola and I were always happy to be left with him if Lisa and Nigel required a break.

We visited Sydney for two weeks in September/October in each of the years 2014 to 2016 and in the latter year enjoyed another few days with the family at Palm Beach. It was wonderful to see the boys maturing. For their ages, all were good swimmers and useful ball players. On these annual visits, I always tried to be in Australia to celebrate my birthday (5 October) with the boys, but in 2015 we were airborne returning to the UK. By chance, the senior steward on the Airbus A380-800 was Ziad, son-in-law of Sean Mahon. We enjoyed excellent service and were served a special celebratory bottle of wine free of charge with dinner.

In 2017 my son, Nigel, accepted a position to work in New Zealand with a consortium of companies involved largely in the reconstruction of Christchurch following major earthquakes. Consequently, our annual October visit required travelling an even greater distance and an additional change of aircraft. However (adding even more travelling time), we spent a very enjoyable week on holiday with the family at the InterContinental Fiji Golf Resort and Spa. This was a new and different holiday experience which we greatly enjoyed. Therefore, in 2018, we agreed to meet up with Nigel and family for a further holiday in Fiji, but this time staying at the Westin Denarau Island Resort and Spa. This was one of the three hotels in line overlooking the beach, which operated together on a "cashless" basis, with residents allowed to use the restaurants, bars, pools, etc. of any of the three hotels, thus providing variety and extending the facilities available.

In 2019, Nicola had commitments which prevented her from making the annual October visit, and Nigel's time was also restricted through having taken a holiday to attend some of the Rugby World Cup games in Japan. Therefore, I decided to stay with Nigel and Lisa for my two-week trip in order to see as much of my grandsons as I could. However, I found that for part of the time, Jack and Sam were competing in a seven-a-side football tournament. Nigel coached the team and was involved in shouting words of encouragement and instruction and in making player substitutions as appropriate.

My role was merely as spectator, while also keeping an eye on Ned (with whom I had established an excellent rapport) to see that he came to no harm from his daredevil antics on various items of playground equipment. Standing on the sideline of the football pitch, I sensed that the young players regarded the "old man" watching them with suspicion. However, as the tournament came to an end, several of the boys smiled and spoke to me. Eventually, my grandson, Jack, came up and said, "Is it true that you were in charge of England's 1966 World Cup winning team, Pops?" Nigel has always been capable of telling a good story!

In addition to my family living in Australasia, in June 2012, when I married Nicola, I became part of her family, comprising her attractive mum, Sheila, adult children, Charles and Sophie, and (added more recently) Charles' wife Veena plus their beautiful little daughter, Meera, born on 6 January 2020.

Nicola is very close to all the above and I have a good relationship with Sheila, dating from the year she spent at Woolley following the death of her husband, Leslie. I had first met Charles and Sophie in late 2003 (when they came with Nicola to live at Woolley) and in the next few years, we enjoyed several overseas holidays together. However, as Charles and Sophie became older, because of boarding schools, attendance at university, career training and, eventually, employment away from South Yorkshire, there have been limited opportunities to spend time with them, although Sophie is aware that there is a home for her with Nicola and myself in Cawthorne whenever she wishes to use it.

Something I have in common with Charles and Veena is that we are all chartered accountants, although (for better or worse?) the profession is now very different from my day. I remember feeling pleased when I passed my exams at the first attempt. However, Charles' route to qualification has been somewhat more impressive with five prizes, including "best performance in the final examination for the degree of BSc in Accounting and Finance" at Leeds University Business School, and 8th place in the Institute of Chartered Accountants International Order of Merit for his performance in the professional stage exams. He is a very trustworthy and bright young man with a great deal of potential.

If my comments in this, and the previous chapter, have seemed less lighthearted than usual, it is possibly because they have been written while in a period of "lockdown" (which is still continuing) during the Coronavirus, Covid-19, situation but on the assumption (or at least in the hope) that everything will return to normal in due course. At this point, "due course" seems long into the future and, on a personal basis, my next opportunity to see Nigel and my grandsons is impossible to predict.

Any readers of these memoirs will probably have their own recollections of living in the time of the virus. Nevertheless, in the next chapter, and for the record, I propose to summarise the challenges and changing circumstance being experienced in the UK in these first few months.

XVIII

The Coronavirus (Covid-19)

I believe that from the end of December 2019 there had been rumours of a strange virus in Wuhan (a city of 11 million people) in China, which was giving rise to a high level of deaths. However, to the best of my recollections, I heard mention of this only in late January 2020. On the 31st of that month, the UK Government made a statement referring to the virus (of which, I think, there was only one case in the UK), to reassure the public that everything was under control.

As the virus spread from China to countries around the world, it was declared to be a pandemic by the World Health Organisation and given the name Coronavirus (Covid-19). However, in certain countries, where (at this stage) there were few infections, there seemed to be a reluctance to take the virus seriously. For example, Donald Trump indicated that there were negligible cases and no deaths in the USA and that he intended to keep it that way – a statement which seemed particularly ironic in June 2020, when deaths in the USA passed the 100,000 mark.

As regards the UK, the decision of the government to allow the Cheltenham Festival Race Meeting to go ahead in the second week of March (by which time infections were starting to increase) came as a surprise to many people.

An even more contentious issue around this time was the theory of "herd immunity", which (in simple terms) appeared to be allowing large numbers of people (particularly young fit people) to contract the virus in the belief that it would be overcome and they would gain immunity. I believe this short-lived theory was abandoned following a study by Imperial College, London, which concluded that the policy must change in favour of "social isolation" in order to avoid the danger of a "quarter of a million" deaths! Matt Hancock, Minister of Health, subsequently denied that herd immunity had ever been official policy.

Very sadly, the situation concerning the Coronavirus deteriorated rapidly from the early events referred to above (both in the UK and the world at large) to be recognised as the greatest crisis, disaster and challenge to be faced since the Second World War. Consequently, with no enthusiasm, I have decided that the subject must be dealt with in these memoirs. However, whereas previous chapters have referred to past events, the matters in this current chapter commenced only a few months ago and continue to develop as I write. With no clear end in sight, or any possibility of assessing the final outcome, I expect to cease my comments on the Coronavirus in a week or so without any conclusions.

As a background to my comments in following paragraphs, I set out below (in respect of the UK) for the dates shown:

- the number of existing cases of Coronavirus,
- the number of daily tests carried out; and,
- the cumulative number of deaths from the virus.

The above information has been taken from the Tuesday editions of the *Daily Telegraph* on the dates indicated and gives the position as at the end of the previous day.

DATE	CASES IN UK	DAILY TESTS	CUMULATIVE DEATHS
17 March 20	1,543	|	55
24 " "	6,650	Negligible in	335
31 " "	22,141	the early	1,415
7 April 20	51,608	weeks	5,373
14 " "	88,621	|	11,329
21 " "	124,743	19,316	16,509
28 " "	157,149	62,976	21,092
5 May 20	190,584	85,186	28,734
12 " "	223,060	100,490	32,065
19 " "	246,406	100,678	34,796
26 " "	261,184	73,726	36,914

DATE	CASES IN UK	DAILY TESTS	CUMULATIVE DEATHS
2 June 20	276,332	128,437	39,045
9 ” ”	287,399	138,183	40,597
16 ” ”	296,857	93,163	41,736

On 17 March, the main information in the press regarding the Coronavirus was the announcement by Boris Johnson, the prime minister, of the biggest ever restriction of civil liberties made in peacetime. These included requirements that:

• everyone must avoid visits to pubs, clubs, restaurants, theatres and other social venues,
• all unnecessary travel must end, and people should work from home if possible,
• anyone of 70 years and over and the millions of people who are younger, but suffer from an underlying health condition, should avoid almost all social contact,
• mass gatherings should be cancelled, and social distancing would be recommended; and,
• whole households must isolate for 14 days if any member has a persistent cough or fever and that no one self-isolating should go out (even to buy food or essentials) other than for exercise.

Professor Chris Whitty, the chief medical officer for England, stated that the country must be prepared for restrictions to be in place for the long haul, and government advisors indicated that, even if the strategy worked, around 20,000 people were likely to die.

Despite the prime minister's comments, my impressions at the time were that the actions being taken and the threats as to the possible consequences of the virus seemed "over the top". How wrong this view proved to be! At the time of writing (16 June), deaths already exceed 41,700 and still counting.

By 18 March, the chancellor of the exchequer, Rishi Sunak, had announced several measures to reassure the public that life could continue despite the restrictions being imposed. These included:

- £330 billion in government-backed loans for businesses,
- £20 billion in grants and business rates relief for hospitality and leisure,
- grants of £10,000 for the smallest businesses,
- all retail, hospitality and leisure businesses to pay no business rates for the next 12 months; and,
- three-month mortgage holidays for homeowners.

Dominic Raab, foreign secretary, advised against all non-essential travel for the next 30 days, because of the risk of becoming stranded abroad, and Boris Johnson indicated that school closures could come soon. In fact, the decision on schools came the following day, with the cancellation of A-Levels and GCSE examinations this summer, although classrooms were to be kept open to look after the children of key workers (such as NHS staff) and vulnerable pupils.

During this period, 19 to 22 March, I felt there was some confusion as to the government's strategy for dealing with the virus. Advice seemed to be changing daily. However, it eventually became clear that:

- no cure for the virus appeared likely to be found for one year to 18 months at least – if ever,
- in what is a traditionally busy period for NHS hospitals, there were major concerns that there would be insufficient beds, ventilators and personal protection equipment for use by NHS staff, to cope with the rapidly growing number of people suffering from the virus.

Against the above background, the simple message became, "STAY AT HOME, PROTECT THE NHS, AND SAVE LIVES."

To reinforce the above objectives, on 23 March, Boris Johnson announced a lockdown for three weeks on the following basis:

- People can leave home for only four reasons – shopping for basic necessities as infrequently as possible; one form of exercise per day (e.g. a run or a walk); travelling for work where necessary and where this cannot be done at home; and for a medical need or to help a vulnerable person.
- Police to have power to enforce the above rules.
- Shops selling non-essentials, libraries, playgrounds, gyms and places of worship must close.
- Gatherings of two or more people in public are banned.
- Weddings, baptisms, etc. are banned – but not funerals.

At this stage, an attack was made on the government's strategy by Jeremy Hunt, the former health secretary. He considered that the UK was wrongly focusing on social distancing, rather than tracking those infected and contact tracing to break the train of transmissions.

I felt that Hunt's above views were very valid. The government's daily target for tests at the time was 10,000 people, which the prime minister promised to increase to 25,000. However, the actual tests carried out seemed to be running at only about 2,000 per day!

I appreciated that the "social distancing" approach during the three-week lockdown should help slow down the spread of the virus and provide some time for hospitals to obtain required equipment. However, it seemed to me that, at the end of the three weeks, there would still be little knowledge of the people infected, with a danger that the spread of the virus could accelerate again.

It was clear that the government were concerned about the lack of facilities for testing, and it was reported that 3.5 million antibody test kits had been ordered from an overseas source. However, I believe that much of this equipment from overseas, when received, proved to be defective and unsatisfactory.

To move ahead on this subject, papers released on 31 May (over two months later) from the Scientific Advisory Group for

Emergencies (SAGE) show that routine testing had stopped because Public Health England were struggling to deal with more than a "handful of cases". Apparently, they could cope with testing and tracing only five cases per week. Modelling suggested that it might only be possible to increase this to 50. In light of this, it was decided to stop routine testing at that stage (12 March). This lack of testing is seen by some people as a key reason why the UK now has the highest death rates in Europe.

After several "missed targets", the current NHS test and trace system, to be rolled out over June, is to be supported by 25,000 "tracers". However, the chief of Public Health England admitted that there may be resistance to the scheme, and, because of some early problems, it is already accepted that the system may not be fully operational for another month.

On 5 April, the Queen addressed the nation, expressing thanks to the NHS and those carrying out essential roles. However, on the same day came the very worrying news that Boris Johnson had been admitted to hospital after failing to shake-off the Coronavirus for two weeks. The following day he was taken into intensive care after the virus symptoms had worsened. Thankfully, Boris eventually pulled through, having been in hospital for a week, but his condition had been serious. He clearly felt very grateful for the dedicated care of the NHS nurses and doctors and, in some respects, I felt that his illness had made him more cautious. A proposed announcement on 9 April with regard to the lockdown had been postponed to await the return of Boris, and on 14 April, it was announced that the lockdown would stay in place beyond the legally required review on 16 April. However, there were signs of government concerns at the financial costs from the virus, which were running at £2.4 billion per day.

It was believed that the "furlough scheme" to subsidise pay during the lockdown could cost £40 billion – four times as much as predicted. The chancellor also admitted that the £750 million package for charities would not be enough to save them.

On 15 April, the Office for Budget Responsibility said that the economy could shrink by 35% in the spring, with unemployment soaring by two million to its highest level since the 90s. It was considered that Britain could suffer its deepest recession for 300 years.

On 28 April, Boris Johnson promised to "fire-up the engine" with plans to refine the lockdown. However, at this time, both new Coronavirus cases and daily deaths were still running at high levels, presenting him with a difficult dilemma. As at the fourth of May, 27 million people (more than half of all adults) were being paid by the state, 6.3 million through the furlough scheme, with others claiming benefits, having become unemployed because of the virus. The remainder were public sector workers and pensioners. Rishi Sunak, the chancellor, admitted that this cost was not sustainable, and that Britain must get back to work.

On the 10 May, there was some relaxation of the lockdown rules. Under this new guidance:

- anyone who cannot work at home should go to work providing the workplace is open,
- people can now meet family and friends from outside their household provided they remain outdoors and sit side-by-side two metres apart.

However, to my surprise, the document did not change the status of the over 70s who (as in my case) do not need to be shielded from society. As a clinically vulnerable group, they were advised to continue to stay at home and minimise contact with those outside the household. This advice stopped short of "formal shielding", a programme for the clinically vulnerable people.

There were claims that the new lockdown rules were confusing and contradictory. However, Boris Johnson defended the strategy with the response that one should "use good solid British common sense".

With the number of UK deaths from the Coronavirus falling (although in excess of any other European country), and the increasing concerns regarding the economy, the government is understandably trying to cautiously ease the lockdown, with the first openings of schools from 1 June, and of shops and shopping centres from 15 June – provided, in both cases, there is adherence to stipulated rules. It has also been announced that before July more concessions are expected, possibly including pubs, restaurants, hair salons, etc.

However, new quarantine requirements introduced in early June, for arrivals from certain countries, with fines for travellers if they fail to fill in online forms on entry, or decline to self-isolate for two weeks (at a time when many other countries are relaxing their entry requirements) are being strongly opposed by the travel industry and some other sectors. Against the background of the government having allowed over 18 million people to enter the UK without health checks and with just 273 being quarantined, between 1 January and 31 March 2020, it is not surprising that many opponents of the new regulations consider it to be a case of "closing the stable door after the horse has bolted".

I believe that as of 10 June, the prime minister has personally taken charge of the situation, which may be calmed by the introduction of "air bridges" in relation to some European destinations.

To date, the heroes of the pandemic have undoubtedly been the National Health Service (NHS) employees – doctors, nurses and other staff, who have been in the frontline of the battle against the virus, often working long hours and genuinely risking their lives. This particularly applied in the early stages, when there were shortages of personal protection equipment for their own use and a lack of essentials, such as ventilators, for treating patients.

The public gratitude for the dedication of these NHS people has been made very clear and, I believe, was important in helping to maintain their morale during a very difficult period.

It is always easy to be wise after the event but, at some stage in the future, there will (one hopes) be an opportunity to look back to determine the lessons which can be learned from events in recent months and to carry out "post-mortems" in respect of areas which appeared to go wrong.

The apparent lack of an action plan to be implemented in the case of a pandemic and the failure to hold (or be able to acquire) adequate supplies of essential equipment may be one matter for consideration. Another important area could be the decision to move hundreds of elderly patients (no longer requiring hospital level treatment) back to care homes without testing for Covid-19. This appears to have been reckless and, at least partly responsible for the high level of deaths of both residents and carers. It is claimed that Public Health England warned against the above actions on 24 February, but it was not until 15 April that the government published its Social Care Action Plan requiring every patient to be tested prior to discharge back to their care home.

Interestingly, Matt Hancock the health secretary, in an interview which was reported in the *Daily Telegraph* on 11 June, insisted that the government's handling of the pandemic in the UK's care homes (where 47% of the overall Covid-19 deaths in England and Wales between 1 March to 5 June took place) was "better than almost any other country in Europe."!

However, the following day's edition of the *Daily Telegraph* refers to a report by the National Audit Office which states that around 25,000 patients were discharged into care homes at the height of the pandemic between 17 March and 15 April without being tested, and that a third of care homes had experienced an outbreak of Covid-19 by the middle of May.

No doubt there will be good reasons for decisions taken under the pressures of the pandemic when actions made with the best intentions will sometimes have resulted in sad consequences. In my view, the important thing should not be to allocate blame, but try to learn from the situation and make plans to be better prepared for any similar situation in the future.

After the foregoing, generally depressing, paragraphs giving my impressions of the development and consequences of the Coronavirus in the period up to mid-June 2020, it is nice to be able to mention two events which, although minor in the scale of things, gave a little pleasure to many people.

On 15 April came the news of a 99-year-old army veteran by the name of Tom Moore, who thought it might be a good idea to get a little exercise by walking around his garden with his Zimmer frame to raise cash for NHS charities. Tom, who was born in Keighley, West Yorks, and served in the Duke of Wellington's Regiment in the Second World War, felt grateful to the NHS for treatment received for skin cancer and an operation to fix a broken hip. Therefore, he set himself the target of completing 100 laps around his garden (at the rate of 10 per day) before his 100-year birthday on 30 April, with the intention of raising £1,000.

Tom raised his target in just 24 hours, but money kept coming in and after one more day, with pledges on his Just Giving crowd funder page, it totalled more than £250,000.

By the time Tom had completed his 100 laps around the garden and reached his 100th birthday, he had raised £29 million for NHS charities and received 120,000 birthday cards. He became No. 1 in the pop charts with Michael Ball singing "You'll Never Walk Alone", was promoted to honorary colonel of his regiment and knighted by the Queen – not bad for an "old man from Yorkshire". You never know, there could be hope for me yet!

No doubt inspired by Tom Moore was another product of Yorkshire – nine-year-old Tobias Weller of Sheffield – nickname "Captain" in honour of the fundraiser supreme. Tobias, who suffers from cerebral palsy, completed his own walking marathon challenge near to his home in Beauchief, to fall into the arms of his mother on completion and raise £46,000 for Sheffield Children's Hospital and Paces School. He attracted support from stars like Olympic Gold medallist Dame Jessica Ennis-Hill and footballer Esme Morgan in the process.

As regards our private lives in these early months of the virus, Nicola's son Charles, with wife Veena and their new arrival Meera (born only on 6 January) had moved into Four Firs on maternity/paternity leave, having given up their rented accommodation in London. They were awaiting completion of a property purchase, for which their offer had been accepted, but was delayed while the vendors finalised an acquisition of their own. Sheila was, therefore, staying at Waterstones with Nicola and myself for this period.

Unfortunately, it was around this time, with the announcement of the Coronavirus pandemic and the increasing numbers of UK infections, that everything started to slow down. As regards property transactions, these almost came to a halt in the next few weeks following Boris Johnson's statement on 16 March with its wide-ranging restrictions on civil liberties, including the requirement for those of 70 years plus (such as Sheila and myself) to avoid social contact.

This latter requirement was strengthened to lockdown in a further statement on 23 March. Effectively, therefore, Sheila and I (together with Nicola, as a member of the household) have now been in some form of lockdown from 16 March to the present time (15 June), a period of 13 weeks, which still continues. There were minor relaxations of the rules on 10 May, but over 70s were advised to continue to stay at home and avoid contact with those outside their household.

Fortunately, Waterstones is well placed to comply with the requirements. The house is quite spacious with an ample garden, and easy access to the parklands of Cannon Hall and its adjacent fields and woodlands. It is a pleasure for us to take the daily exercise walk and observe the ducks and geese, with their newly born offspring, and to watch the herons catching their prey. However, I feel sorry for those millions of people in lockdown who reside in built-up areas.

As regards food and provisions, we are able to phone or email our requirements to Cannon Hall Farm shop, or to Hillary or Andrew, the proprietors of Cawthorne Village Store, from whom we have received excellent service with free deliveries throughout the lockdown. In addition, the efficient young woman who would normally visit us a couple of times per week for cleaning and gardening (but is now unable to enter the house), has shopped for us when necessary at the major food stores. She has also devoted additional time to gardening (in liaison with Nicola), with the result that the garden is better kept than at any time I can remember.

Nicola is an excellent cook and ensures that we have a variety of dishes to suit our various tastes – although we tend to eat at different times. Sheila takes an early evening meal, which she sometimes prepares herself. She is the first to retire for the night, but the earliest riser. Nicola is the second one to have an evening meal (but appears to follow with later snacks!). I eat quite frugally during the day, but dine very well in the evening, usually around 8pm. Nicola retires at various times depending upon programmes on TV (which we usually watch together) or how tired she feels. I seem to need less sleep than the others and rarely head for the bedroom until the early hours of the morning. All this may sound rather disjointed, but it works quite well.

As regards household chores, without the usual cleaner, we have all taken a share but with Nicola having the main role. She has also displayed hidden skills as hairdresser, chiropodist, beautician and general factotum. However, I believe that I have the worst jobs, as operator of the main vacuum cleaner and person in charge of bins. I am also the most efficient "stacker" of pots and pans in the dishwasher. These are not roles I had planned for my retirement.

One major benefit of the lockdown for Nicola and Sheila is the opportunity to see more of adorable little Meera in these early months of her life. However, for myself, the opposite situation applies with regard to my grandsons. At this time of the year, planning for the next visit to Australasia would normally be in process, but in the current circumstances it is difficult to envisage when (or even if) a trip is likely. Of course, we Facetime Nigel and the boys each week, but this is a very poor substitute for being with them.

With the continuing restrictions placed upon people in my age group, the likelihood of stringent travel and entry rules when flights recommence, and the possible higher costs made necessary from "distancing" and insurance, I find this a most depressing situation.

However, at least the average UK daily deaths from the Coronavirus appear to be falling. One can only hope that this continues and the famous words of Winston Churchill in November 1942, following the Battle of Egypt, will also apply in this case –

"This is not the end. It is not even the beginning of the end. But it is, perhaps, the end of the beginning."

XIX

Interesting Experiences

In the concluding paragraph of Chapter XVI, in which I referred to events attended when serving as a non-executive director, I commented that there had been several other experiences, with little relevance to business activities, which may also be worth mentioning. These remained in my memory because of the interesting people encountered and the iconic nature of some of the venues at which they took place.

One of the earliest of these experiences (although quite low key) was an opportunity in February 2002, which Sean Mahon had set up, for us to tour the Houses of Parliament. Our guide and host, Lord Roger Freeman (a corporate finance specialist in the consultancy department of PWC) had served as a Member of Parliament before his elevation to the Lords. Consequently, he had access to both Houses. We found that Roger had a deep knowledge of the history, traditions and paintings, which made our visit particularly interesting and enjoyable.

After the tour, Roger entertained us for drinks in the Houses of Parliament bar, followed by dinner, at which I believe we were joined by Philip Kendall, a director of the investment bank, Hill Samuel. It was the perfect end to the evening.

In March 2002, I was contacted by Alderman & Sheriff Michael Savory of the City of London to see if I would like to join the judges of the Central Criminal Court, the Old Bailey, for luncheon and, if of interest, stay on to attend a court afterwards.

I was unaware that the City of London Alderman have a responsibility for the criminal courts when in session, and that one of their tasks is to obtain suitable luncheon guests to provide conversation for the "entertainment" of the judges, who are not allowed to discuss the cases in which they are involved.

I was pleased to accept the invitation, which I felt would be interesting and, as instructed, duly arrived at the Lord Mayor's Entrance of the Old Bailey at 12.30 on the 25 April, to be received by Mr Savory and one other Alderman, for pre-lunch drinks. Shortly afterwards we were joined by the 15 judges, who (so far as I could tell) drank only water! Luncheon commenced without delay, in order to be concluded promptly at 2.00pm, so that the judges could return to their courts.

In view of the limited time available, the judges dined in their wigs and full court regalia. The only exception being one judge, wearing a lounge suit, whose case, apparently, involved several juveniles.

In addition to myself, there were three other guests:

- Dr Josef Baxa, first deputy minister of justice – Czech Republic, vice chairman of the Regional Court in Plzen and author or co-author of several legal books and publications,
- Miss Vackova, interpreter for Dr Baxa; and
- Sir Peter Davis, chairman of Sainsbury's Supermarkets, previously group chief executive of Prudential plc and a non-executive director of Boots, Cadbury Schweppes, Granada and BSB and the holder of numerous other prestigious City appointments.

However, despite this impressive gathering, conversation was entertaining and quite lighthearted. One of the judges, seated across the table from myself, was a Liverpudlian, so at least I had someone with whom to discuss football. I greatly enjoyed the experience, which was not what I had expected, and hope that the judges returned to their afternoon duties suitably relaxed and refreshed.

In December 2003, I received a letter from Sir Michael Perry, GBE, who had accepted an invitation to become chairman of the Olympic Appeal to British Industry. He explained in his letter that, although the British Olympic Association's plans for sending a team to Athens for the Games in August 2004 were well advanced, the government provided no funding for this purpose and everything depended upon the success of an appeal, which was relaunched every four years.

As with previous years, Sir Michael's proposal was "to invite a number of prominent personalities to join an Appeal Council, the members of which would, in turn, be asked to approach a small number of business leaders who were well known to them."

Sir Michael promised that there would be no council meetings to attend (but several fundraising events which should be of interest). He hoped, therefore, that I would feel able to join the Appeal Council and attend the launch of the appeal by Her Royal Highness, The Princess Royal (President of the British Olympic Association – the BOA) to be held at the Savoy Hotel on 5 February 2004.

I had always taken a close interest in the Olympic Games (I remember my school homework suffered in 1948 when I was glued to the radio) and the prospect of joining the council was attractive. However, I wished to have more information as to what was expected from members, and also to obtain the views of my executive board colleagues at Cattles and SIG (of which companies I was chairman) before accepting.

In a subsequent letter from Sir Michael, I found that the approach would be for council members to nominate 15 to 20 business contacts, who they would be willing to approach for a donation. However, to ensure that no one was contacted by more than one council member, the BOA would "re-confirm" the list before actual approaches were made. The target for each council member would be to raise £20,000 and experience had shown that the approach to nominated contacts was made easier if the council member (or their organisation) had already made a commitment to contribute. This seemed more demanding than simply joining the council, but I was not deterred.

I spoke to my executive board colleagues at Cattles and was pleased to find the unanimous feeling that for me to become a member of the Council, which would include distinguished City individuals from several prestigious organisations, could help lift the profile and status of Cattles itself. Consequently, they would be happy for me to become involved and would support Cattles committing to a donation of £10,000 towards the appeal.

Very encouraged by this reaction, I next consulted the executive directors of SIG. I was pleased that their response was similar to that of the Cattles directors, with the promise of a donation of £5,000.

Having obtained the support of my colleagues and the promise of donations, which would guarantee £15,000 towards a £20,000 target, I contacted Sir Michael and confirmed that I would be pleased to become a member of the council. I also informed him that in discussions with nominated contacts, it could be disclosed that Cattles plc had already pledged a donation of £10,000.

As regards the list of nominated business contacts to be approached for donations, I consulted with Sean Mahon and we produced the suggested 15 names. After review by the BOA, this was reduced to 12. Sean and I then decided which people on the revised list each of us would contact and 10 out of the 12 (which included Cattles and SIG) made donations to reach a total sum of £22,525. This was respectably in excess of the £20,000 target and Sean's help had been invaluable.

If anyone is interested, the members of the Appeal Council, together with their companies or organisations, are shown in the Official Olympic Report on the 2004 Games. Membership totalled 45 individuals, including 8 Lords, 15 Knights, Lord Mayor of the City of London and many other distinguished figures (I wondered who had suggested my name?).

In addition to the monies raised through members' targets, several fundraising events were held in the build-up to the Games and I comment upon these below. In total, over £1 million was raised by the council in support of Team GB, which was acknowledged as having "really made a difference". The Games had become extremely competitive, as illustrated by Simon Clegg (chief executive of BOA) in his subsequent "Chef de Mission's" report which disclosed that 0.545 of a second was the cumulative difference between five of Team GB's gold medals and what would otherwise have been silver medals.

As regards fundraising events initiated or supported by the Appeal Council in the build-up to the 2004 Games, the first was a reception, at the Savoy Hotel on 5 February 2004. We had gathered for cocktails, together with many distinguished guests, at 6.30pm and awaited the arrival of the Princess Royal, who had agreed to launch the appeal. While waiting, I had met Duncan Goodhew, the swimmer and 100 metre breaststroke gold medallist in the 1980 Olympics and found him to be an interesting and very likeable person. Deep in conversation, we failed to notice that the Princess had joined the event and was being escorted towards the microphone. However, in passing, she recognised Duncan, her fellow Olympian (possibly from his bald head!) and said, "Good evening Duncan." Caught unawares, Duncan turned and stuttered, "Oh, good evening, Your Majesty." Smiling, the Princess said, "I think you have got that wrong, Duncan."

The incident reminded me of my first meeting with the Princess Royal, some years earlier, at a reception given by the Royal Bank of Scotland at the Queens Hotel in Leeds. In company with one of the bank's important customers, we were standing on crosses, chalked on the floor near to the entrance of the banqueting room, so that we could be immediately found and "casually" introduced to the Princess on her arrival.

I was the first to be introduced as "the senior local partner of Cooper Brothers & Co" and I think that the Princess said something like, "Oh, the accountants." She was next introduced to my colleague, who informed her that he "farmed in Yorkshire to the north of Leeds." The Princess said, "Do you keep horses?" With his answer of, "Yes, ma'am," I realised that my opportunity for further conversation had ended!

On 27 May 2004, the main fundraising event of the Appeal Council – the Gala Dinner and Auction – was held in the wonderful facilities of Sotheby's in New Bond Street. Several Olympic Gold Medallists attended to give their support, including Steve Redgrave (chairman of the Appeal), Lord Sebastian Coe and Duncan Goodhew. Also present was Martin Bayfield, the England rugby lock-forward, who later in the proceedings made a very amusing after-dinner speech.

Sotheby's had generously made the whole of their premises and facilities available for the function free of charge and, prior to dinner, there was the opportunity to visit the "Galleries" to view their collection of Modern British Art, which included works by Spencer, Munnings, Lowry and many others.

At the dinner, council members acted as "table hosts". In addition to Nicola and myself, Cattles table included James Corr (finance director) and his wife Brenda, Mark Collins (treasury and risk director) and wife, Lis, together with our guests, Nick Donald (HSBC) and Alison, and Geoffrey and Lois Pelham-Lane. Geoffrey was the founder and managing director of Financial Dynamics.

Sir John Beckwith made a speech of welcome to the guests, explaining the purpose of the council, with the objective of ensuring that the athletes of Team GB were able to compete on equal terms with the best in the world.

Following the dinner, Henry Wyndham, chairman of Sotheby's (at 6ft 6in, almost the height of Martin Bayfield!) conducted the auction. The items were mainly of a sporting nature and generally impressive. For example:

- A three-day package for four people at the British Grand Prix at Silverstone as guests of the British Racing Drivers Club. Racing to be watched from the club grandstand with meals and refreshments taken in the exclusive Club House,
- A place in the 4-man bobsleigh with Team GB as they trained for the Winter Games, staying with the team in their accommodation in Austria. The successful bidder would join three team members in the bobsleigh for a full run. The prize included flights, transfers, accommodation, equipment and insurance for two people, both of whom could take part in a bobsleigh run,
- A day with five-times Olympic Champion, Steve Redgrave, joining Steve and two other rowers on the Thames as a passenger in the coxless 4, followed by lunch: and,
- A visit to the 2004 Olympic Games as a guest of Team GB. A three-night package for two people at the 4-star Mare Nostrum Hotel in Athens. The package included seeing the

rowing finals, the 100 metre men's track final and lunch or dinner with Team GB athletes.

Bidding for any of the above would have been beyond my means (or at least, more than I could reasonably afford). I entered the bidding for one other item, an England rugby shirt, signed by the 2003 World Cup winning squad, but was unsuccessful. A novelty item was a pair of boots (to be suitably personalised for the successful bidder) comprised of Jonny Wilkinson's left foot and David Beckham's right foot!

It was an interesting and enjoyable evening and very successful in raising monies for the appeal.

The final event, before the Games commenced, took place on 13 July 2004, and was "a small private dinner for council members who have been particularly supportive of the appeal". This was held in the Chinese Dining Room of Buckingham Palace and was attended by the Princess Royal. I do not know the criteria for falling into membership of the above group but was delighted to be included. As the evening was intended to be "relaxed and informal", dress was lounge suits.

My only previous visits to Buckingham Palace had been simply to pass through in order to attend garden parties, and it was interesting to be able to gain an impression of its size and splendour.

Following completion of the Games in August 2004, a formal dinner was held at the Mansion House to celebrate Team GB's performance (they had won 30 medals of which 9 were gold). Members of the Appeal Council were guaranteed a medallist (together with spouse or partner) to join their table for the dinner, after these successful competitors had been announced to the assembled company. The name of the Olympian who would be joining each table was not disclosed in advance.

In addition to Nicola and myself, the Cattles plc table of 10 included Mark and Lis Collins, James Wight (of our brokers) and his wife, Ann, and Nick Marshall (from our investment bankers) with his wife, Jill. It was an excellent and friendly group of people. James Wight, I had known for many years, as he was the son of my good friend and former C&L partner, Robin. We awaited announcement of the medallist who, with partner, would join us. This proved to be cyclist Bradley Wiggins (gold medal winner in the Individual Pursuit) accompanied by his wife, Cath. Both were charming people and fitted well into our party. I know that Nicola, seated next to Bradley, particularly enjoyed her conversations with him.

If one moves ahead, by 2012 Bradley Wiggins had become Sir Bradley, the first ever British winner of the Tour de France, holder of seven Olympic medals and, I believe, voted TV Sports Personality of the Year.

The 2004 Games having been held and the Appeal Council having served its purpose, I assumed that my involvement with the BOA was at an end. However, in 2005, I was contacted to see if Cattles would support a fundraising event at the London Guild Hall on 4 October, at which the Princess Royal would again be present. I was still chairman of Cattles at the time and we agreed to take a table for 10, which number included an Olympic guest and partner, the identity of whom would not be revealed in advance.

On this occasion, our "surprise" Olympian was Duncan Goodhew, with whom I had become quite friendly, so, perhaps, it was not such a surprise after all! I know that Nicola had been hoping that it would be Duncan. They shared an interest in dyslexia and she wanted to discuss her dyslexia website with him.

It was another enjoyable evening and financially successful for BOA in raising over £100,000, which was used in providing "elite level service for future Olympic athletes".

My last (and rather unexpected) contact with BOA came on 2 October 2007. By this time I had completed my period of service as chairman of Cattles but, partly I think because of my previous involvement, the company had taken a table for eight people for the Olympic Gold Ball at the National History Museum and invited Nicola and myself to join the party.

The event was again being held in the presence of the Princess Royal but was supported by the attendance of 41 Olympians from various Games over the years, including such luminaries as Steve

Redgrave, Seb Coe, Mary Peters, Matthew Pinsent, Lynn Davies and Kelly Holmes.

I had not previously visited the museum and was impressed by the ornate architecture of the building and its internal range of galleries and halls, commencing with the vaulted central hall, where "Dippy", the 105-foot-long replica of a *Diplodocus* skeleton dinosaur, was on display, a copy of the real fossil in the Carnegie Museum in Pittsburgh, USA. I believe that Dippy was replaced by "Hope" in 2017, the genuine skeleton of a blue whale, which now hangs from the ceiling.

In addition to Nicola and myself, the Cattles table included my previously mentioned friends and former colleagues – James and Brenda Corr, and Mark and Lis Collins, but also David Postings, the recently appointed chief executive of Cattles, who had succeeded Sean Mahon. David was not accompanied and Nicola's friend, Virginia Walker (who was working in London at the time) completed the party.

Attendance at the event was in excess of 330 people, accommodated on 22 tables of various sized parties. Proceedings commenced at 7pm with a champagne reception, which was followed by dinner and dancing. Presentation of the evening's events was by BBC's Hazel Irvine and Olympic medallist Steve Cram and there was a piano bar in a separate location, which continued until 1am.

I was delighted to be back with my former Cattles colleagues, with whom, by necessity, I had spent many evenings in London over the years, when dealing with banks and institutions.

As I move towards the end of this chapter, another event, which I think worth mentioning, was not in London. This was a dinner held on 3 September 2004 at Harewood House (home of the Lascelles family since 1760s), situated in 100 acres of gardens north of Leeds and one of my favourite stately homes. The invitation to Nicola and myself had come from Sir Timothy Kitson (who was attending with his wife, Sally). Tim appeared to be organising the event on behalf of his old colleague, the former prime minister, Sir John Major, who would be accompanied by his wife, Norma, and be speaking at the event.

Attendance totalled about 20 to 24 people, comprised mainly of chairmen or chief executives of Yorkshire companies, together with their spouses. I was privileged to be seated next to Norma Major, who was delightful and had an interesting and amusing fund of anecdotes. John Major spoke well and passionately. It was not a political speech, but concerned his commitment to the Hope and Homes for Children charity, which worked alongside governments and civil society organisations in several countries in Central and Eastern Europe and Africa, to dismantle orphanage-based care systems and move children back into family-based care. Cattles was subsequently pleased to make a donation in support of the charity. It was an enjoyable occasion.

Moving several years ahead, I was pleased (and surprised) to receive a letter, dated 4 March 2015, from David Cameron, the prime minister, thanking me for the voluntary work which I carried out. I found that this followed a letter he had received from Bob Dyson, a former deputy chief constable of the county and the current chairman of Boys & Girls Clubs of South Yorkshire.

In May 2017, I was even more delighted to be informed that I was to be appointed a Member of the Order of the British Empire (MBE) in the 2017 Birthday Honours List. This honour followed the submission of a nomination (together with numerous supporting documents) by Sean Mahon, my friend and colleague over many years.

The documents included letters from Sir Norman Adsetts and Gordon Bridge (who are mentioned in these memoirs in chapters XVI and XVII respectively) and also from:

- Mark Brine, general manager of Boys & Girls Clubs of South Yorkshire,
- Philip Bartey, group chief executive of Autism Plus; and,
- Robert Rabone, chief financial officer, of the University of Sheffield.

I was very grateful to all of the above for the help they provided to Sean.

The presentation of my award took place at Buckingham Palace on 7 December 2017. Three guests were allowed to attend the ceremony, and in my case, these were Nicola, my stepdaughter Sophie, and Nigel, who came from Australia especially for the event.

Nicola, Sophie and I travelled to London by car the previous day, meeting Nigel at the Goring Hotel where we were all staying. We were driven to London by Ian Staniforth, whose services I used quite often. Ian stayed the night in London with friends, so that he was available to transport us the short distance to the Palace the next day and, in due course, take us back to Yorkshire.

On arrival at the Palace, I was directed into a room containing other award recipients, while the remainder of our party took seats in the chamber where the ceremony was to be held. As one might expect, everything was well organised, musicians were playing and various military types taking up positions. In due course, Prince Charles arrived, flanked on both sides by equerries, and commenced the handing out of awards.

The procedure for recipients was to march into the room, halt on reaching the Prince, turn to face him, make a slight bow, take two steps forward, enter into brief conversation and, still facing the Prince, take two steps back, make another slight bow, turn and exit the room in the opposite direction from that of arrival.

It was during the brief conversation with the Prince that he would hang the award on a small hook, which had been placed in position on the recipient's clothing by an equerry just before entry to the chamber. Prince Charles was obviously well practiced in this procedure, which he carried out quite surreptitiously, to the extent that, when I looked up after my farewell bow, on noticing that the Prince had a medal in his hand, I momentarily thought that it must be mine and took a half step forward! The equerry said, "No, no, you have had your turn."

I had hoped that no one had noticed this minor faux pas, but the first thing Nigel said (grinning like a Cheshire cat) when we met after the ceremony was, "I could have died laughing when you tried to go back for another medal."

By the time we were leaving the Palace, the weather had deteriorated, and it was raining quite heavily. Official photographers were available in the foyer but use of private cameras was allowed only in the courtyard. Fortunately, there was a covered area of "no man's land" outside the entrance to the Palace which we made use of for additional photographs. Ian was on hand with the car and we returned to the Goring. I had reserved a table for lunch and insisted that Ian should join us – although, disciplined as always, he drank only water.

After lunch, we bade goodbye to Nigel, who was meeting up with his mother to spend a couple of days before returning to Australia. Nicola, Sophie and I boarded the car, but this was where the mistake of the day occurred. Sophie had decided to stay a few days with Charles at an apartment he was renting south of the Thames. Nicola had arranged with Ian that he would take us across the river to drop off Sophie before we returned to Yorkshire.

Travelling south of the river, late in the afternoon, only to return north again, proved to be bad news and we should probably have sent Sophie by taxi, but it seemed too late to start making changes.

I could write many pages on the problems we encountered, starting with traffic delays and congestion south of the river, aggravated by the closure of one of the road bridges following an accident. Back on the M1, Ian's car broke down (only days after it had been serviced), necessitating Nicola and myself abandoning the vehicle (for safety). We were left standing on the hard shoulder for almost one hour (I was still wearing my morning suit and Nicola was dressed in her Palace finery), while waiting in the rain for a taxi from Leicester. Farther north on the M1, we were brought to a standstill for a time as the rain turned to heavy snow.

We eventually arrived home in the early hours of the morning and I gave the taxi driver a good tip – which he deserved. Despite everything, I was still in high spirits. It was a day to remember.

XX

Sheffield United FC

My father first took me to Bramall Lane to see Sheffield United when I was about six or seven years old. This was probably the time when I became a Blade, which I remain these 80 plus years later. In the above days, Bramall Lane (currently the world's oldest football stadium which is still in use as a professional match venue) was a three-sided ground with viewing from the Spion Kop or Terrace (both for standing spectators only), or from seats in the wooden stand. On the fourth side of the ground, some distance back, was the cricket pavilion, leaving plenty of space alongside the football pitch for the roped-off cricket strips which, in season, had been used by Sheffield Cricket Club since 1855, and where the Yorkshire County Team played one or two games each year.

At the age of 87, I still support Sheffield United and have season tickets for the stand (now on the side of the ground where the pavilion used to be). I attend most games, although, for the occasional midweek fixture, in the winter with an 8pm kick-off and a 15 mile drive each way, I sometimes make the cowardly choice to remain at home and watch sport on TV.

I suppose that few readers will be interested in hearing about Sheffield United, even though we are now a Premier League Club. However, for these memoirs, there was one traumatic period in the history of the Blades in which I was involved and consider worth mentioning, even if only for my own satisfaction.

In January 1996, Reg Brearley, chairman of Sheffield United Football Club Ltd (SU) sold his 60% shareholding to Manchester-based Texas Holdings plc (Texas), in which company A.M. McDonald held a very substantial financial interest. McDonald replaced Brearley as chairman of SU and immediately appointed his associate, Charles Green, as chief executive.

Green soon began taking decisions which appeared beyond his expected remit – including running the SU first team itself! This led to unrest amongst supporters and staff. The situation deteriorated even further when Green sacked popular manager, Dave Basset, only to become embroiled in a dispute over compensation. Howard Kendall, a former Everton and England international footballer, was appointed as successor to Basset but remained only briefly, his assistant, Nigel Spackman, taking over the role. However, Spackman resigned in March 1998, citing interference in team affairs by Green and players being sold without any consultation.

In the same month, the dissatisfaction of supporters with the way SU was being run came to a head when, following a 1–0 defeat by Ipswich at Bramall Lane, 1,000 fans gathered in the car park to confront Green and McDonald. Shortly after this demonstration, McDonald resigned, with Green following several weeks later.

Kevin McCabe became executive chairman of SU, and supporters were pleased to see a genuine Blade in control. On 18 December 1996, during the above-mentioned "reign" of McDonald, an offer (the SU Offer) was received by shareholders of SU on behalf of another Manchester-based company, Conrad plc (Conrad), for the acquisition of the entire ordinary and original share capital which comprised:

- 2,883 ordinary shares of £500 each; and
- 477 original shares of £100 each

For information only, SU shareholders also received a copy of a second Offer document, which was being sent from Conrad to its own shareholders, with details of the above SU Offer together with a Proposed Placing and Open Offer for 20,840,000 new Conrad shares at 60p per share.

The SU Offer included a letter from McDonald stating that the directors supported the takeover by Conrad, having been advised by investment bank, Singer & Friedlander (S & F), and unanimously recommended shareholders to accept the SU Offer as they and related trusts, associated companies and certain others, had irrevocably undertaken to do in respect of their holdings.

The above documents had been posted to SU shareholders on 18 December 1996, but (by accident or design?) were delayed in the Christmas mail and not delivered until 31 December. As acceptances were required "no later than 13 January 1997", this substantially reduced the time for shareholders to consider the Offer.

In view of the size of the transaction, trading in Conrad shares was being suspended and, together with the proposed new shares, would be relisted on the London Stock Exchange on 16 January. The name of Conrad would be changed to Sheffield United plc.

On receipt of the SU Offer, the holders of original shares, which in the past had changed hands at prices well in excess of those for ordinary shares, were shocked to find that the consideration for an original share would be only one-fifth of that being offered for an ordinary share.

This massive difference in value appeared to result from the exclusion of two benefits and rights, which had previously been enjoyed by the original shareholder, but had not been included in the terms of the Offer from Conrad. These were:

- Firstly, a free season ticket for a seat in the stand, which benefit had existed for original shareholders for at least 50 years. The Articles of Association gave the SU directors discretion to "suspend or vary this privilege", and it came as no surprise to me that, under McDonald's chairmanship, it was being removed.
- Secondly, the right of one vote per share, regardless of class. Until 1982, when new Articles of Association were adopted, the above right had not been in doubt and still appeared to exist under the wording in the 1996 audited accounts. However, in the 1982 Articles, it was stated that ordinary and original shares "rank equally in all respects in proportion to their respective nominal values". On the basis of this wording, nominal values had been taken into account in computing the consideration being put forward for the

two classes of shares in the SU Offer. This treatment was strongly contested by the original shareholders (of which I was one).

On the basis of the above, and assuming a value of 60p for each Conrad share, the SU Offer could be summarised as follows:

Class of Shares	Number in Issue	Offer per share (£)	Total Consideration (£)
Ordinary	2,883	3,324.00	9,583,092
Original	477	664.80	317,109

As the directors of SU with their related trusts, associated companies, etc., owned 91.33% of the ordinary shares, but only 1.68% of the original shares, it was not difficult to see which category of shareholders would be the beneficiaries from the decisions which had been made in formulating the SU Offer.

At this point, I was contacted by William Beckett, an original shareholder and Sheffield businessman, who I knew socially. He suggested that we call an informal meeting of original shareholders to discuss the SU Offer. A meeting was duly held and very well attended, with the outcome of three people (the Representatives) being appointed to deal with the SU Board in order to express the concerns of the original shareholders and question the validity of certain aspects of the SU Offer.

The three Representatives were William, myself and Paul Southern, my friend and former C&L partner, specialising in corporate finance. I recognised that we would also require legal advice and Michael Jelly, an experienced commercial lawyer, agreed to assist – even though I warned him that we may not be able to pay any fee! Michael's help proved most valuable.

Shortly after appointment, the Representatives contacted the London Stock Exchange, the Panel of Takeovers & Mergers, the Department for Trade and Industry, the Football Association and the Football League, in connection with our concerns on the

Offers and requesting advice or preferably intervention to delay proceedings and provide more time for investigation. None of these bodies felt able to become involved in any way and (probably for the first time) I recognised how difficult it is for minority shareholders (with little financial resources) to make an effective challenge to the actions of management with a controlling interest.

The next step was for me to speak to the director at S&F, who had advised the directors of SU and enabled them to express the opinion that the Offers were "fair and reasonable". I informed him of my particular concerns that the voting rights of shareholders, which had been assumed in the documents, were incorrect. Understandably, his response was guarded, but it appeared that S&F had relied largely on the interpretation of the solicitors to the Offers on the wording in the 1982 Articles. I informed him of my understanding that it would have required a separate General Meeting of the original shareholders to approve the 1982 Articles, in order for any change to be made in their class rights. I said that from my enquiries (which included contact with the company secretary of SU), I had found no evidence that such a meeting had been held. Therefore, I felt that he should consider this matter together with the SU directors.

Arising from the above conversation, over the next week or so, in the run-up to the relisting of Conrad shares on 16 January 1997, I had two meetings with directors of SU. The first was attended by McDonald and the second by Green, and representatives from S&F were present on both occasions. I again expressed my concerns on the terms of the Offers and particularly the validity of the voting rights which had been assumed. However, in the absence of firm proof that no class meeting had been held, I could make no progress in delaying events to allow for further consideration. I had hoped that S&F might withdraw the advice they had given to the SU Board, but they used this uncertainty and the previously mentioned views of the solicitors not to do so.

On 17 January 1997 (sadly, the day after the relisting), I climbed a ladder and spent one hour in the dusty loft of an elderly SU shareholder's house. He had contacted me to say that the documents relating to the EGM, at which the 1982 Articles of

Association had been considered, may be stored there. Eureka! I discovered the letter which had accompanied the notice of the meeting and this stated – "there is no variation of the Class Rights of Shares". This information, which seemed to confirm the views of the Representatives on voting rights, was conveyed to S&F by Michael Jelly without delay.

On 20 January, I met with two SU directors, who were accompanied by three people from S&F (which organisation now seemed more concerned) and a partner from Hammond Suddards, the solicitors providing advice to Conrad on the Offers. Neither McDonald nor Green were able to attend the meeting! I again made it clear that the Representatives of the original shareholders were strong in their views that the Offers were incorrect in several respects and particularly with regards to the voting rights of the two classes of shares. However, unsurprisingly, in the absence of McDonald, there was no formal acceptance of these views by the SU directors.

Little happened with regard to our protests over the next few weeks, in which period, the various parties presumably considered their positions. A major problem for us was that Conrad's Offer to SU shareholders had inevitably been accepted by virtually all the ordinary shareholders, but also by over half of the original shareholders. Consequently, Conrad had been relisted and become the holding company of SU and renamed Sheffield United plc. The remaining original shareholders (even with equal voting rights to ordinary shareholders) would constitute only a very small minority group in SU with little influence.

The Representatives discussed the position with Michael Jelly, including the possibility of taking legal action. Although we did not immediately dismiss the idea, it was recognised that it could be a difficult case to pursue, time-consuming and expensive. Furthermore, there would be a need to find some source of funding. The ideal would have been an investigation by a regulatory body, but from earlier contacts, there seemed a negligible chance of this.

At some stage in this period, the SU directors contacted us and came up with the proposal that, in addition to the Offer terms for the original shares (and without any admission that these were defective) they would be prepared to provide a free season ticket for each original shareholder for a seat in the stand for the next 25 years. This entitlement (reduced for the value of certain benefits which had already been taken) would also be granted to the former original shareholders who had already accepted the Offer. The directors also agreed that they would pay any legal costs incurred by the Representatives, which (in the main) was a fee for Michael Jelly.

We were somewhat hurried into making a decision when it was announced that the Offers, which had been extended to allow for any late acceptances, were to close on 20 June 1997. However, by this stage, we had already decided to recommend acceptance of the Offer, together with the additional benefit of a free stand seat. After all, we were Blades and the proposed loss of our regular seat in the stand (now effectively to be reversed for 25 years) had been a greater issue for many of us than the price at which we could dispose of our small shareholdings. Consequently, we called a meeting on 17 June of the remaining original shareholders and expressed our views. Inevitably, a few diehards considered that we should continue to fight for a better deal, but the bulk of attenders supported acceptance of these amended terms and our duties came to an end.

Dealing with the above matter had been an interesting experience. I could not remember any previous time of being on the side of the "little men", against someone with such complete control as was held by McDonald in this case. I think it was inevitable from the start that, unless the "professional advisors" had been prepared to withdraw their opinions, when new information was emerging, we would eventually be defeated. However, I felt that we had put up a good fight and won an important concession. I also considered that the press publicity, relating to our opposition to the SU Board, had added to the general discontent of the fans with the way in which the club was being run, which had resulted in the departure of McDonald and Green in March 1998.

I made no effort to track the actions of either McDonald or Green after they had departed from SU. However, from 2012, for the next three years or so, Green's name was mentioned quite regularly on BBC Sport and BBC News, particularly in connection with his role in leading a consortium, which acquired Scottish football club, Rangers, together with its assets, out of administration. On 3 September 2015, an article in the *Daily Telegraph*, under the heading "Rangers pair charged" reported that: "Former Rangers owner Craig Whyte and chief executive Charles Green have been charged with serious organised crimes offences in relation to the alleged fraudulent acquisition of the club in 2012. They have been given bail, but no date has been set yet for their next court appearance."

I did not see any subsequent articles or hear any reports regarding the above matter and have no idea how it ended.

Postscript

On the 2 September 2020, an article appeared in the *Times* under the heading: "Wrongly prosecuted ex-Rangers boss Charles Green seeks £20 million and an enquiry." The article commented as follows:

"A former chief executive of Glasgow Rangers is to seek £20 million in damages and will call for an enquiry after Scotland's most senior law officer admitted that he should never have been prosecuted.

"Charles Green (67) was arrested five years ago over the "alleged fraudulent acquisition" of the club in 2012 but the prosecution was later abandoned.

"Yesterday it was announced that the businessman would receive a public apology from James Wolffe, QC, the lord advocate.

"Mr Green has maintained that the wrongful arrest and prosecution ruined his life, and the *Times* understands that he will seek damages in the region of £20m."

XXI

Miscellany

As I move towards the closure of these memoirs and look back on the events recorded and people mentioned, I feel that there is much more which could have been said. However, there has to be a limit. Therefore, in this chapter, I have merely picked up a few items which, on reflection, might conveniently have been included elsewhere.

Sir Henry (later, Lord) Benson

In earlier chapters, I have mentioned Henry Benson (HAB), the firm's senior partner at the time of my admission, and the doyen of the accountancy profession in his day. Quite recently, when going through some old papers, I found a copy of HAB's "Notes for a junior partner on joining the firm", which I believe had first been prepared in February 1968 and were sent to all new partners for several years thereafter.

Never one to skimp, HAB's notes (on foolscap-sized paper) comprised seven pages, plus another seven pages of "further notes", to which were attached four pages of appendices and two pages on the justifications for and charging of fees to clients (a subject which was always close to HAB's heart).

The notes included many words of wisdom and guidance for a wide range of situations, but always with the underlying message of a requirement to observe the high standards and principles which were expected of a CB&Co partner, who (in those days) was likely to serve in this role for the remainder of their working life. HAB acknowledged that his words may sound "priggish and pompous", but he made no apology for this. Personally, I found a re-reading of the notes a poignant reminder of 37 satisfying years, spent with talented and highly principled colleagues for whom I had great respect.

Certain recollections of working with HAB in my early years of partnership are still clear in my mind. Although he was always exacting (even demanding) in his requirements, I welcomed these experiences and felt that I learned a great deal.

On one occasion, which involved my review of a profits forecast, in my draft report, I used the word "anticipate". HAB informed me that "what I meant to say" was "expect"! I didn't argue but checked definitions in the Oxford dictionary afterwards – it was a close call but of course HAB was right.

Probably the largest assignment on which I provided support to HAB was the review of a feasibility study for a major rolling mill expansion at Park Gate Iron & Steel Co in Rotherham. The estimated capital cost was £100 million, which would be about 18 times higher in current day values. My draft report exceeded 200 pages and the Sheffield office typists stayed on until 9.30pm, with other staff remaining to call over each page as it was completed, so that I could take the document with me on the 7.20am "Master Cutler" Pullman train to London next day for my appointment with HAB.

I was pleased and relieved to find that HAB liked the report and also that I was able to answer any questions asked. However, in stating my sources of information for verifying the build-up of estimated costs, for one difficult category of items I had accepted "broad-based engineers estimates". HAB did not question my acceptance of this source, but disliked the description, which he considered sounded as if we had obtained the information from (in his words) "fat-arsed engineers"! He considered that a more appropriate wording would be "engineers broad-based estimates".

Readers can imagine the delight of the Sheffield office typists on my return (in these days before we had word processors) in having to retype numerous pages to change the words "broad-based engineers" to "engineers broad-based".

People

In previous chapters, I have mentioned meeting several interesting and sometimes famous (in their own fields) people. There were other occasions when such meetings were quite fleeting and occasionally (for me) embarrassing. On one occasion, shortly after I became a partner, Kath and I were invited to a function in support of the Prince's Trust. We felt honoured to be introduced to the Duke of Edinburgh and Prince Edward during pre-dinner drinks, shortly after which, guests were requested to go through to take up their seats in the dining room.

At this stage, some late arrivals from Sheffield (with whom we were quite friendly) appeared and, as we greeted each other, I was unaware that the Duke and Prince Edward were waiting for everyone to go through into the dining room before making their entrance. However, after a dig in my back, I turned to find the Duke, who, pointing to the dining room door, said, "Shouldn't you be going in there?"

Around this time, I also met Edward Heath (former prime minister and, until a few years before, leader of the Conservative Party). He had been speaking at a dinner held at the Queens Hotel in Leeds and, afterwards, was brought into the CB&Co entertaining room by Peter Schofield, chairman of family owned Schofields, the largest department store in Leeds at the time.

Mr Heath accepted "a small malt whisky" and I congratulated him on joining the board of the accountancy firm Arthur Anderson. A number of the other large firms were making similar appointments of prominent "non-accountant" business leaders to their boards, but CB&Co were being more cautious in this respect. I tried to make a joke by saying that we had thought of appointing Mike Yarwood (a talented and very popular impersonator at the time, appearing regularly on TV) to see what style of person would suit us best. However, I recognised immediately that this was an inappropriate quip, which I regretted as soon as I made it. Fortunately, Edward Heath seemed not to take any offence, but responded by telling a story of his own, which, although not very funny, put me at ease.

Many years later (in November 2009) I was contacted by Alan Young, my friend and the former senior tax partner in CB&Co's North East region. Alan was serving his year as president of one of the Sheffield Rotary Clubs and their annual dinner, which always had a strong charitable fundraising bias, was approaching. It was Alan's right to choose the charity which should benefit, and he kindly offered to select Boys and Girls Clubs of South Yorkshire (BGCSY) of which I was president.

Alan and I discussed a possible speaker for the event. Most of the affiliated BGCSY clubs were situated in depressed areas of the county and, after some consideration, we decided that if he could be persuaded, David Blunkett, MP for the Sheffield Brightside and Hillsborough constituency and a past holder of several important positions (including home secretary and secretary of work and pensions) in Tony Blair's Cabinet, would be ideal. Coming from one of Sheffield's most deprived districts and being blind from birth, we considered that David would be well aware of the difficulties and problems encountered by many of the young people the clubs tried to serve.

We telephoned David's constituency office and arranged to see him. It was a pleasant meeting and, after giving him a short briefing, he agreed to speak at the dinner. At the event, he made an excellent and humorous speech, which was perfect for the occasion and completely free from any political bias. We were very impressed.

These days David (now a Labour peer) writes a regular weekly article for the *Yorkshire Post*, which I always read and find knowledgeable and well balanced.

Two people I should probably have mentioned in Chapter XVII are Andrew and Sue Coombe. However, since 2015 when Andrew became the very busy and conscientious Lord Lieutenant of South Yorkshire, there have been limited opportunities to see them.

Andrew was my first articled clerk in 1964, when indentured service to a practising chartered accountant (together with passing the examinations) was necessary to qualify. I think that the original contact with Andrew had been through his father, who I believe was sales director of our client Spear & Jackson.

Even in these early years, Andrew was a confident and pleasant young man with the ability to "keep below the radar" where partners were concerned – not a talent possessed by all his contemporaries. However, I remember one occasion when he almost came unstuck. This followed a short period of secondment to our Cardiff office, in order to assist during their peak period.

I was with Ray Emmitt in his office when, following a knock on the door, our rather nervous cashier entered. He was bearing an expense voucher which he wondered if "one of us should approve!" The voucher was for a dinner, which Andrew and a colleague had enjoyed one evening when in Cardiff, at what must have been the most expensive restaurant in the city!

Not a person normally interested in approving expense vouchers for articled clerks, Ray, nevertheless, took an interest on this occasion and Andrew was duly summoned to appear before us. Ray had decided to give Andrew "enough rope to hang himself" and, after confirming that he had dined at home the previous evening, Ray's first question (without any mention of the expenses voucher) was "What did you have for dinner last night, Coombe?"

At this Andrew's face lit up and he proceeded to describe a four-course menu in detail (throwing in the names of a couple of expensive wines for good measure), which could not have been bettered at the Savoy.

I could sense that Ray felt that he was being outmanoeuvred, but he controlled his temper (just) and enquired, "Is that the sort of dinner that you have every evening?" "Oh no," said Andrew, "but my father was entertaining the company's director in charge of European operations, who was visiting head office."

"Get out," said Ray – unaccustomed to being defeated and feeling that he had wasted too much time already.

My subsequent enquiries indicated that there were some "mitigating circumstances" for Andrew's apparent excesses, but I thought it best not to bother mentioning the subject to Ray!

Cancer

Most of these memoirs have been concerned with my business or leisure-related activities, but one personal matter of significance, which I feel warrants mention, occurred in 2009. Since my days as chairman of Cattles, I had attended annually for a medical examination at the London Endocrine Centre in Harley Street.

In general, I am fit and healthy for my age but, in the above-mentioned year, tests identified low-grade cancer of the prostate. Although it was believed that this was confined to soft tissue, there were concerns regarding a possible leakage. Therefore, the required action was for three months of hormone treatment to shrink the cancer back into the prostate, followed by a course of "intensity modulated radiation therapy", which would take place every weekday over a period of seven and a half weeks.

Initially I was informed by the consultant, Dr Plowman, that the 7 ½ weeks of radiation treatment would need to be carried out under his supervision at St Bartholomew's Hospital in London. However, thankfully, it was found that it could be dealt with by one of his former colleagues, Dr Kirkbride, who was based in Sheffield and consultant to Weston Park Cancer Hospital.

I was warned that over the period of treatment, I would gradually become less well and should not expect to be able to drive myself to and from the hospital. I was reluctant to heed this advice, but Nicola took charge of the situation and acted as chauffeuse every day. This proved to be particularly helpful as, because of a shortage of parking places, there was usually a queue of cars waiting for vehicles to leave. Through Nicola's help, I was able to report for my appointment on time and leave her in the car to park and join me when possible. She was supportive throughout the ordeal and never complained.

To ensure that the radiation equipment could be accurately targeted, I was tattooed with a couple of dots either side of my prostate gland, and required to drink six glasses of water in the 30 minutes before a session, so that my bladder would always be full. Whenever I mention this, people seem to find it amusing, but it was no laughing matter for me, especially if (having drunk the water) there was a delay! A rush to the loo, with the hope that it was not in use, was always my first act after a session.

A particularly sad side to these visits to Weston Park was seeing many people who were clearly much worse off than myself.

One of these was a young boy of about eight or nine years, called Jack (the same as my own grandson), who was obviously very ill. He was there on several occasions when we were visiting and always brought tears to the eyes of Nicola. We can only hope that he recovered.

On completion of treatment, my PSA readings were monitored, initially six monthly and then annually, for a total period of five years, before I was discharged. The experience now seems like a bad dream. I have sometimes thought of discontinuing my annual visits to the London Endocrine Centre, which are expensive and rather inconvenient. However, Nicola has always felt that I should continue. She believes that the early diagnosis of my cancer saved my life.

XXII

Concluding Remarks

In a speech made by Winston Churchill in 1949, he commented:
"Writing a book is an adventure. To begin with it is a toy and an amusement. Then it becomes a mistress, then it becomes a master, then it becomes a tyrant. The last phase is that just as you are about to be reconciled to your servitude, you kill the monster and fling him about to the public."

I would not deem to compare my feeble efforts in these memoirs with the numerous and impressive literary contributions of Churchill, but I have sympathy with the sentiments he expresses and recognise that, in my case, the appropriate stage for closure has been reached.

Unfortunately, I will have to terminate the memoirs when there is still no conclusion in sight to the Covid-19 pandemic, which I discussed in Chapter XVIII. Although, in the three months since writing that chapter, progress has been made in the UK in containing the virus with, thankfully, a reduction in the death rate, outbreaks continue in various parts of the country. These are giving rise to the imposition of localised restrictions and lockdowns, while concerns exist that the coming winter months may see a further deterioration in the situation.

The actions taken to restrict the virus have resulted in massive damage to the economy and, as of 22 August 2020, Britain's national debt had surged past £2 trillion for the first time and reached 100.5 per cent of GDP, a level not seen since the 1960s. One can only await the next stage which, I fear, will be higher taxation and cuts in services.

Of course, the Covid-19 crisis applies worldwide. While New Zealand has fared well to date, major outbreaks are being experienced in Australia (to which country Nigel and family plan to return at the end of 2020) and, as in the case of the UK, these are giving rise to major economic problems.

On a personal basis, I find it depressing that there is no realistic prospect, at this time, of planning a future visit for Nicola and myself to see Nigel and family.

On a change of subject, as indicated in the Introduction to these memoirs, a main objective has been to give support to Nigel in ensuring that my grandsons gain some knowledge and pride in their British roots and heritage and (although not stated, but my own hope) that they find their grandfather had rather more spirit and ability than might be indicated by the "old man" who visits them each year. I accept that this latter mentioned hope might be something of a long shot.

Except possibly for Jack, it will probably be a few years before the boys will be old enough to read (and appreciate?) the memoirs, but hopefully there will be a few anecdotes, which will be useful for Nigel. However, writing is a poor alternative to the usual privilege of grandfathers for face-to-face indoctrination of their grandsons on important matters such as (in my case) Sheffield United and Yorkshire cricket teams.

On my last visit to Christchurch, Jack apologised to me saying that his favourite football team was now Manchester City! I felt that this must result from a dereliction of duty by Nigel, but it could have been worse – he might have become a "Wednesdayite".

In conclusion, I will resist any temptation to give words of advice to my grandchildren. They have excellent parents, who will continue to provide all necessary guidance. However, looking for the longer term, I will quote Confucius, "Choose a job you love, and you will never have to work a day in your life" – it worked for me.

With Cousin Ian and his son Chris at Wembley for the Burnley v Sheffield United play-off game in May 2009.

The wedding of Lisa and Nigel in January 2009.

Robin and Sheila Wight at the marriage of their son James to Ann.

"The ladies" at York Races in 2012 – Janet Bridge, Pauline Mahon, Jo Wood, Bev Grayson and Nicola.

Nigel and Lisa with "new arrival" Jack in August 2009.

Jack and Sam with the clowns at Luna Park.

Visiting Luna Park Fairground with grandsons Sam and Jack in 2016.

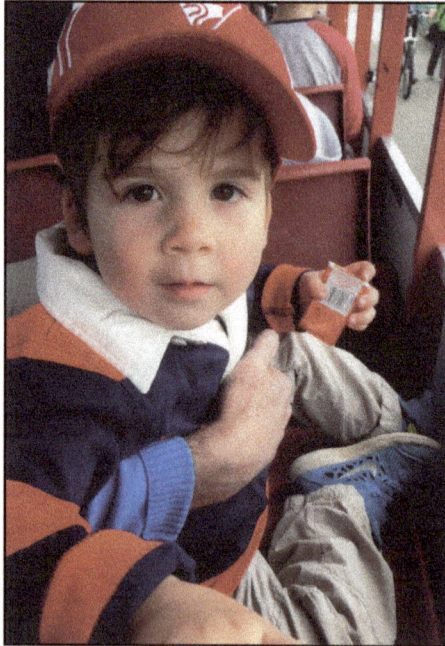

Ned – three years old and too young for the Luna Park visit.

"Bikers" in Sydney. My surprise birthday gift from
Nigel and Lisa on 5 October 2012.

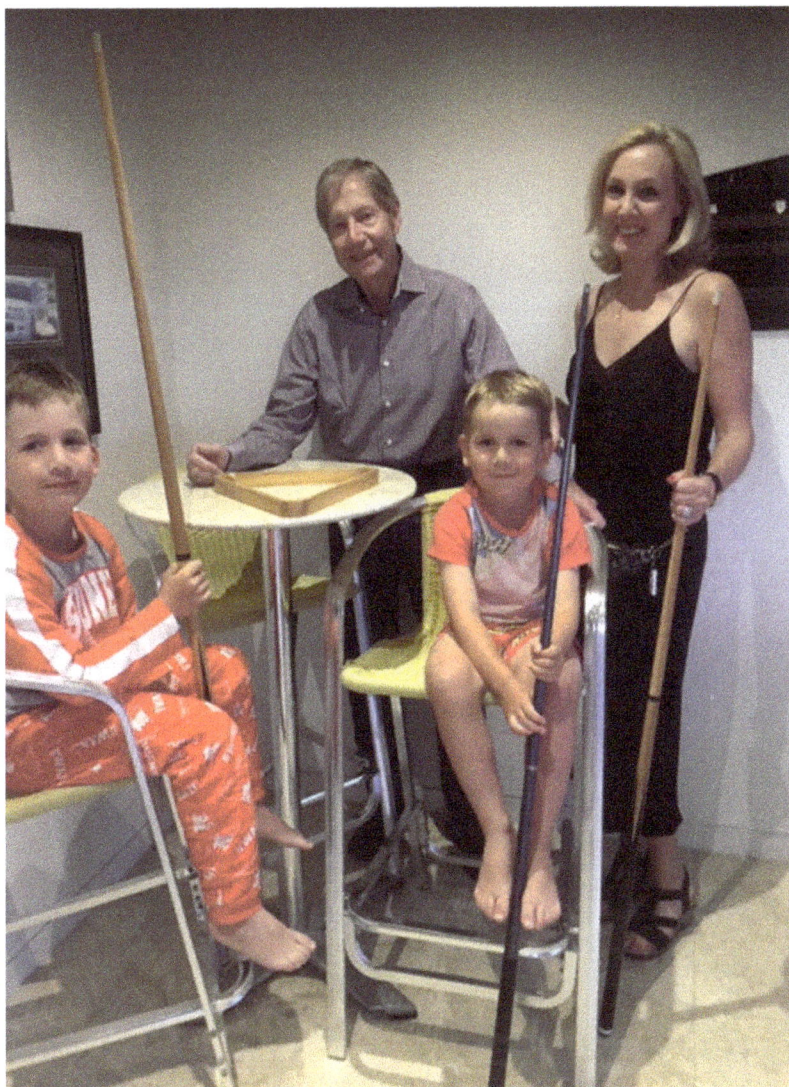

Snooker with Jack and Sam – 2016.

My grandsons – Jack, Sam and Ned in 2019.

Faith Douglas with Hugh Grayson and Nicola. Faith (who took the Group Wedding Photograph) had her own way of making the boys smile!

The Wedding Guests.

The family group at our wedding on 27 June 2012. Left to right –
Nigel, Sheila, Nicola and myself, Sheila's friend Peter, Sophie
(Bridesmaid) and Charles.

At Buckingham Palace to receive my MBE from Prince Charles, in the
presence of Nicola, Nigel and Sophie.

Nicola and myself at the Canton Orchard restaurant with a group of close friends, celebrating the award of my MBE announced on 16 June 2017.

Nicola's son Charles and new wife, Veena, in 2017.

Our first granddaughter, lovely little Meera, born on 6 January 2020.

Nicola's daughter Sophie on holiday in Mykonos in 2017.

Photographs

FIRST GROUP

1. The author at six years of age – Loose leaf cover (Front)

2. Mum and Dad – 1931

3. Family guests at Mum and Dad's wedding in 1931:

   Back row – Harry King, Alex Nussey, Arthur Fairbrother, Clara Darley, Frank Darley, Emily King, Alice Sleighford, Elsie Needham, Jessie Nussey with male friend, and Nelly Fairbrother

   Centre row – Connie Price, George Nussey, Esther Cottingham (my grandmother), Dad and Mum, Amelia Price and Walter Price (my maternal grandparents), Great-Grandma Frith

   Front row – John Robert Cottingham (my grandfather), Dolly (Dad's youngest sister), Donald Nussey, Walter Price, Amy Price (my favourite aunt) and Eliza Nussey

   Children in Front – Ron Fairbrother, Esther Needham and Stanley Price.

4. On holiday with my maternal grandparents about 1943.

5. In 1948 with my maternal cousins – John (aged 1 ¾ years), Ian (1 year) and Linda (2 ½ years).

6. Walter Price in Egypt during WWII.

7. Carfield School 1st XI in 1949. I am the last seated person at the end of the front row.

8. Blackpool, 1953, left to right – Gordon Dorling, Tony Worthington, Ted Machon, Myself, Bernard Gaffney and Frank Gunby.

9. At Royal Air Force, Leconfield, in1956. Commissioned at last.

10. Sports Day at Leconfield, 1957. Sqn Ldr Harrison (on my right) joins the athletes of the Accounts Section, the "backbone" of the victorious Administration Wing Team.

11. The ascent of Mount Kilimanjaro in 1960, accompanied by Keith Traynor.

12. Crossing the "Saddle" between Kilimanjaro's twin peaks of Kibo (19,340 feet) and Mawenzi (16,900 feet).

13. A brief respite with Helmut Schwarz and Wolfgang Heiduk, Germans we met on the climb.

14. Bismark Hut with porters and our guide, Aleapende.

15. "Tossing the coin" – Mombasa Sports Club versus a combined Kenya Schools XI in 1960.

16. C&L Mombasa Office Fishing Trip in 1960. Left to right – Self, Tom Winning, Bill Andress (kneeling), Malcolm Pedlow, Neil McCormick and Bob Whall. The catch included two sailfish of 87lb and 58lb. We gave everything to the African market.

SECOND GROUP

17. 1973 – Nigel and Michelle on holiday in Venice.

18. With Kath, Michelle and Nigel visiting my cousin Ian and wife, René, in Hong Kong (where they resided for some years) in 1988.

19. 1983 – Michelle's "VIP Day" at Sheffield Wednesday's Hillsborough Stadium to celebrate her 21st birthday. "All smiles" receiving her cake from Bob Grierson, a Wednesday Director. By kind permission of Steve Ellis, Photographer.

20. Michelle with "The Great Derek Dooley". Sheffield born Dooley scored 62 goals in 61 league games for the Owls between 1950 and 1953, powering their promotion to the First Division

(the top division in English football at the time). Sadly, in a collision playing against Preston on Valentine's Day 1953, when still only 23 years of age, he sustained a double fracture of the right leg, which, following a gas gangrene infection, resulted in amputation above the knee. Dooley subsequently became manager of Wednesday, before leaving to join Sheffield United, where he served in various executive roles. He was awarded the Freedom of Sheffield in 1993, an MBE in 2003, and remained a hero to both sides of the city.

21. Michelle in 1979.

22. Visiting my cousin Linda in Heidelberg, where she resided for several years, in 1990.

23. My cousin John Strafford at Christmas in 1990.

24. The Croft, my home for 26 years until December 2002.

25. Aunt Connie and Mum outside The Croft in 1996 – "Will you drive, or shall I?"

26. With Sir Stanley Matthews in 1998 in the Sheffield Wednesday Directors Suite. Stanley was widely regarded as having been the greatest player in the British game. By kind permission of Steve Ellis, Photographer.

27. With Nigel and Lisa.

28. Peter and Pat Allen at an outdoor party during the C&L European Partners Meeting in Stockholm in 1990.

29. With Kenneth Clarke, Chancellor of the Exchequer, at Number 11 Downing Street in 1994.

30. Nicola's parents, Leslie and Sheila Scahill with their grandchildren in 1994.

31. Nicola at "Sweet Seventeen" – 26 years before we met in May 2004.

32. Dinner at Harewood House, at which we met John and Norma Major, in September 2004.

33. Nicola and her mother, Sheila, on holiday at Lake Como, Italy, in 2006.

34. Hugh and Beverley Grayson, Tony Wood, Jane Gibbs and Jo Wood attending my "Cattles" retirement party at the Devonshire Arms, Bolton Abbey, in 2006.

35. Nicola and myself with former England rugby lock-forward, Martin Bayfield, who spoke at my Retirement Dinner held in the Chinese Suite of the Dorchester Hotel in 2006.

36. Sean and Pauline Mahon attending a farewell party for Nigel and Lisa on their return to Sydney in 2008.

THIRD GROUP

37. With Cousin Ian and his son Chris at Wembley for the Burnley v Sheffield United play-off game in May 2009.

38. The wedding of Lisa and Nigel in January 2009.

39. Robin and Sheila Wight at the marriage of their son James to Ann.

40. "The ladies" at York Races in 2012 – Janet Bridge, Pauline Mahon, Jo Wood, Bev Grayson and Nicola.

41. Nigel and Lisa with "new arrival" Jack in August 2009.

42. Jack and Sam with the clowns at Luna Park.

43. Visiting Luna Park Fairground with grandsons Sam and Jack in 2016.

44. Ned – three years old and too young for the Luna Park visit.

45. "Bikers" in Sydney. My surprise birthday gift from Nigel and Lisa on 5 October 2012.

46. Snooker with Jack and Sam – 2016.

47. My grandsons – Jack, Sam and Ned in 2019.

48. Faith Douglas with Hugh Grayson and Nicola. Faith (who took the Group Wedding Photograph) had her own way of making the boys smile!

49. The Wedding Guests:

Back row – James Corr, Clive Gibbs, Sean Mahon, John Swynnerton, Hugh Grayson, Tony Grant and Paul Southern

2nd from back – Pauline Mahon, Donna McDonald, Kevin McDonald, Tony Wood, Ted Machon, Richard Walker, and Margaret Machon

3rd from back – Beverley Grayson, Liz Swynnerton, Darel Grant, Jane Gibbs, Jo Wood, Brenda Corr, Liz Atkinson, and Sally Southern

Front row – Charles McMullan, Sophie McMullan, Self and Nicola, Bryan Hancock, Sheila Scahill, Peter Bailey, and Nigel Cottingham

50. The family group at our wedding on 27 June 2012. Left to right – Nigel, Sheila, Nicola and myself, Sheila's friend Peter, Sophie (Bridesmaid) and Charles.

51. At Buckingham Palace on 7 December 2017, after receiving my MBE from Prince Charles, in the presence of Nicola, Nigel and Sophie.

52. Nicola and myself at the Canton Orchard restaurant with a group of close friends, celebrating the award of my MBE announced on 16 June 2017.

53. Nicola's son Charles and his wife, Veena, on their wedding day in November 2017.

54. Our first granddaughter, lovely little Meera, born on 6 January 2020.

55. Nicola's daughter Sophie on holiday in Mykonos in 2017.

56. Nigel, Lisa and the boys on the glaciers in New Zealand, 2020 – Loose leaf cover (Back).

Bibliography and Additional Sources

Books and Reports

A Century of Sheffield. Geoffrey Howse. Sutton Publishing Limited, Stroud, Gloucestershire. 1999.

A Man of Sheffield. Sir Norman Adsetts OBE. RMC Media, Sheffield. 2017.

A History of Cooper Brothers & Co 1854 to 1954. London. 1954.

Battle of Britain. Patrick Bishop. Quercus Publishing plc, London. 2009.

Battle of Britain. Len Deighton. Book Club Associates, by arrangement with Johnathan Cape Ltd. 1980.

Battle of Britain Remembered; Issue 4. Bill Bond (Ed.). Battle of Britain Historical Society, The Production House, Norwich. 2002.

Chronicle of The Second World War. Jacques Legrand. Chronicle Communications Ltd, Farnborough. 1994.

Collections – Bomber Air Crew and Fighter Pilot Profile. The Military Gallery, Bath. 1984.

Defeating Mau Mau, Creating Kenya. Daniel Branch. Cambridge University Press, Cambridge. 2009.

East African Statistical Department. Population Census. 1948.

East African Statistical Department. Statistical Abstract. 1960.

Feet First. Stanley Matthews. Even and Dale Ltd, London. 1948.

Goodbye to Yorkshire. Roy Hattersley. Penguin Books Ltd, Middlesex. 1976.

Great Sporting Quotations. David Pickering. Cassell & Co, London. 2001.

Hand Book and Gazetteer of East Africa. Royal East African Automobile Association. 1958 – 1959.

Heroes of the Skies. Michael Ashcroft. Headline Publishing Group, London. 2012.

Imperial Reckoning. Caroline Elkins. Henry Holt & Company, New York. 2005.

Jambo Kenya. Patrick Orr. David Bruce & Watson Ltd, London. 1970.

National Organisation for Rare Disorders – Synonyms of Prader-Willi Syndrome. 1984.

New 2018 UK Corporate Governance Code – Overseen by Financial Reporting Council. July 2018.

Pevsner Architectural Guides Sheffield. Ruth Harman and John Minnes. Buildings Book Trust. 2004.

Reflections. PWC Magazine for Former Partners. Spring 2015.

Sheffield Blitz. Paul License. A Star Publication, Sheffield Newspapers Ltd. November 2000.

South Yorkshire Mining Disasters – Volume 2. Brian Elliott. Warncliffe Books. 2009.

The Few. Peter Kaplan and Richard Cottier. Blandford Press, London. 1989.

The Hunt for Kimathi. Ian Henderson with Robert Goodhart. Hamish Hamilton, London. 1958.

Yorkshire Cricketers 1839 – 1939. Peter Thomas. Derek Hodgson Publishers, Manchester. 1973.

Newspapers, Magazines and Journals –

The Daily Telegraph – Obituaries

- Sir Brandon Gough – 19 June 2012
- Ian Henderson – 23 April 2013
- Sir Robert Atkinson – 3 February 2015
- The 8th Marquis of Waterford – 17 February 2015
- Sir Hugh Neill – 29 November 2017
- Sir Timothy Kitson – 23 May 2019

The Daily Telegraph – Re: Kenya. Tear gas chaos and killings as Kenyatta sworn in as president. 29 November 2017.

The Daily Telegraph – Re: The Hillsborough Disaster. Articles on 23 February 2019 and 9 April 2019.

The Daily Telegraph – Re: National debt passing £2 trillion for first time. 22 August 2020.

The Daily Telegraph and *The Sunday Telegraph* – Reports and article on the Coronavirus (Covid-19). From 1 March to 30 June 2020.

The Sunday Telegraph – "Fame and Fortune Interviews". Ted Dexter. 5 August 2018.

The Telegraph online. Courage above all. Lord Ashcroft. 9 September 2012.

C&L Journal – Number 31. 125th Anniversary Issue. June 1979.

Contract Journal – *The Realist*. Stuart Doughty, Chief Executive of Costain. 21 July 2004.

Yorkshire Post – The Yorkshire Business Awards: Sir Kenneth Morrison – Executive of the Year; SIG – Yorkshire Board of the Year. 2000.

Online

Periodic references have been made to the Internet in order to access the vast amount of information available. In particular, the following sites have been consulted in connection with these memoirs.

en.wikipedia.org/wiki/
- Sheffield Blitz
- Great Depression in the United Kingdom
- List of World Organisation of the Scout Movement
- Hugh Cholmondeley, 3rd Baron Delamere
- Ted Dexter
- Godfrey Evans
- Stanley Matthews
- Basil D'Oliveira
- Hugh Neill
- Prader-Willi Syndrome
- British Steel (1967 – 1999)
- Pan's People
- Serlby Hall
- Jayne Mansfield
- Prince Philip, Duke of Edinburgh
- David Blunkett
- Sir Norman Adsetts
- Lord Sebastian Coe

www.chrishobbs.com/nunnerypit1923.htm
The Nunnery Pit Accident – Sheffield. 3 December 1923.

www.bbc.co.uk/bitesize/guides/zsxyhv4/revision/2 The General Strike 1926.

www.sheffieldhistory.co.uk/forums/topic/69-the-story-of-the-sheffield-blitz/ The Story of the Sheffield Blitz.

journeysbydesign.com/experiences/wildlife-of-the-maasai-mara-and-great-rift-valley The Great Rift Valley.

inflation.stephenmorley.org/ Inflation Calculator.

www.bbc.co.uk/news/business-39932653/comments?post Id=127079061 UK inflation rate at highest level since September 2013.

www.thoughtco.com/world-war-ii-sten-2361239 World War II Sten.

www.thisismoney.co.uk/money/news/article-1581679/Polypipe-flush-with-163337-million-sale.html Polypipe flush with £337 million sale.

Index

I am aware that most learned books contain an index (often of great length and detail) to facilitate reference to the important information they contain. My personal memoirs are clearly not in the above category. The events recorded (which may, hopefully, raise an occasional smile) are unlikely to be of more than passing interest to readers and, as regarding the people included, most of my current friends are already mentioned in Chapter XVII. Consequently, although I have prepared the following index, it has been restricted to:

- A small number of close friends, who have figured in some detail or been mentioned in several chapters throughout the memoirs.
- A few other friends or colleagues, who I feel have had an influence on my career over the years.

Close friends

Names	Chapter in which mentioned
Gordon and Janet Bridge	XVII, XIX
Hugh and Beverley Grayson	XVI, XVII
Bryan and Liz Hancock	II, III, X, XVII
Ted and Margaret Machon	III, X, XVII
Sean and Pauline Mahon	X, XI, XII, XIII, XVI, XVII, XIX
Kevin and Donna McDonald	XI, XIII, XIV, XVI, XVII
Paul and Sally Southern	XI, XII, XVII, XX
John and Liz Swynnerton	XVII
Tony and Jo Wood	VIII, IX, XI, XII, XIV, XVII
Alan and Sue Young	XII, XVII, XXI

Other friends or colleagues who influenced my career

Names	Chapter in which mentioned
Sir Norman Adsetts	XVI, XIX
Peter Allen	XII, XIII, XVII
Sir Robert Atkinson	VIII, XI
Lord Henry Benson	VIII, XI, XII, XXI
Ray Emmitt	IV(C), VIII, XI, XII, XIII, XXI
Sir Brandon Gough	XII, XIII
David Hobson	XII, XIII
Wilfred Molyneux	VIII, XI, XV

About the Author

Born in 1933, the only child of loving working-class parents, the early recollections of Barrie Cottingham are of life in World War Two, and particularly of the Sheffield Blitz, when serious bomb damage to the homes of relatives resulted in a total of 11 family members living together for several weeks in the small terraced property (with no bathroom and only an outside toilet), which his parents rented.

These reminiscences are an appropriate introduction to the main stated objective of the memoirs, to provide the author's Australian born grandsons with some knowledge of their British heritage and ancestors. However, as the recollections unfold, they also give a record of the period from the end of the Second World War when changes in British society (possibly the most rapid ever) provided opportunities for working-class people to move up the social scale.

The author completed his state school education at the age of 15, obtaining the best examination results of his year. These, together with a testimonial from his headmaster, resulted in the grant of articles with a small Sheffield firm to study accountancy, without payment of the premium which was normally required at that time. Qualifying at the age of 21 years, he was called up for national service in the Royal Air Force where, after appropriate training, he obtained a commission, the first person from his family to have risen from the ranks.

On completion of RAF service, and with a wish to see something of the world, he joined the international accountancy firm of Cooper Brothers & Co (subsequently to become Coopers & Lybrand – "the firm") to spend three years in Kenya. This proved to be one of the most interesting periods of his life.

Returning to the firm in the UK at the age of 27, he was admitted to partnership three years later, and subsequently became the youngest member of the Executive Committee (effectively the Managing Board) at the age of 40 – remaining in this management group (with its various changes of name over the years) until the retirement age of 60 years.

Following Coopers & Lybrand, he enjoyed a second career, extending over the next 20 years, as a non-executive director on several company boards, including the chairmanship of two public listed groups. The greater flexibility of time when carrying out these duties enabled him to also undertake a number of unremunerated and charitable activities. In relation to one of these, he was awarded an MBE in 2017.

However, these memoirs are not confined to a review of the author's professional, business and charitable activities. Aspects of his private life are interwoven throughout, including the tragic death of his daughter Michelle (suffering from birth with Prader-Willi syndrome) at the age of 35, despite the devoted care of his first wife, Kathleen, his close relationship with his son Nigel, and meeting and marrying his current wife, Nicola.

His pride in Sheffield and lifelong interest in sport also receive mention. A "Blade" for 80 years since first being taken to Bramall Lane by his father as a small boy, he still holds season tickets – although these are of little current value in the days of Covid-19.